Smart Working

This book is dedicated to my family – brother, sisters, nieces and sister-in-law – all of whom are nurses. Each one of them brings deep humanity, caring and integrity to the work they do.

I am in awe of them all.

Smart Working

Creating the Next Wave

ANNE MARIE McEWAN

Routledge
Taylor & Francis Group

LONDON AND NEW YORK

First published in paperback 2024

First published 2013 by Gower Publishing

Published 2016
by Routledge
4 Park Square, Milton Park, Abingdon, Oxon OX14 4RN

and by Routledge
605 Third Avenue, New York, NY 10158

Routledge is an imprint of the Taylor & Francis Group, an informa business

British Library Cataloguing in Publication Data
 McEwan, Anne Marie.
    Smart working : creating the next wave.
    1. Organizational effectiveness. 2. Employee motivation. 3. Work environment.
    I. Title
    658.4–dc23

Library of Congress Cataloging-in-Publication Data
McEwan, Anne Marie.
    Smart working : creating the next wave / by Anne Marie McEwan.
       p. cm.
    Includes bibliographical references and index.
    ISBN 978-1-4094-0456-9 (hbk. : alk. paper) – ISBN 978-1-4094-0457-6 (ebook)
  1.   Organizational effectiveness. 2.   Flexible work arrangements. 3.   Performance.
4. Diffusion of innovations. 5. Manpower planning. I. Title.

    HD58.9.M423 2013
    658.3'01–dc23

                                                                                    2012025341

ISBN: 978-1-4094-0456-9 (hbk)
ISBN: 978-1-03-292357-4 (pbk)
ISBN: 978-1-315-60940-9 (ebk)

DOI: 10.4324/9781315609409

Contents

List of Figures

List of Tables

Acknowledgements

This work owes a debt of acknowledgement to so many people. While wishing to avoid the gushing acknowledgements that regularly accompany acceptance speeches at the Oscars, in which all and sundry are thanked, I am afraid this is how this acknowledgement might read. One of my reasons for writing the book is my perception that academic thinkers and their theoretical perspectives are largely being overlooked online, where the search for the next new big thing can seem to take precedence over the search for knowledge, and that this ought not to happen because I believe their work to be practically relevant for today's complex, uncertain and highly connected global contexts. My heartfelt thanks go to these authors, whose works have for a long time inspired me, and continue to do so.

There are many members of staff at Kingston University to whom I am grateful. I am particularly indebted to Professor Richard Ennals for his patience, generosity and insights, many of which I only recently began to appreciate beyond my previously superficial understanding. I am also grateful for the opportunities he created. Professor Robin Matthews similarly gave me the opportunity of being involved in developing an innovative work-based strategic programme for senior executives, through a partnership between Kingston University and the Academy of National Economy in Moscow (now the Russian Presidential Academy of National Economy and Public Administration). The book would not have been possible without either Professor Ennals or Professor Matthews.

My thanks to all who agreed to let me interview them over the years, and to Roman Markov for letting me reference his unpublished Master's thesis.

Finally, my grateful thanks go to Dr Marie Puybaraud, Director of Innovation at Johnson Controls. Marie and I have been co-facilitating the Johnson Controls Innovation Network (previously the Global Mobility Network) since 2006.

I have drawn heavily on the white papers that we have co-authored following the network meetings, which bring together experts from a range of diverse disciplines connected with the workplace and the changing world of work. Again, this book would not have been possible without my involvement in this network, and being exposed to such energetic and exploratory conversations.

Introduction

Overview

This overview condenses the book's main arguments. It was written out of frustration at Enterprise 2.0 and social business discussions online, and dismay at proclamations of 'smart working' as a new paradigm. Of course technological, demographic and economic developments are causing turmoil and opportunity in global and local business environments. Uncertainty and increasing complexity are now the norm.

However, the lack of reference in blog posts and online articles to foundation knowledge and principles, which link the design of social, technical, organisational and physical performance environments to foundation literature on high-performance, innovation and adaptation, impoverishes the discussions of how best to adapt work environments and working practices. A number of contentions underpin *Smart Working: Creating the Next Wave*, including these:

- Knowledge about the components of smart working and making the transition to new ways of working, including practical tactics and theoretical perspectives, is widely available but overlooked in practice.

- As a result, an abundance of potential and capability in people is wasted.

- People participate in shaping their own realities. This is not easy, but social and networking technologies that connect us to each other, and are used without permission and for our own ends, are transformational. It is more possible than ever to influence and shape our working environments, our experience of work and of each other.

- Although people are not prisoners of organisational systems and processes, the pull towards the status quo is strong. Existing knowledge is useless until it is experimented with and applied through 'chaotic action' (Weick 2001).

- We need to act our way dynamically and continuously into the next wave of doing better or doing differently. The tools, technologies, methods, knowledge and systemic approaches are all there for the discovering and using.

Rationale

Recent events in the global business environment indicate two things happening simultaneously:

- a range of systemic failures at international and organisational levels;

- profound economic, technological, demographic, structural and environmental developments.

In the face of this environmental turmoil, there is a gathering consensus that working practices and management approaches need to adapt radically to reflect increasingly complex and uncertain operating environments. One specific response is a call for 'smart working'. The term is beginning to appear in articles and research reports (CIPD 2008a, CIPD 2008b, Pearson et al. 2010). What others are saying about smart working and how they define it will be explored more fully in Chapter 1.

What can be said for the moment is that smart working is an outcome of designing organisational systems that are adaptable, 'fit for purpose' and that are built around harnessing workforce knowledge, skills, potential for learning and require everyone's participation in innovation.

Smart working is claimed as a 'new paradigm' (CIPD 2008a). The tendency in management literature is to talk of twenty-first-century management and new paradigms. This 'delusion with novelty' (Pettigrew and Fenton 2000) risks overlooking fundamental insights of trail-blazing theoretical thinkers from decades ago, and from years of academic research and lessons learned from process innovation methods that took root in manufacturing from the 1980s onwards.

Social computing and collaborative communication technologies are now creating immense possibilities for stimulating and harnessing collective intelligence within and beyond organisational boundaries. They provide unprecedented opportunities to discover this legacy of learning and to provide creation spaces (Hagel et al. 2010) inside and outside of organisational boundaries where people can come together to learn, share, connect, experiment and reflect.

Building on what is already known about creating systems and performance environments compatible with smart working practices, social and collaboration techniques give us powerful new tools to explore the implications and requirements for contemporary management capabilities and systems design.

There are therefore two reasons for writing this book. The first is to alert practitioners to the fact that what is already known about the management systems, processes and practices associated with process innovation and control methods from the first wave of smart working, and from a plethora of other research that lies hidden from view in academic journals, remains highly relevant for current conditions. They are associated with high performance, business benefits and more satisfying work for people.

Discovering old knowledge and systemic approaches is only part of the story. They need to be interpreted, contextualised and put into practice. The second reason for writing this book is strongly to suggest that creating the next wave of smart working will require 'chaotic action' and experimentation. One of the key lessons in making the transition from traditional manufacturing to lean and quality approaches is that it was challenging and that businesses 'failed their way to various levels of success' (Randolph 1995). Those that failed to make the transition ceased to be viable. The pull of the status quo is strong, and can only be overcome by determined action.

It is more possible than ever for us to influence and shape our working environments, our experience of work and of each other. A major benefit of social technologies is that they connect us to knowledgeable people who can tell others where to find relevant information, and to peers who provide each other with support as they engage in the often challenging experience of making the transition to new ways of working. These technologies can now be included within a range of formal and informal approaches to learning by doing and learning together, two of which are described later in the book.

Objectives

The objectives of the book are to:

- review what we already know about effective management and high-performance work methods; this includes evaluating what others are saying about smart working, and extending it to include design principles that are missing from current interpretations;

- review current workplace trends (in people, technology, place and space);

- show how insights from what we already know can be interpreted and used to business advantage in contemporary turbulent, fast-changing and global business environments.

Smart Working: Creating the Next Wave is a reflection of my experience over the past fifteen years. Arguments, observations and conclusions throughout the book are drawn from multiple primary and secondary sources.

Literature Review

Much of what business leaders need to know to create adaptive responsive organisations, the effectiveness of which is dependent on the active and willing contributions of people's knowledge and skills, is already well documented and evidenced. The literature reviewed here has been surveyed over an extended period and carried out in connection with different research projects and work activities.

Senge (1993) says in his well-known book *The Fifth Discipline* that he takes no credit for inventing the five disciplines he explores and expands on in that book. They represent the work of many people. This is also the case here. Drawing from a broad range of organisational design and theoretical perspectives – including social psychology, organisational learning, systems thinking, process perspectives like lean and quality, socio-technical systems theory and more – *Smart Working: Creating the Next Wave* explores issues around formal systems design and organisational capabilities needed to support smart working.

These capabilities include the ability to identify key principles, which can then be interpreted and applied to unique operating contexts in the pursuit of viability, adaptation, innovation, performance and integration.

Research Sources

On the research side, my unpublished doctoral research provides useful insights on the basics of first wave working practices, especially focusing on the pivotal contribution of shop floor operator tacit knowledge, and participation in continuous improvement and problem-solving activities (McEwan 1999). An additional key source for analysis of first wave smart working is past participation in the UK Work Organisation Network.[1]

A more recent source is a five-year-long collaboration as co-facilitator with Dr Marie Puybaraud, Director of Workplace Innovation of the Johnson Controls Global Mobility Network. This is a learning network to explore global workplace trends and their impact on the workplace (Puybaraud and McEwan 2007). Unpublished white papers documenting key issues that arose within network meetings provide insight on a variety of topics on global workplace trends, which contribute to defining second wave smart working.

For the practical transition to reflections on new ways of working, these are drawn from activities with practitioners and senior executives on a work-based Master's degree at a UK university. The approach was subsequently developed through a partnership between the university and an academic institute in Russia.

Part I: Legacy of Learning

Theoretical and research perspectives on organisational dynamics and associated systems design considerations are reviewed in Part I, which are then used to reflect on first wave smart working practices. This lays the foundation for comparison with a second wave of smart working practices that are currently emerging in response to turbulent environmental conditions.

---

1   http://www.ukwon.net/ [accessed: 31 March 2012].

CHAPTER 1: SETTING THE CONTEXT

Chapter 1 expands on the systemic failures at international and organisational levels, and briefly references the global trends that are explored in detail in Chapter 5. Responses to the complexities and uncertainties in the external operating environment include calls for smart working. The chapter reviews who is talking about smart working and what they are saying. Altogether, the analysis in Chapter 1 provides initial justification for proposing that principles and practices from the past remain highly relevant for the current context.

CHAPTER 2: HOW ORGANISATIONS WORK (AND DO NOT WORK)

This sprint through the basics of organisational systems and dynamics provides a platform for exploring in later chapters how organisations are changing and what this means for organisational systems, working practices and leadership skills. The chapter reviews fundamental concepts in organising dynamics. It then uses the analysis to assess the formal systems that enterprises put in place to co-ordinate complex interactions arising from organising dynamics.

This review serves another purpose, which is to remind the reader that the current hoopla about organisations being networks of formal and informal relationships is only a re-discovery of something we have always known. Organisations have always consisted of networks of inter-related relationships, despite repeatedly overstated pronouncements about the supposed dominance of hierarchy. It is through these informal networks of relationships, connections and knowledge that adaptation of rigid, formal systems takes place – if, in fact, adaptation does occur.

CHAPTER 3: FIRST WAVE SMART WORKING

Chapter 3 reviews a number of statements being made about transformations in working practices, management practices and performance cultures that need to happen in response to current global competitive pressures, in particular the need to make innovation everyone's business and to empower workforces to 'take action that will benefit the customer without layers of bureaucratic approval' (Nayar 2010).

This is exactly what happened through process innovation and control methods, which if implemented in ways that recognised the primacy of people's skills and tacit knowledge, represented the first wave of smart working.

Chapter 3 summarises the components of these practices and systems. Making the transition to new ways of working was problematic for many enterprises. Those that did manage to make the transition left a legacy of learning on which we can now draw.

CHAPTER 4: DESIGN PRINCIPLES FROM THE FIRST WAVE

Chapter 4 reviews two theoretical perspectives, the Viable System and Socio-technical Systems theories. Principles from both models provide insights for practical systems design to address some of the challenges that were revealed through the analysis of first wave smart working in Chapter 3. Four particular design principles emerge from the analysis:

1. designing for adaptability;

2. designing for integration;

3. designing for disciplined collaboration;

4. designing for innovation and knowledge-sharing.

Part II: All Change

Part II shifts focus to detailed examination of current global workplace trends and implications for working practices, organisational re-design and leadership development. Characteristics of second wave smart working are compared to first wave characteristics to suggest that the design principles identified in Chapter 4 remain relevant, and to identify any additional principles.

CHAPTER 5: WHAT IS HAPPENING?

Chapter 5 reviews current workplace trends and concludes that the conditions exist for the next iteration of smart working to take off. A recurring topic throughout the chapter is the implications of social computing and collaboration technologies for second wave smart working, particularly their role in:

- discovering, sharing, co-creating and distributing knowledge within knowledge networks;

- breaching geographical, cultural and functional boundaries across increasingly fragmented and globally distributed enterprises;

- energising and harnessing collective intelligence.

CHAPTER 6: SPACE, PLACE AND KNOWLEDGE FLOWS

The CIPD/Cap Gemini four-pillar model of smart working includes the physical work environment as one of the core elements (CIPD 2008a). The case studies identified the role of physical workplaces in catalysing flexible space usage like hot-desking, typically a source of significant cost saving. They also identified the need for collaboration, implying the crucial role workplaces play in knowledge creation, and in communicating management values and company culture. This chapter expands on these themes and explains why physical and virtual workplaces are becoming key enablers of knowledge-creation.

CHAPTER 7: PATTERNS AND PARALLELS

Chapter 7 proposes insights and principles from first wave smart working to provide guidance on systems design and practices for working and managing in fragmented, connected, fluid, uncertain and boundary-crossing business environments. The initial design principles from first wave smart working are reviewed and assessed against the characteristics of second wave smart working.

Part III: Creating the Next Wave

Part III proposes practical approaches to making the transition to new ways of working and managing, including suggestions for tools and frameworks to get started.

CHAPTER 8: DO BETTER OR DO DIFFERENTLY

Chapter 8 focuses on factors that need to be in place to create the next wave of smart working. The importance of creative leaders who are distributed throughout organisations is highlighted, as are formal and informal approaches to nurturing their learning and development.

The chapter draws on examples of practitioners who took it on themselves to instigate new ways of working, one through particularly chaotic action – discovering, experimenting, persevering and muddling through – and the other through a more formalised and structured approach. The chapter then adds insights arising from their experiences to all the analysis so far, to suggest what all this implies for leadership skills and capabilities.

CHAPTER 9: DIAGNOSING, DESIGNING AND LEARNING

Outputs from Chapter 9 include the Smart Work Framework, the Diagnostic Grid and the Diagnostic Checklist, which are all based on core topics in smart working and theoretical design principles. They are intended as resources to help leaders to instigate change, and as aids to dialogue and informal conversations around shared reflective practice. The chapter concludes by describing an experimental learning community currently in development, where people can meet in an online environment to discover, explore, share ideas and experiment with smart working practices.

CHAPTER 10: TOOLS, TECHNIQUES AND RESOURCES

The final chapter suggests tools, techniques and resources to get going on creating the next wave of smart working. As knowledge becomes more distributed, conceptual and emergent, people need tools to make their thinking visible to themselves and their colleagues. People also need tools to have conversations about the different ways in which they see the world. The chapter points to a software tool and two approaches for making intangible business processes visible and transparent.

Chapter 10 also makes suggestions for resources: sources of research and insight that can help in applying smart working principles, including details of institutions and online learning communities. More information about tools, techniques and resources is available through The Smart Work Company learning communities.

PART I
Legacy of Learning

1

Setting the Context

Introduction

The objective of this chapter is to provide initial justification for proposing that principles and practices from the past remain highly relevant for the current context. This theme will be further developed throughout Part I.

The global business environment at the beginning of the second decade of the twenty-first century is evolving simultaneously on many fronts: economically, technologically, demographically, structurally and environmentally. Some of these issues are coming over the horizon. Others are already here and gathering pace. Yet others will be increasingly felt in the coming decades, and include energy, waste, climate change, acidification of the oceans, water, food and urbanisation.[1]

> *China and India are phenomenal innovators. We won't just go down, we'll go down big time if we don't watch out. We have to think of the clever new ideas and be ahead of the game while we have the affluence and economic growth to invest in way-out concepts. That includes the way we work. (Cooper 2005)*

There is urgency in recognising a changing economic world order. The affluence and economic growth conditions that Professor Cooper spoke of at the beginning of 2005 are now fond memories for many Western businesses. The Confederation of British Industry (CBI) in the UK concluded in 2009 that post-recession operating conditions would continue to be volatile and risky. This was partly attributed to more expensive and regulated capital conditions, linked to constrained capacity to fund innovation, and the longer-term and inevitable shift to low-carbon energy usage (CBI 2009).

---

1   http://www.driversofchange.com/ [accessed: 9 March 2012].

Business leaders, who were caught unprepared for a global financial crisis, need to adopt new mindsets to cope with the extreme short-term and long-term pressures that are creating harsh operating environments (PWC 2009). These are exacerbated by many governments being saddled with unprecedented levels of debt and a consequent need to consider how to deliver public services more cost-effectively, which is creating further potential difficulties and uncertainties for the private sector as governments reduce spending and consider raising taxes to fund their deficits. What the CBI could not predict as a further contributing factor to volatility was the crisis in the Eurozone, triggered by fears over national debts. At the time of writing, this is ongoing and adding to economic uncertainty and disruption.

Meanwhile, the signs are that Asian economies continue to prosper, led by India and China, with home markets providing strong drivers of business expansion.[2] The emerging economies have the benefit of large domestic markets, growing consuming middle classes, and young populations at a time when populations in the West are ageing. If clever, well-educated Indian, Chinese and other emerging-economy workforces have phenomenal innovation capabilities and are eager for economic success, businesses in the developed economies are going to have to mobilise all the energy, passion and knowledge available to them to stay in the game, never mind being ahead of it.

Writing this book has been like trying to analyse a rapidly moving target. The one thing that is clear is that complexity, instability and uncertainty are the new norms. How well equipped are enterprises to deal with these potentially overwhelmingly complex environmental conditions, which require vigilance, agility, adaptation of systems, management practices, attitudes and methods to cope with increasingly unpredictable global business environments? The signs are not good.

Failure of Governance

One consequence of the crisis has been widespread reflection on and analysis of what went wrong in the global financial system and what it all means for business. Reading surveys of CEOs and discussion documents, you could be forgiven for thinking that developments in the external environment are entirely responsible for current pressures.

---

2   http://www.ft.com/cms/s/0/7530f484-f8da-11de-beb8-00144feab49a.html?catid=15&SID=google.

This obviously, and unfortunately, is not the case. Commenting on his experience of trying to report his concerns over decisions being taken and policies being pursued at UK bank HBOS plc, Paul Moore, ex-head of Group Regulatory Risk at HBOS, said:

> *I strongly believe that the real underlying cause of all the problems was simply this – a total failure of all key aspects of governance. In my view and from my personal experience at HBOS, all the other specific failures stem from this one primary cause. (Moore 2009)*

A review of corporate governance in UK banks supports his view. In his foreword to the review, Sir David Walker says that he was asked to review corporate governance in UK banks 'in the light of the experience of critical loss and failure throughout the banking system' (Walker 2009). He continues:

> *The fact that different banks operating in the same geography, in the same financial and market environment and under the same regulatory arrangements generated such massively different outcomes can only be fully explained in terms of differences in the way they were run ... how banks are run is a matter for their boards, that is corporate governance.*

Failure to Adapt

At the time General Motors filed for bankruptcy in June 2009, the rash of commentary on the company's troubles is without a doubt linked to its iconic status; it represents a metaphor for the mighty fallen. There is shock that this could happen to an apparently invincible corporation. It is not as though the signs were not there. This is not being wise after the event.

Senge (1993) was writing almost 20 years ago, when the first edition of his widely known *The Fifth Discipline* came out, about the company's inability to change its way of thinking and doing. Tactics that had served General Motors well in a previous era were even then no longer appropriate.

Hamel (2009c) compares General Motors to a 'two pack a day smoker committing suicide by degrees'. He notes that its failure was the result of many decisions over a long period, and wryly concludes that 'the company didn't jump off a cliff. Instead, it meandered into mediocrity, one small short-sighted step at a time.' To Kay (2009), 'the history of modern business is the history of

GM, and vice versa ... if the success of GM defined the management agenda for 20th century, then its failure defines the management agenda for the 21st'.

The ability to sense and respond to threats and opportunities, it will be argued later, is a core element of smart working. Two short quotes from an article in the *Financial Times* sum this up for General Motors:

> *Organisations fail not because they stray from their core, but because they stick to it too closely as circumstances shift ... the idea that focusing on the core is the best defence against failure is too simplistic for these complex and turbulent times.*[3]

In an article following the filing for bankruptcy, the then CEO, Fritz Henderson, is reported as saying that the New GM would be 'dedicated to building the very best cars and trucks – highly fuel efficient, world-class quality, green technology development and with truly outstanding design. Above all, the New GM will be re-dedicated in its entirety to our customers'. The article pithily observes that 'quite why this wasn't the case with the old GM will no doubt become the subject of many books and academic theses to come' (Kahl 2009).

Failure of Systems

The environmental and public relations disaster associated with the BP oil spill in the Gulf of Mexico happened since writing the first draft of this chapter. As with the financial crisis, there is much wisdom after the event. From the final report into the incident:

> *The immediate causes of the Macondo well blowout can be traced to a series of identifiable mistakes ... that reveal such systematic failures in risk management that they place in doubt the safety culture of the entire industry. Fundamental reform will be needed in both the structure of those in charge of regulatory oversight and their internal decision making process to ensure their political autonomy, technical expertise, and their full consideration of environmental protection concerns.*[4]

---

3   http://www.ft.com/cms/s/0/56c9b7e6-4c56-11de-a6c5-00144feabdc0.html?ftcamp=rss.
4   http://www.oilspillcommission.gov/sites/default/files/documents/FinalReportIntro.pdf [accessed: 9 March 2012].

Systemic failures happen within organisations, across eco-systems of supply networks and in the external environment, and within national and international contexts. The global financial system is obviously the outcome of complex interactions between systems of systems, which cross national and cultural boundaries. Failure to think and act systematically contributed to the global financial crisis.

Gillian Tett of the *Financial Times* was one of the few to warn of impending dangers (Tett 2009). She saw that financiers operating within silos of specialised knowledge failed to understand how they interacted with each other and with the rest of society. An IBM global survey of CEOs agrees that thinking and acting with regard to systems dynamics is a crucial requirement, concluding that 'our world is increasingly subject to failures that require cross-systems-level thinking and approaches' (IBM 2010a).

Systems inter-connect and interact with each other in complex and uncertain ways, making it difficult to see what is going on. Take the Toyota product recalls of 2009. According to this report:

> *Experts say the sudden acceleration problem that has put the brakes on Toyota sales and production is likely not a single problem but an alignment of complicated interconnected conditions. 'You've got a multitude of problems that are coming to the surface that result in one thing: unintended acceleration.'*[5]

Failure of governance, adaptation and systems are in addition to the global workplace trends that were already unfolding and driving the next wave of process innovation and organisational reconfiguration, which are reviewed in detail in Chapter 5.

Smart Working

What should businesses be doing to prepare leaders and managers operating within increasingly complex, uncertain and highly connected external environments? And what help are they getting from management thinkers, academics and consultants in improving their capabilities to adapt rapidly? How are they being equipped to perform within environments that consist of

5   http://www.msnbc.msn.com/id/35110966/ns/business-autos/ [accessed: 9 March 2012].

systems of systems, where complex inter-personal dynamics are influenced by those performance environments?

Among the responses to current conditions are calls for smart working. Some use the term to describe flexible 'anywhere, anytime' ways of working. For example, a smarter working initiative by Hampshire County Council in the South East of England was based on smart work as 'meaning all forms of Flexible Working (flexible hours, job share etc.) with a major focus on ICT enabled occasional or permanent Home or Mobile based Teleworking'.[6] Working remotely is linked to smarter working practices in an article from the Department of Transport in the UK, although the article does also stress that remote working needs organisational cultures to change.[7]

Although flexible working, or smart working as understood in this specific and limited way, has been the focus of interest for a long time (Huws et al. 1990), it is enjoying a resurgence in the public sector as deep cuts to public services are anticipated and attempts are made to reduce the overhead costs of property.

PERFORMANCE ENVIRONMENTS

More holistic views than a narrow focus on flexibility of time, place and employment contracts are emerging, encompassing psycho-social attitudes to work and relationships (CIPD 2008a, CIPD 2008b) and re-configuring business processes (Pearson et al. 2010). The Chartered Institute of Personnel Development (CIPD) in conjunction with CAP Gemini focus their interpretation of smart working on organisational systems that create enabling performance environments, which influence psycho-social attitudes to work and working relationships.

Smart working in this view is about 'managing and optimising both the physical and philosophical work environment to release energy that drives business performance'. They say: 'In particular, we believe that a focus on the core beliefs and culture of the organisation is the underpinning factor that makes an organisation "smart". It is a "smart mindset".'

---

6   The initiative was part of the MATiSSE project. The link is no longer available but this link describes savings in business travel suggested by the project: http://www.governmenttechnology.co.uk/features2/item/1319-reducing-the-cost-of-business-travel [assessed: 31 March 2012].

7   http://www.dft.gov.uk/publications/smarter-working/ [accessed: 31 March 2012].

The CIPD proposes a four-pillar framework of multiplicative relationships, which can alternatively be seen as interacting sub-systems (see Table 1.1).

Table 1.1   CIPD four-pillar framework of multiplicative relationships

Management Values	×	High-performance System	×	Enabling Technology	×	Physical Workplace

Source: CIPD (2008a).

The authors' depiction of their framework in the conclusion as multiplicative relationships among sub-systems is conceptually similar to the Matthews model of organisational strategy.[8] The CIPD/Cap Gemini framework is a very useful tool in identifying high-level topics that can be drilled down to greater detail, allowing links and dependencies to be mapped. Systems, working environments and governance principles are more likely to lead to effective performance if they are designed in a way that is consistent with self-determination and choice for people in where, when and how they work. These in turn are determined and influenced by organisational culture and core beliefs.

DYNAMIC, DISTRIBUTED PROCESSES

Whereas the CIPD proposes smart working in terms of enabling systems, the authors of an IBM research report define smart working in terms of dynamic, distributed business processes and knowledge flows (Pearson et al. 2010). They identify 15 smarter working practices that are crucial in making enterprises more:

- **dynamic** – enabling people, processes and information to adapt rapidly;

- **collaborative** – facilitating learning and problem-solving;

- **connected** – enabling access to timely and appropriate information.

---

8   http://robindcmatthews.com/lecdocs/documents/31/original_the%20meta%20model%20 october%202010.pdf [accessed: 8 March 2012].

Both the enabling performance environment and the dynamic interactions perspectives provide a foundation for further detailed analysis as specific components and interactions among them are considered in greater detail in later chapters.

For the moment, it is enough to conclude that smart working practices are agile, dynamic and emergent. They are outcomes of designing organisational systems that facilitate customer-focused, value-creating relationships that are good for business and good for people.

Delusion with Novelty

In the face of tumultuous environmental change and organisational dysfunction, there are voices calling for management re-invention and new paradigms (Hamel and Breen 2007). Things we already know are presented as though they are new. Pettigrew and Fenton note that this obsession with novelty is delusional. Robert Sutton is a well-known Professor of Management Science at Stamford University in the USA, and he writes a popular blog. In one of his posts, he cites another respected management thinker, James March, as saying 'most claims of originality are testimony to ignorance and most claims of magic are testimony to hubris'.[9]

Acknowledging that there is much more yet to be done in clarifying what is involved in smart working, the authors of one of the reports from the CIPD two-part investigation into smart working say that: 'This second report draws on wide evidence to convincingly conclude that "smart working" represents a new organisational paradigm.'

FIRST WAVE SMART WORKING

The claim that smart working is a new paradigm is not helpful and is open to considerable debate. For example, the CIPD views high-trust management cultures and values as the cornerstone of smart working, where people are regarded as crucial to the success of the business, are given freedom to work out among themselves how, where and when work is best organised, and where recognition and rewards are assessed according to outcomes.

---

9   http://bobsutton.typepad.com/my_weblog/2008/12/good-to-great-more-evidence-that-most-claims-of-magic-are-testimony-to-hubris.html [accessed: 31 March 2012].

In lean and agile manufacturing two decades ago, there had already been a first wave of smart working based on 'high-trust management cultures and values as the cornerstone of smart working, where people are regarded as crucial to the success of the business, are given freedom to work out among themselves how, where and when work is best organised'. Exactly as the CIPD says about smart working, first wave smart working involved managing and optimising the work environment for employees 'in such a way that it releases energy and therefore drives business performance'.

Lean and agile approaches require the engagement of machine operators in continuous improvement and problem-solving. This involves sharing knowledge across distributed business processes within and across organisations. 'A fundamental change to the assumptions that govern and shape the working relationship' – a condition essential for smart working, according to the CIPD – had to take place for this level of engagement to be achieved.

If a key objective in the first wave was to gain the willing compliance of operators in knowledge-sharing, there had to be a new deal in relationships between management and operators. For many managers used to monitoring and policing in highly controlled traditional manufacturing environments, this was a real mind shift.

Even where management values were trusting and participative – in other words, where the mental models had already changed – making the transition to new working practices was still challenging, and involved a lot of trial, error, admitting mistakes, give and take, trying again and moving forward. Autonomy, discretion, open and trusting relationships, a philosophy of empowerment, high-performance teams and multi-skilling are all core features of the first wave of smart working.

EXISTING KNOWLEDGE

As well as the considerable body of research and literature that exists on first wave working practices, a wealth of research findings already exist on high-performance management systems (Huselid 1995, Pettigrew and Fenton 2000, Guest 2006, Tamkin et al. 2008, Totterdill et al. 2009). This is one of the components the CIPD/CAP Gemini research identified in their four-pillar framework of smart working. It may be tentatively concluded from the high-performance research that:

- A range of performance benefits are associated with high performance when they are implemented in complementary bundles of structures, processes and policies.

- Take-up of high-performance work systems is consistently low.

We already know what smart, high-performance working practices and systems look like. Too many businesses are just not putting this knowledge into practice. The elements of high-performance working will be considered in great detail in Chapter 2. It is noted for the moment that a core element of high-performance work systems is the need for businesses to invest in learning and skills development.

International research shows that a large number of business leaders are failing to create learning environments and work that people find engaging (Towers Perrin 2007). Skills, eagerness to contribute and creativity are wasted. This squandering makes no business sense at any time, but is particularly perverse in the face of relentlessly challenging global business conditions and competition from emerging economies.

Business leaders who do manage to set the initial conditions and create engaging, meaningful work through organisational design and ways of working that make the best use of the knowledge and creative potential of their workforces will be the ones who succeed in staying ahead of the game. If people's desire for learning, meaningful work and opportunities to contribute are going unheeded and ignored, this cannot be good for business. It is certainly not good for people.

Social Technologies

Social networking and collaboration technologies, including the opportunities and challenges they represent, really are new. What are these technologies? How are they used? Which technologies are used for what purposes? What are the social protocols associated with them? What implications are there for new ways of working, and what does their use imply for skills development?

Castells et al. (2007) tell us that all technologies diffuse only when they resonate with pre-existing social structures and cultural values. Social networking and digital collaboration technologies might be new, but knowledge around social and organisational issues are not. I would argue that we already know a lot about the social structures, organisational design and cultural conditions that have to exist to support these technologies in practice.

Technologies change, but people essentially do not – or if they do, they change much more slowly. Many of the people promoting Enterprise 2.0 technologies and working practices – for example, blogs, wikis, micro-blogging and discussion forums – come from a technology background. While these professionals appreciate the need to understand how people engage with their work, how they work together, and what helps or hinders this, they may not be fully aware of the abundance of well-documented research that exists around work organisation design principles that would support these new technologies in use.

Concluding Remarks

OPPORTUNITIES FOR CHANGE

A meeting of 'a group of renowned scholars and business leaders' came up with 25 'Moon Shots for Managers', ten of which were regarded as uniquely critical.[10] Many of these challenges to management practices are derived from existing theoretical perspectives. What appears not to have been reported was whether the assembled thinkers addressed why these 'uniquely critical' principles had not made more practical impact, and how they proposed to change that.

How are people to discover overlooked patterns and insights from decades of research and use it in practice for the benefit of themselves, their colleagues and their businesses? Social technologies are hugely significant in enabling us to discover long-forgotten or overlooked insights. Here is Chris Anderson, one of the authors of The Cluetrain Manifesto, talking about the 'Long Tail' in music:

> ... you can find everything out there on the Long Tail. There's the back catalog, older albums still fondly remembered by long-time fans or rediscovered by new ones. There are live tracks, B-sides, remixes, even

---

10 http://blogs.hbr.org/hbr/hamel/2009/02/25_stretch_goals_for_managemen.html [accessed: 31 March 2012].

(gasp) covers. There are niches by the thousands, genre within genre within genre ....[11]

The Long Tail does not only apply to books, films and music. There is also a long tail in academic research. Hagel et al. (2010) propose that the value of social technologies lies in the possibilities they create for connecting us to knowledge flows and collective discovering and sharing of insights for mutual advantage.

PAST REMAINS RELEVANT

It is precisely because there is so much actionable knowledge apparently being overlooked and not being heeded in practice that I wrote this book. I propose that there are first principles of organising, and that these have to be constantly assessed, interpreted and applied according to what is happening in the external environment. These include designing for adaptation, designing for complexity and designing for high performance, which are all familiar themes from the past. Designing for autonomy, integration, collaboration, and creating performance environments to enable knowledge sharing and innovation are all particular themes of lean, quality and agile. Looking backwards to inform the present would seem to be profitable.

---

11 http://www.longtail.com/the_long_tail/2005/02/index.html [accessed: 31 March 2012].

2

How Organisations Work (and Do Not Work)

Introduction

This chapter is an exploration of a number of diverse topics concerning the basics of organisations and organising, which are structured around three themes.

The first theme is a review of how organisations work, where 'how they work' is understood in the sense that people create value through the work they carry out within their networks of relationships and social interactions. The resulting relationship dynamics are highly dynamic, fluid and complex. It is therefore unsurprising that the issues arising from complex relationship dynamics include dysfunctional as well as creative behaviours. Themes arising from relationship dynamics include psychological needs, culture, emotion, power, collaboration, conflict and the influence of context.

The second theme is how organisations do *not* work. The formal systems that enterprises put in place to mediate relationship dynamics change at a much slower rate and are resistant to adaptation. The topics of control, high-performance work systems and employee engagement are explored to illustrate deep-rooted inability or unwillingness within enterprises to act on research evidence, even where business benefits are associated with specific working practices.

There is a link between the two enduring management obsessions with control, which alienates people, and the desire to increase employee engagement. Close surveillance and social control are the precise opposites of the self-determined control that is needed for high performance.

The third theme is how people have to make deliberate and determined efforts to overcome the forces of inertia that pull systems towards stability and the status quo. The suggestion is that systems adapt through reciprocal determinism, where people interact, and in the process change their environments. How people interact with their environments through 'reciprocal determinism' is a significant point that will be taken up as a thread throughout the book.

How Organisations Work

Both sides of Figure 2.1 represent a range of research and theoretical perspectives from various literatures. Rather than review vast literatures across a number of knowledge disciplines, a few key sources are concentrated on to illustrate themes.

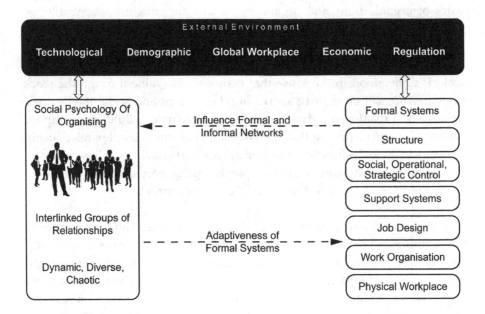

Figure 2.1   Organising dynamics and formal systems

One of the key sources consulted was Pettigrew and Fenton (2000), who have provided an enormous service by conducting a comprehensive literature review to support their 'multi-disciplinary, multi-time methods and multi-research study' into the characteristics of innovating global organisations. The following sections concentrate on the left-hand side of Figure 2.1 and review:

- how elements of organising integrate to become flows of behaviour;

- themes arising from flows of behaviour among people;

- how contexts influence flows of behaviour.

SOCIAL AND COMPLEX

Organisations are essentially dynamic networks of relationships. Weick (1979) provides strong thought leadership in understanding how complex social interactions among people play out. He speaks about organising as flows of behaviour, and describes the basic building blocks of organising in terms of 'individual behaviours interlocked among two or more people, who change each other's behaviour'.

When two people engage, he calls the act of one person responding to another an 'interact'. If the person who instigated the exchange then further responds, this is a double interact (see Figure 2.2). Weick tells us that the double interact is the stable component in organisational growth and decay, and that inter-locked behaviours are the elements that make up dynamic processes.

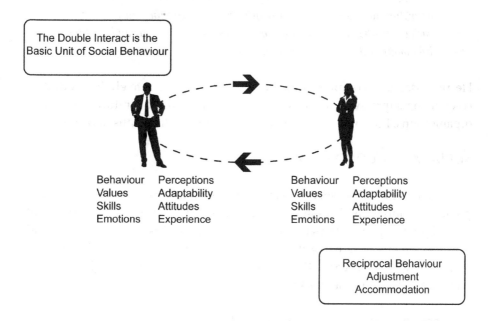

Figure 2.2   Weick's concept of the double interact

We are all individually complex to begin with, and we constantly change: our moods fluctuate, we feel more or less at ease in different places and with different people, we have sensitivities, agendas, positions to defend, cultural biases, cognitive biases, decision-making biases and personal values that influence how we communicate, how we react and so on. Add to this fluctuating and fluid personal change the influence we are able, or unable, to exert on each other and it is not difficult to see what happens when complex individuals try to communicate with and manipulate other equally complex individuals.

Weick was far from alone in focusing on the highly dynamic and social nature of human systems. Argyris and Schon (1978), for example, recognised organising as active and cognitive, and Schoderbek et al. (1975) described groups interacting within 'organised complexities', which they describe as 'phenomena composed of a very large number of parts that interact in a non-simple way'.

Conceptualising social organisations as complex adaptive systems is well-trodden ground (Stacey 1996, Dooley 1997, Palmberg 2009). Stacey explains complex adaptive systems as:

> A number of components, or agents, that interact with each other according to sets of rules that require them to examine and respond to each other's behaviour in order to improve their behaviour and thus the behaviour of the system they comprise.

He proposes that complex adaptive systems can alternatively be viewed as co-evolving supra-systems, which 'learn their way into the future'. Too many organisations, however, are not adaptive. The pull of the status quo is strong.

SOCIAL AND NETWORKED

Weick makes the important observation that relationships are the crucial control point in organisations. This insight is fundamental to a number of different but related process perspectives of organising. Relationships and interactions, and the events they create being the basic elements of organising, lead inevitably to consideration of organisations as value-creating entities through processes, knowledge flows and networks.

Denison's critique of process-based perspectives of organisations is comprehensive and useful (Denison 1997). As well as summarising the emergence and development of a range of process perspectives, he sets them within the context of the value chain: managing, organising and designing it.

The value chain concept, originating in Porter's work on competitive strategy (Porter 1985), is about how enterprises systematically organise resources, people, business units and partnerships with suppliers to deliver customer value. According to Dennison, an organisation has to 'first define a value chain, and then to establish the relationships to exploit these potential advantages in the workplace'. More recently, Osterwalder and Pigneur (2010) talk about business model innovation, rather than value chains, 'embracing new and innovative models of value creation'.

VALUE NETWORKS

According to Denison, managing the value chain is concerned with control and innovation – for example, eliminating waste from processes and applying quality approaches through continuous improvement and problem-solving. As Denison admits, the distinction between managing and organising the value chain is 'fuzzy'. He nevertheless defends the inclusion of the category in his analysis because: 'An important insight is introduced: the value chain is fluid and abstract, and a multitude of potential value chains exist that can deliver the same product to the same customer.'

Choice over the design of value chain is the defining feature of Denison's third category of process-based perspectives. Methods and approaches associated with designing the value chain are about configuration, flexibility, agility, customisation and differentiation. Methods include mass customisation, partnerships and alliances, knowledge networks, virtual organisations and the knowledge-based organisation.

What is really interesting now is how the process-based perspectives are evolving towards re-conceptualisation as networks (Castells 2004, Benkler 2006). Peppard and Rylander (2006) link this shift from a value chain to a value network perspective to the emergence of 'new economy' industries like telecoms. Networks are self-configurable, complex structures of inter-connected nodes that absorb and process information. Human networks communicate, co-operate and compete with each other (Castells 2004). According to Castells, knowledge and information have always been crucial sources of economic activity. He says that 'we must let the notion of an information society or of a knowledge society wither' in favour of speaking of a network society.

Castells says that re-conceptualising matters because of practical implications. Social networking and collaboration technologies enable the 'extension and augmentation of the body and mind' so that networks of interactions now have global reach. People outside businesses are connecting, self-organising and doing what they want, without leadership and at will. Social networking and collaboration technologies provide people with 'new ways to imagine our lives as productive human beings' (Benkler 2006). This includes self-directed, informal social learning and knowledge acquisition through networks and communities.

Converging trends linking knowledge networks, strategic partnerships and collaboration across multiple boundaries are driving the emergence of new value network configurations, powered by social and collaboration technologies. Considering the opportunities value networks present for creating economic value, it very quickly becomes apparent that people, their relationships, capabilities and knowledge need to be pivotally engaged in value creation processes.

Technologies are much more than communication devices, software and machines. They include methods and techniques, like those associated with managing, organising and designing the value chain. It is people working together to engage with methods and with each other – generating, sharing and applying knowledge – that really matters. It almost seems so obvious as not to be worth saying, but the focus is too often on shiny communication technologies, and not what people actually do together. Social networking and collaboration technologies draw renewed focus onto what has always been true: that business organisations are social entities first and last.

There is widespread discomfort in business circles about using the word 'social' in connection with work. Rather than avoid it, it is time to insist on using 'social' in recognition of the fact that networked, distributed and connected forms of organising are so instrumental in creating new potential for economic, customer and social value. Social relationships therefore need support and nurturing rather than to be denied. How purposeful sociability is nurtured in increasingly knowledge-intensive economies will have to become a core management capability.

Themes Arising

Many themes emerge from people's relationship with their work and with each other. These include (and the topics are in no way exhaustive): power, culture, conflict, collaboration and social learning. Returning to Weick, he recommends adopting a minimalist approach to understanding organisational dynamics. He proposes that if you can understand what happens when nine people work together, you can understand what can happens with thousands. We already know that two people create interdependence and reciprocal behaviour.

The addition of one more person increases the complexity of inter-personal dynamics. Three is a key transition point because now there is the possibility of alliances between two against one. Issues of power, control, co-operation, competition, manipulation and influence emerge. Although they already exist between two people, 'these phenomena, formerly suppressed, now become more visible and subject to manipulation and sanction' when three people interact. At seven people, groups as well as individuals form alliances and partnerships.

The next key transition is from seven to nine, when there is the possibility of coalitions between pairs of triads, groups of three, as well as within. With just nine people, it is easy to see how this complexity rapidly has potential to increase exponentially. It is unnecessary to spell out to anyone with management responsibilities – or indeed anyone who has ever worked with colleagues – that relationships at work can be fraught and the cause of many, if not most, of managers' day-to-day problems.

This is hardly surprising when we stop to consider that people who work together, and who might not otherwise have anything to do with each other, have such diverse beliefs, perceptions, interpretations, cultures, attitudes, emotions, capabilities, personalities and ways of communicating. The resulting delights or frustrations are the lived experience of everyone in the workplace. The wonder is that any productive work gets done – which, of course, it does.

PSYCHOLOGICAL NEEDS

Warr's edited collection of contributions on a range of topics associated with psychology at work is a useful place to start. This summarises a range of psychological themes connected with emotional well-being, performance, learning, job design, change, leadership and team-working. Warr (2002) identifies ten key psychologically important attributes of work associated with job-related well-being, and claims that there is 'considerable evidence for the importance of all those job features'.

Psychologically significant features include opportunities for personal control, opportunities to learn and use skills, supportive leadership, access to a safe, facilitating environment, and opportunities for social interaction and social recognition. A brief review of topics across literatures confirms that key recurrent topics are the need for autonomy and self-determination, social status, the opportunity for social support and good personal relationships, rewarding work and performance feedback. These psychological traits are inter-related and mutually reinforcing.

Rock (2009) is one among a number of management, psychology and medical researchers and practitioners who have expanded on these themes. He claims that neuroscience research is revealing the social nature of workplaces, with people seeking to minimise threat responses and maximise reward. Rock cites Professor Sir Michael Marmot's research on the health impacts of status on health, concluding that 'in short, we are biologically programmed to care about status because it favours our survival'. Status is intimately associated with position in social hierarchies, and this in turn influences the degree to which people experience autonomy, control and self-determination.

Marmot (2006) writes that he has been researching the link between the risk of early death and position in social hierarchy for almost thirty years. The accumulation of this research supports the relationship between control, social engagement, ill-health and early death, in the context of the workplace and wider societies. He says: 'As evolved beings, we are social animals ... the other important human need, after autonomy or control, is to be socially engaged.' Marmot suggests that esteem of self and others is part of social engagement, as is participation in social networks for social support and affirmation of social standing.

Warr's inclusion of opportunity to learn and use skills as a psychologically significant feature of work resonates with the management literature. The newest generation coming into workplaces the world over is causing a stir, for reasons that will be explored in Chapter 3. Among the plethora of articles and blogs discussing who they are, what they like and what they dislike there are claims, counter-claims and contradictions.

One feature on which there is consistency, and about which data is now being collected (McCrindle Research 2006, London Business School 2009, Deloitte 2009), is the fact that young people value and seek challenges. They prize opportunities for learning and development.

Valuing opportunities for learning is not unique to this new generation. A survey of 88,600 employees in 18 countries found that challenging work and opportunities for learning were the most powerful influencers of engagement (Towers Perrin 2007). Dr Marie Puybaraud, in her role as Director of Global Workplace Innovation, set out to discover what young people want from their workplaces, but she also collected data from people of other generations (Johnson Controls 2010). As with the Towers Perrin survey, opportunity for learning was found to be a key preference in choosing an employer, and this was the case across all demographics in the workplace.

A word of caution is offered at this point. Much of the research and writing about core human and psychological needs has been from a Western perspective. Are autonomy, self-determination and choice really universal human needs? Culturally derived values can shape attitudes and behaviour towards a more collective, social orientation. And even within more collective cultures, individual preferences might be strongly in the direction of self-determination.

A Russian colleague pointed out that following the financial crisis in 1997, when many lost businesses and all their money when banks collapsed – and this on top of the collapse of the Soviet Union some years earlier – people in general were not seeking autonomy. Rather, the view was that they were looking for direction and strong leadership. Was this view valid and based on informed, lived experience? The comment was not made in isolation, and was one of a number of similar opinions expressed in conversations over several years with other Russian people.

Staying with Russia, another dimension of culture – generational – arose in a heated exchange between a young executive and an older colleague. The older of the two was putting forward the view that young people had lost many of the cultural values he and people of his generation recognised. She strongly disagreed with this development, and argued for continuity of national cultural values despite fundamental changes in the wider social, political and economic environment.

CULTURE

Trompenaars and Hampden-Turner (1997) comment that culturally influenced management attitudes of even close national neighbours can be very different:

> The average Belgian manager has a family idea of the organisation. He or she experiences the organisation as paternalistic and hierarchical; father decides how it should be done. The Belgians see the Dutch manager as overly democratic; what nonsense that everybody consults everybody.

National cultural tendencies are not the whole story. They become mixed in with professional cultural identities. Norms, values and 'the way we do things around here' can be so deeply embedded within specific groups that even tactics for increasing social interaction among these groups, like physical co-location, can be ineffective.[1] Challenges in communicating across groups of knowledge specialists, which are increasingly distributed across national boundaries, are intensifying as businesses become more knowledge-based and organisational boundaries more porous.

What is it?

What is culture and how can we better understand it? Culture would appear to be an academically contested concept, with a range of perspectives, including integrationists, differentiationists, fragmentationists, interpretive perspectives, postmodern perspectives, managerially oriented and critically minded organisational researchers (Hatch 1994). For Schein (1996), culture is 'shared tacit, taken for granted, ways of perceiving, thinking and reacting'.

Schein's model (Schein 2009) proposes that culture can be visible and represented through artefacts that communicate cultural norms. Less easy to discern are cultural values that can be inferred from behaviour, and then there is a third level of culture, represented by hidden and deeply held assumptions. Schein contends that it is this hidden and deeply embedded level of culture that drives behaviour, rather than professed values.

---

1   J.H. Heerwagen, speaking at the BASS (Building and Social Science) Group, London, 2007. Minutes of the meeting available online at: http://api.ning.com/files/ErLtUFRZ0JIgwA*23 T8pdXOlyZjW5t2PRwWPvQRDVt83F4FMAgnktSwYnhSNDELSYZUyRb0LzfvGkfAfW-o3iazvLBTGHRc6/BASS1Minutes29Nov07.pdf [accessed: 8 March 2012].

Stable and dynamic

According to Hatch (2004), management thinkers tend to represent culture as stable and resistant to change. She comments that 'only a handful of organisational studies since the 1980s, when organisational culture came into its own, mentions the dynamic properties of culture', and argues persuasively that culture is both stable and dynamic.

Moffat and McLean (2010) also see culture as dynamic and socially constructed, emerging in time through participation, dialogue and shared meaning. They stress that culture is not a product; rather, it is a dynamic outcome of the struggle to live and work the way we want. Although culture is dynamic and subject to change, Schein talks about tensions between restraining forces and driving forces for change. He describes how stable cultures provide meaning, predictability and security, and the anxieties adults experience in having to unlearn current beliefs and ways of thinking.

Culture is crucial

Hofstede (1999) argues that managers and theorists have neglected to recognise the extent to which 'managing' and 'organising' are culturally dependent. Trompenaars and Hampden-Turner agree, saying that managers see culture as a 'dish on the side', when in reality a complex mix of cultural influences pervades social interactions within organisations.

EMOTION

Briner and Totterdell (2002) say that 'emotion at work is a relatively new topic within psychology' and that attention has been paid to the topic only in the past ten years. Sociology and management researchers have been more active, in their view, but Ashforth and Humphrey (1995) are critical of the attention paid to emotion in the management literature, concluding that: 'The relative neglect of the role of everyday emotion in mundane organisational life is surprising because this role has been a more or less implicit feature or research since the dawn of the human relations perspective.'

Ashforth and Humphrey note that researchers and management thinkers appear to assume that 'emotionality is the antithesis of rationality' and that the dominant tendency towards rationality has been a defence against the perceived dysfunctions of emotion. They go on to describe four ways in which emotion at work is regulated. Only a limited range of emotional responses are deemed socially acceptable in the workplace, which in turn is linked to cultural climate.

Cultures – whether societal, organisational, occupational, departmental and so on –provide beliefs about emotional states. The breadth of emotional states (fear, love, hate) and the depth of the states (that is, the number of nuances) that are included differ across cultures.

Ashforth and Humphrey have interesting observations to make on the role of leaders in influencing shared meanings to encourage engagement in co-ordinated behaviours. Hosfstede's view that culture involves manipulating symbols that have meaning for the people being managed or organised is highly relevant. Ashforth and Humphrey explain that managers communicate values and beliefs through action, interactions, use of metaphor, stories, myths and rituals. Calling this symbolic management, they say that:

> We contend that the success of symbolic management is largely dependent upon the evocation of emotion. Symbolic management is effective because it draws on the qualities of the heart and of the head – and at times, it entirely bypasses the later for the former.

The conclusion of this exploration of culture and emotion is that relationships and interactions among people are saturated with and deeply influenced by both, despite the relative neglect of both in management research and in management practice.

POWER

In his quest to promote civilised workplaces, Sutton (2007) explores abuse of power. He says that even normally well-behaved and sensitive people can turn nasty given even small amounts of power. He cites 'a huge body of research' showing that once people are put in positions of power, they become more self-centred, ignore how less powerful people react to their behaviour, and treat others as a means of getting what they want.

Bandura (1999), as an example of one of the contributions to this body of theory and research, explores how people behave towards each other within the context of 'moral disengagement' from self-sanction for inhumane treatment of other people. Although much of the paper is concerned with extreme cruelty and inhumane behaviour, like the My Lai massacre for example, Bandura also says that many things in contemporary life are conducive to impersonalisation and de-humanisation. It is through the constant reminder that we are dealing with human beings that the temptation is subdued to abdicate from personal obligation for moral behaviour.

Power and social alienation

Among conditions of the modern world that Bandura sees as contributing to social alienation are bureaucratisation, automation and urbanisation, where 'strangers can be more easily de-personalised than can acquaintances'. Interestingly, he includes geographical mobility in the list of factors that contribute to de-humanisation. Bandura also blames social practices that divide people into in-group and out-group members. He continues:

> *Under certain conditions, wielding institutional power changes the power holders in ways that are conducive to de-humanisation. This happens when persons in positions of authority have coercive power over others with few safeguards for constraining their behaviour. Power holders come to devalue those over whom they wield control.*

The physical workplace environment is becoming a crucial component of knowledge-creating systems support by providing opportunities to meet psychological and social needs – for example, social inclusion or communicating reduced power distances. The workplace can also powerfully communicate cultural values and provide opportunities for symbolic management. The emergence of the physical workplace in social knowledge generation is addressed in Chapter 6.

Abuse of power

Bandura's focus on minimising the de-humanising effects of the environment and social relations finds an echo in Sutton's solution of reducing power distances in organisations between those in power and those on whom their power has an impact. Sutton says of learning lessons from observing primates: 'When the social distance between higher- and lower-status mammals in a group is reduced and steps are taken to keep the distance smaller, high-status members are less likely to act like jerks, too' (Sutton 2007).

Abuse of power can happen at all levels and among peers. It is so insidious at the top, however, because bad behaviour at this level, and tolerance of it, sends out messages throughout the organisation about what you can get away with and creates a model for others to copy. As Garratt observes (2003), a fish rots from the head. His writing about a failure of boards to enforce effective governance was more recently addressed in the Walker review of governance in the UK banking and finance industries (Walker 2009).

In the extreme, the cost of unchecked power is the eventual viability of the business when people feel unable to challenge those in positions of power. In a statement on his experience of trying to raise his concerns over the risk profile of a UK bank, Moore said that 'there is a natural tension between the need to raise legitimate challenge on the one hand, and the likely reaction of those individuals who are the subject of the challenge', and spoke of alleged threatening behaviours by executives when he and his team were attempting to fulfil their legitimate roles.[2] He concludes that 'openness to challenge is a critical cultural necessity for good risk management and compliance'.

COLLABORATION

It follows from Weick's analysis of the social dynamics of organising that collaboration was always a core organising activity. It will become clearer in Chapter 5, which analyses current global workplace trends, why effective collaboration is now such a crucial competitive capability.

Collaboration can be challenging in the extreme. It can also be intensely rewarding. Hirsch et al. (2005) make explicit that collaboration can be an emotional roller-coaster for people, who need to be able to tolerate ambiguity and uncertainty, plus have the necessary inter-personal and political skills to mediate among conflicting perspectives and agendas. Whereas Hirsch et al. approach collaboration from a context of partnerships and alliances among networks of different organisations, Hansen (2009) explores collaboration within organisations and across organisational units.

He says that collaboration rarely happens naturally because of barriers that get put in the way, often unintentionally. This leads him to ask: 'How do we cultivate collaboration in the right way so that we achieve the great things that are not possible when we are divided?' Hansen explores 'disciplined

---

2   http://www.publications.parliament.uk/pa/cm200809/cmselect/cmtreasy/144/144w243.htm
     [accessed: 31 March 2012].

collaboration', which is: 'The leadership practice of properly assessing when to collaborate (and when not to) and instilling in people both the willingness and the ability to collaborate when required'.

One point he makes – and one that will become a core focus when we examine the conditions associated with smart working and managing – is that disciplined collaboration 'requires that organisations be centralised and yet co-ordinated'. This comment highlights the fact that a major business response in attempting to direct and control behavioural outcomes is to create underpinning structures of roles, responsibilities and distributed authorities for decision-making.

How organisations are structured does not determine behavioural outcomes, but it can create significant barriers and enablers to collaborative action, and ultimately threaten the organisation's viability. Failure of organisations to collaborate effectively with external regulatory bodies was a factor in the recent global financial crisis. It is once more being considered as a contributing factor, as questions emerge about the relationship between the regulatory bodies and the oil and gas industry in the fall-out from the BP environmental disaster in the Gulf of Mexico.[3]

Factions and group identities develop internally along functional lines within organisations. Silo mentalities lead to short-sighted and self-interested behaviours rather than behaviours in the interests of the business. Whereas failure to collaborate at an organisational level with regulatory bodies has led to excessive risk-taking, failure of collaboration within organisations is also associated with perceptions of risk that reinforce risk-averse attitudes and behaviours. While the link between risk-averse behaviour and absence of collaboration across organisational boundaries may not be direct and causal, a mentality of risk-aversion does not create fertile conditions for cross-boundary collaboration.

CONFLICT

Given the complexity of interactions among people, ambiguity and conflict are inevitable. They are also desirable and necessary for learning and adaptation, according to Dr Frances Westley[4] in a keynote address at a conference exploring Canada's response to global trends and how Canadian companies will compete

3   http://www.oilspillcommission.gov/final-report [accessed: 9 March 2012].
4   http://sig.uwaterloo.ca/people/frances-westley [accessed: 9 March 2012].

and collaborate in a workplace landscape that is becoming increasingly fluid and unpredictable. The main theme of her presentation was the need to integrate knowledge and purpose. She spoke about traditional discipline-based knowledge and the need to move to transgressive, trans-disciplinary, collaborative and reflexive knowledge-production.

The skills required to engage in new knowledge-production include deep knowledge, risk-taking, making judgements, pattern discernment, inter-personal skills, negotiation, active listening and conflict management. Dr Westley maintains that constructive conflict is a critical element in surfacing knowledge; learning how to engage with conflict is crucial.

People have to learn how to listen, negotiate and adapt. She linked collaboration and culture, saying that learning to crack the code of other cultures would have to become a core capability in engaging in collaborative knowledge-creation. People hold their beliefs deeply. Values and beliefs need to be surfaced, and people need to be aware that they work from cultural values and assumptions. Being an outsider can help people figure it out, crack the cultural codes and recognise patterns to assist integrative thinking.

CONTEXT

Contextual and environmental factors influence how people experience work and how they experience each other under different circumstances. Stress, excessive workload and time constraints are common for many. According to a European Agency for Safety and Health at Work report on stress (Milczarek et al. 2009),[5] throughout the 27 countries of the EU, for example:

> *The changing world of work is making increased demands on workers; downsizing and outsourcing, the greater need for flexibility in terms of both function and skills, increasing use of temporary contracts, increased job insecurity, higher workloads and more pressure, and poor work-life balance are all factors which contribute to work related stress. Studies suggest that stress is a factor in between 50% and 60% of all lost working days. This represents a huge cost in terms of both human distress and impaired economic performance.*

---

5   http://osha.europa.eu/en/publications/reports/TE-81-08-478-EN-C_OSH_in_figures_stress_at_work [accessed: 9 March 2012].

This was true before the global financial crisis. Unless management attitudes and behaviour begin to change, it is not unreasonable to suppose that stress and unreasonable workloads are likely to continue as organisations – especially in the public sector – face stringent cost-cutting and belt-tightening. Businesses need a different response to conducting business within challenging operating conditions such as we are currently experiencing. They need to engage with their workforces, supply networks and other stakeholders to nurture goodwill towards the business.

There are many factors inside and outside businesses that create context at any given time, and of course, context is dynamic and rapidly evolving. In an external environment that is turbulent on many fronts, business contexts are shifting at warp-speed. An optimistic perspective is that the 'great reset' (Florida 2010) presents businesses with a tremendous opportunity to rethink how they do things and to create the conditions for smart working and managing to emerge.

How Organisations Do Not Work

Relationship complexity is increasing significantly as a result of developments in the wider operating environment. Given the normal complexity of relationship dynamics within organisations and the now increasing levels of relationship complexity, what sort of formal systems do enterprises put in place to co-ordinate, facilitate and mediate complex social dynamics? How are flexibility and adaptability built in? How are formal systems configured such that they meet both the needs of people and the enterprise?

As Figure 2.1 above shows, these interacting systems are a mix of structures, processes, technologies, functional support systems and the physical workplace. To be fit for purpose, formal systems must be:

- designed in accordance with performance requirements;

- sufficiently flexible and adaptable so that they provide an effective performance environment within which complex, dynamic relationships play out;

- adaptable and congruent with the external operating environment;

- agile and emergent to keep pace with change on multiple fronts.

This section reviews evidence of the sort of formal systems enterprises typically put in place in their attempts to co-ordinate and make sense of organisational dynamics.

The assessment of effective formal systems design begins with a consideration of the influence leaders have in shaping formal organisational systems, which can be significantly influenced by the values they hold. In their international research on the characteristics of innovating organisations, Pettigrew and Fenton (2000) found that although 'innovation journeys are initiated and sustained by cocktails of internal and external pressures', leader effects in championing organising innovations could be 'highly value laden'. Two topics illustrate that those who design support systems have choices, which emanate from their beliefs about people. One is pay and remuneration, and the other is management control systems.

Pay and Remuneration

How pay and remuneration are distributed can signal values and beliefs. Sutton, commenting on the link between power and remuneration, says that remuneration is a potent symbol of power, and that reducing the scale of differences between executive pay and low-paid staff yields business benefits. Unfortunately, this is not happening.

Benkler (2009), although speaking of General Motors, could have been talking of many workplaces where bonuses are paid to attract and retain senior staff when he said that 'they incentivise at the top and monitor at the bottom'. Debates and controversy over executive pay continue to reverberate. Particularly for senior executives, in finance and other sectors, many continue to regard bonuses and high salaries as crucial in attracting talent. On the opposite side, there are growls from those who would regulate and restrict what they regard as excessive rewards.

The issue of remuneration is complicated and contested. Ghoshal (2005) was critical of agency theory, which assumes that managers act in their own divergent interests. Since their primary responsibility is to maximise shareholder value and they cannot be trusted to do this of their own volition, they have to be incentivised through bonuses and share options. He argues that theories in social sciences, through a process he describes in detail, tend to become self-fulfilling, and that bad management theories destroy good management practices.

Davis et al. (1997) propose stewardship theory as a way of explaining that divergence from company and shareholder interests might not apply to all managers. They are careful to say that they make no assumption of the inferiority or otherwise of agency theory, only that there are situations in which executives are motivated to act in the best interests of the company – to act as stewards in the best interests of the company. In this view, collective behaviours are more satisfying than individual, self-serving behaviours. It is not difficult to see that different approaches to designing rewards and remuneration could differ according to whether core values about executive behaviour were driven by an agency theory or stewardship theory perspective.

Control

Control means different things to different people, depending on the perspective and values of the person using it. Godfrey et al. (1997) demonstrated this from a manufacturing case study, where output from a machine was constantly monitored so that the final product was traceable back to a specific operator. The research team members from a human resources (HR) background thought that this demonstrated unacceptable and obtrusive surveillance. The researchers from a quality management perspective viewed the procedure as part of acceptable process control measures designed to facilitate continuous improvement.

A good place to start in looking at control is cybernetics, originally explained as the science of control and communication in the animal and the machine (Ashby 1956). Cybernetic systems are goal-seeking and self-regulating, using information to communicate among a system's components, and between the system and its environment. Control and adaptation are regulated through information about performance, which is fed back into the system and compared to pre-specified goals.

Ashby (1956) saw cybernetics as offering 'the hope of providing effective methods for the study and control of systems that are intrinsically extremely complex'. Cybernetic control can justifiably be seen as mechanistic: 'Cybernetics deals with all forms of behaviour in so far as they are regular or determinate or reproducible.'

There is nothing regular, determinate or reproducible about human behaviour within social systems. This has not stopped behaviour control from being a dominant business concern over the decades, as this quote from Tannenbaum (1968) illustrates: 'The theoretical analysis of control in social systems has a long and venerable history. Control helps circumscribe idiosyncratic behaviours and keep them conformant to the rational plan of the organisation.'

Except that it obviously does not. Behaviour control has been tried through control mechanisms that might have been appropriate for machines, but certainly not people. As Robb (1984) put it: 'An engineer who understands how to control a complex physical system also understands how to control an analogous managerial system: all he requires to do is to generalise his engineering knowledge and then transport it to his managerial problems.'

Management attempts to exert zealous control can be not only ineffective, but counter-productive. There are numerous examples of subversive rebellion on manufacturing shop floors (Delbridge 1998). According to Hitchins (1997): 'Engineering managers seem so obsessed with exerting and maintaining control that they disregard the havoc that excessive control wreaks on the business.'

TYPES OF CONTROL

Figure 2.3 summarises social, strategic and operational control.

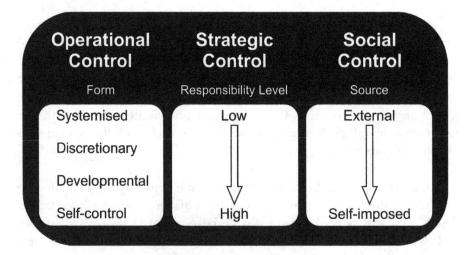

Figure 2.3   Types of control

Social control

As already noted, considerable attention has been devoted over the years to controlling behaviour (Mills 1983, Manz et al. 1987). Despite criticism of the extent to which behaviour control has been the focus of management attention over the decades, this is not to say that behaviour cannot or should not be influenced. Belief systems are often used in distributed organisations to influence enactment of core organisational values. One tactic to influence behaviour is negatively stated boundary systems that tell people what they are not allowed to do. Boundary systems give scope for innovation and are critical where trust is a key competitive asset (Simons 1995).

Social control can also be self-determined. In fact, it could be argued that all control is self-imposed. People assess external control mechanisms and decide the extent to which they will comply (Manz et al. 1987). Mills (1983) stresses that self-controlled employees remain very much controlled through self-imposed norms.

Self-control and group self-management turn out to be more controlling than anything that management could ever impose. Barker calls this 'concertive control', which is social control exerted by peers who force compliance through consensus on shared values. The combination of peer pressure and self-regulation can produce powerful social control (Barker 1993).

Individual self-control is mediated through personal disposition, psychological perceptions of control, and attitudes towards the consequences of non-compliance with performance indicators. It is also influenced by cultural tendencies. A French colleague claims that rules are there to be broken and that tax avoidance in France, if you can get away with it, is a national sport.

Strategic control

Strategic controls – internally and externally directed – keep track of the strategic position of the business, providing managers of subunits with information on performance criteria that are consistent with current strategy (Daniel and Reitsperger 1991).

Strategic control has been further categorised as informational (Picken and Dess 1997) and interactive (Osborne 1998). Informational control is used to scan and continually assess external environments to evaluate and adapt strategic assumptions, goals and objectives. Interactive control systems look inwards to operations, and are used to surface and act on strategic opportunities from monitoring activities, creating mechanisms for debate that challenges assumptions and declared objectives (Simons 1995).

Operational control

An alternative to controlling behaviour is controlling outputs. Attention is drawn here to two particular features of controlling outputs. The first is differing degrees of discretion in decision-making and the other is what constitutes an output in service-based knowledge work.

Systematised, discretionary and developmental operational control describe differing degrees of decision-making discretion (Van de Ven and Delbecq 1974). Systematised control consists of detailed procedures applied to repeatable tasks. With discretionary control, a limited range of options for action is defined in advance. Developmental control describes the greatest degree of decision-making autonomy, enabled by rules and behavioural expectations. This mode of control is most relevant for complex tasks.

Not only are attempts to micro-manage behaviour ineffective, the approach is inappropriate for complex and uncertain work (Ouchi 1977), which is increasingly the case in the knowledge economy. Output control and outcome management become more appropriate under these circumstances. As increasingly complex work becomes more mobile, flexible and distributed across time and geographical location, a key responsibility when managing and leading within mobile and distributed work environments is to ensure that people have all that they need to get on with their work when they are out of sight.

One of the objections to output control is the difficulty of identifying and measuring outputs in service and knowledge-based work, where intangible outputs related to productive relationships like conversation and feedback are important, and tangible outputs are often difficult to assess accurately. Acquiring the ability to do so is becoming a key capability in increasingly distributed workplaces.

A major sticking point in implementing home-working can be the attitude and skills of some line managers. In an interview with a senior BT executive, she said that managers had to learn to put the customer at the centre of decision-making.

As long as customer needs were met, staff had discretion to deliver work how and when they chose.[6]

OBSESSION WITH CONTROL ENDURES

A 'considerable literature' has emerged on management controls and their fit with structure and context (Selto et al. 1995), and this continues right up until the present. White et al. (2004) concluded from the Future of Work research, which was conducted over a period of six years and involved 22 universities in the UK, that:

> One area where ICT is rapidly expanding management choices is in monitoring and control systems. If ICT-based control continues to be seen as a management prerogative, and the monitoring information is not shared with employees, then this is likely to become a divisive and damaging issue.

Evidence of continuing interest in control comes from a 2007 *McKinsey Quarterly* article on informal networks in organisations, which 'typically fly under management's radar, they elude control' and 'the greatest limitation of these ad hoc arrangements (informal networks) is that they can't be managed' (Lowell et al. 2007). Of course, control and co-ordination are entirely valid management concerns. It is how these processes are designed and monitored that matters. It is a mistake to see social systems as deterministic and biddable.

Feedback 'pushes a fluid, changeable system towards a goal' and 'is a way of transforming a complex system into a complex adaptive system' (Johnson 2001). People don't always follow rules, though, and they can choose, intentionally and unintentionally, to disregard feedback (Nadler 1977). This is important. The distinction between feedback in mechanical and social systems is that it does not automatically create change in social systems.

The volume of writing on control and the fact that it can be traced back decades is an indication that attempting to maintain control is problematic and is an illusion. Management fears about losing control (Fenton-O'Creevy 1996) are misplaced since they never had control in the first place. As argued below in the discussion about shadow systems, people will take control for themselves if they are officially denied self-determination.

---

6   South East England Development Agency (SEEDA) Healthy Working Centres research conducted by the Centre for Working Life Research, Kingston University, 2004.

Tannenbaum was prescient in claiming that control is not a zero-sum game. There is not a fixed quantity of control within organisations. Devolving control to others does not result in a loss of control at higher management levels – in fact, it is deemed to be a control-enhancing action (Tannenbaum 1968: 20). Paradoxically, managers need to let go if they want to gain control. People will do the monitoring and co-ordinating for them.

The role of leaders and managers is to influence the environment that allows people to self-manage and to co-ordinate their outputs. Many enterprises seem doomed repeatedly to design and impose control systems that are based on mechanistic assumptions in the face of overwhelming evidence that people choose whether to comply or not, or appear to comply and use 'consent and evade' tactics.[7]

CONTROL AND AUTONOMY

One of the management values that the CIPD associates with smart working is 'a high degree of individual freedom to act, discretion and autonomy in work practice'. We saw in Chapter 1 that personal autonomy and self-determination are widely seen as essential for emotional, physical and psychological health.

Besides being psychologically desirable, operational responses to current workplace trends commonly include calls for increased workforce autonomy, with the need to shift from command and control to greater degrees of freedom, flexibility and collaboration (CIPD 2008a). Similarly, in an article commenting on a survey on knowledge work, Brinkley said that companies should aim for 'more autonomy for people and less intensive management'.[8]

Maintaining a balance between autonomy and control has long been an understandable management concern (Baker 1994, Brown and Brown 1994, Kinlaw 1995, Simons 1995, Robinson 1997). Evidence from a number of sources suggests that management obsession with exerting control endures, and runs counter to workforce needs for autonomy and self-determination.

---

7   V. Newman, at the Henley KM Forum 10th anniversary conference: 'Celebrating Connections: Evocations and Provocations for the Future', 2010.
8   http://www.hrreview.co.uk/articles/hrreview-articles/hr-strategy-practice/businesses-urged-to-give-employees-more-autonomy-and-less-intensive-management/2179 [accessed: 31 March 2012].

RIGID CONTROL SYSTEMS

Pearson et al. (2010) conclude that there is a major problem in adapting to agile working environments because 'the tools for getting things done, like business processes, people and support systems, are too rigid and static'. The relative unresponsiveness of organisational and behavioural systems is noted in other articles and research studies.

British businesses have unusually high rates of technological adoption, but 'lower than average ability to achieve the managerial innovations that could exploit it to the full'.[9] This echoes a conclusion from the Future of Work research which was referenced earlier. Taylor (2002) reports dramatic take-up of communication technologies in a wide range of jobs and occupations, but less dramatic advances in the management of people.

Poor capability in managing and engaging people is not just an issue for enterprises in the UK. The Towers Perrin survey referenced earlier reported widespread failure of businesses to create engaging, high-performance work systems (Towers Perrin 2007). Skills, eagerness to contribute and creativity are wasted. This squandering makes no business sense at any time, but is particularly perverse in the face of relentlessly challenging global business conditions and competition from emerging economies.

Castells (2004) maintains that 'technology can only yield its promise in the framework of cultural, organisational and institutional transformations'. This is where the problem starts for many organisations seeking to shape new behaviours through technologies. Too many organisational cultures are still characterised by obsession with control, along with inability or unwillingness to act on research findings even where business benefits are demonstrated. A review of research on high-performance work systems and employee engagement in the following sections will illustrate this.

High-performance Work Systems

The CIPD/CAP Gemini reports on smart working identify high-performance work systems as one of the elements of their four-pillar model. The high-performance work practices they specify include:

---

9   Mobile Work Futures research for Microsoft, conducted by the futurelaboratory, January 2007.

- a philosophy of empowerment;

- investment in skills development and talent enhancement;

- high levels of employee engagement.

The first wave of smart working practices was founded on a philosophy of empowerment, and issues arising from this are discussed in much greater detail in Chapter 3. This review of the high-performance work systems research focuses on what others say high-performance systems are and the performance benefits claimed for them. Despite corroborating evidence from a range of sources of business benefits, take-up of high-performance work systems is low.

How systems are designed influences behaviour. According to Senge (1993), 'systems cause their own crises, not external forces or individuals' mistakes'. Conversely, systems do not cause high performance, but they do set the initial conditions for high performance to emerge. Research supports the facilitating influence of systems. For example, a large-scale survey on attracting and engaging talent that collected responses from 88,600 people in 18 countries found that the organisation, 'a whole system of leadership, learning, empowerment and corporate social responsibility', is the most powerful influence on what people find engaging about their work (Towers Perrin 2007).

Although there are diverse views on what constitutes high-performance working, two recurring themes in the literature are consistent. These are that the take-up of high-performance work systems is low, and that the range of practices that make up these systems increase in effectiveness when implemented together as bundles of practices and support strategies. Pettigrew and Fenton (2000) found nine indicators of change, encompassing structures, processes and boundaries. Organised in a mutually supporting and holistic way, they are associated with superior business results. In their words, doing more of one thing increases the returns from doing more of another. Pettigrew and Fenton call these change indicators 'complementarities'.

Interestingly, Pettigrew and Fenton found evidence of negative performance outcomes when complementary structures and processes are approached unsystematically and in piecemeal fashion. The mutually supporting aspect of bundles of complementary strategies and systems is supported in other research studies. Huselid (1995), for example, suggests that performance benefits occur where HR interventions and policies are implemented together, and has published a table summarising the outcomes of 158 studies published between 1995 and 2003 that explore the link between firm performance and human resource management systems. Indicators include operational performance, staff turnover, quality, productivity, job satisfaction, innovation and profitability. While some of the studies showed no effects or weak effects, the majority did show performance effects.

More recently, Tamkin et al. (2008) conducted a review of existing research on high-performance work systems. The theoretical framework they used was constructed from an 'extensive' literature review, and resulted in what they call the 4A Model, incorporating 12 indicators of access, ability, attitude and application. The indicators are: access (recruitment, roles and succession planning), attitude (engagement, involvement and motivation), ability (skills, learning and development) and application (business strategy, organisational structure, environment, job design and work environment). Tamkin et al. similarly conclude that: 'Organisations that adopt an integrated range of HR practices are likely to perform better on key indicators like profit and sales growth.'

As well as being significant for their link to superior business performance, complementarities are also crucial in negotiating what Pettigrew and Fenton call 'dualities'. Thompson (1998) prefers to talk about 'paradoxes' to describe these phenomena. These are conflicting demands that need to be met. Pettigrew and Fenton found that ability to accommodate dualities successfully was a key characteristic of innovating organisations, meaning that people constantly had to make decisions in the face of multiple dilemmas and deploy integrative thinking skills that are akin to having an 'opposable mind' (Martin 2007). Examples of dualities are given in Table 2.1.

Table 2.1   Examples of dualities

Hierarchies and networks	Stability and innovation
Standardising and customising	Centralise and decentralise
Control and autonomy	Order and disorder
Continuity and change	Complexity and simplicity
Diversity and common vision	Conflict and agreement

It is commonly assumed that hierarchy was a dominant twentieth-century structural form, whereas in reality multiple forms of organising like networks and hierarchies have simultaneously co-existed within innovating organisations. In practice, structures are connected with the values and visions of the chief executive and senior management, whose attitudes and beliefs significantly influence choice of policies, processes and work practices.

Guest (2006) describes high-performance work systems as typically having four core components, which are in line with the Tamkin et al. 4A Model: building workforce competence, creating environments and jobs that provide people with opportunities to contribute, workforce motivation for continuous learning, and organisational commitment.

He places great emphasis on the ability and willingness of the workforce to learn continually and for enterprises to encourage this, since it is a core organisational competency for business effectiveness and is also the mechanism for creating meaningful, challenging and psychologically satisfying work for people. He says that organisations that invest in their workforces are unwilling to see the investment wasted, and therefore demonstrate commitment to their people through setting realistic expectations and meeting them, and providing indications that people are valued. A key indicator is job design: 'Jobs should be designed, either singly or in team-based groups to provide sufficient autonomy, control and responsibility to make full use of knowledge and skills, and to permit on-going learning and adjustment.'

Guest points out that the concept of reciprocal organisational commitment is complex because people have competing commitments to family, friends and a life away from the workplace. A really interesting phenomenon to note is young people coming into the workplace, who have yet another source of commitment – their social networks. According to digital ethnographer danah boyd, young people are committed to, even addicted to, their personal social networks (boyd 2007).

EMPLOYEE ENGAGEMENT

Engagement is an outcome of the strength of feeling we have towards work, our colleagues and our physical surroundings, all of which interact in non-simple ways. It is influenced by having the opportunity, desire and the right sort of environments to allow us to connect with work and each other: 'It is a concept that places flexibility, change and continuous improvement at the heart of what it means to be an employee and an employer in a twenty-first century workplace' (CIPD 2008c).

Engagement is a topic that is attracting a lot of attention. Although it is being treated here as a separate topic, it is synonymous with Guest's organisational commitment component of high-performance work systems. Like high-performance working, it is difficult to find agreement on how it is defined. In fact, in a report for the UK government on employee engagement, Guest suggests that engagement 'needs to be more clearly defined or it needs to be abandoned' (MacLeod and Clarke 2010). MacLeod and Clarke comment that there is too much good work and momentum in the UK to let it go. They believe it is helpful to see engagement as: 'A workplace approach designed to ensure employees are committed to organisation's goals and values, motivated to contribute to organisational success, and are able at the same time to enhance their own sense of well-being'.

They stress that engagement is two-way. Organisations, they say, must work to engage employees. MacLeod and Clarke's report makes the business case for engagement. Like high-performance work systems, they provide evidence of a positive link with performance and innovation, but say that there is an 'engagement deficit' in the UK.

LOW LEVELS OF ADOPTION

Take-up of high-performance working practices is low (Guest 1996). Tamkin et al. (2008) state: 'The doubts of practitioners reflect concerns over what it might mean for individual firms and sectors, and confusion over which people management practices are likely to show the greatest link to performance.'

Guest considers why the prevalence of high-performance work systems is so low, highlighting as possible reasons a lack of management awareness of the concept, and the fact that high-performance work systems challenge management skills and capabilities. He comments that high-performance management 'is a complex business', and identifies job design and skills development as good places to start in efforts to increase take-up of high-performance work systems. Job design, he says, is the cornerstone of high-performance working.

This is indeed a problem. In one of the CIPD reports (2008b) on smart working, approximately 10 per cent strongly agreed that their company deliberately designed job roles that reflected high-performance and smart working principles. A little over 35 per cent of respondents 'somewhat agreed'. The report's authors admit that they found this one of the most surprising results.

Reciprocal Determinism

In Bandura's social cognitive view of human activity, events are the outcomes of continuously interacting behavioural, cognitive and environmental influences, which are inter-locked and mutually shaped (Bandura 1978).

This 'reciprocal determinism' is a core feature of Bandura's work, whose stance is very much in opposition to behaviourist theorists who believe that behaviour is causally determined by what is happening in the environment so that the environment becomes 'an autonomous force that automatically orchestrates and controls behaviour'.

Bandura disputes this. Although the environment does influence behaviour, people choose through cognition what they want to see and how they perceive their environment. He proposes that people learn in four ways:

1. **actively** – by doing and experimenting;

2. **vicariously** – by watching other people's experiences;

3. **socially** – through conversation and by listening to the judgements of others;

4. **logically** – by developing rules of inference and deriving new knowledge from reasoning.

As Bandura says: 'by their actions, people play a role in creating the social milieu and other circumstances that arise in their daily transactions'. Self-regulating, self-organising and self-reflecting are core concepts in his accounts of the constantly shifting, mutually adapting and dynamic engagements of people with each other and their environments. Bandura points out that complex interaction among behaviour, cognition and environment lead to probabilistic rather than deterministic outcomes. If what Bandura proposes is valid, then this means that people are not prisoners of rigid systems, and that they can adapt their environments through their actions.

SHADOW SYSTEMS

Stacey's position is consistent with Bandura's processes of 'reciprocal determinism'. He proposes that an organisation's legitimate system is the sum of the officially sanctioned formal systems and control mechanisms. Shadow systems, on the other hand, are informal and can be influenced, but they are beyond the control of an organisation's formal management systems. He says that every organisation possesses a shadow system of unofficial and spontaneous relationships among people, who are engaged in self-determined actions directed towards self-seeking objectives that can support or sabotage the legitimate system.

Destructive activities can take place within shadow systems. Treat people badly and coercively control them and they will wreak their revenge through resistance and non-compliance. Cause and effect become intertwined, and it is not difficult to see that even more repressive and equally ineffective legitimate behavioural control measures might be the response. Shadow systems can also be creative. This is what Stacey says about them: 'I am arguing, then, that it is primarily the state of the shadow system that determines whether or not an organisation operates in the space for creativity ... the space for creativity lies at the the edge of disintegration or anarchy.'

Shadow systems depend on prevailing organisational cultures, how people are treated, and how formal systems support self-directed, creative action. People will connect and communicate within informal networks at will and as they see fit, with or without technology. Politics, jockeying for position, cliques, cabals, skulduggery, the exercise of subversive power, resistance, creativity, collaboration – it's all there in the dynamic, self-organising shadow system. Stacey comments that there is a 'murky relationship between legitimate structures and shadow systems ... the shadow system is in effect, seeking to destroy the current legitimate system in the interest of creativity and thus better long-term prospects of survival'.

He describes a state of tension between the legitimate system, which is an organisation's dominant schema, and the recessive schema of the shadow system. Given management preoccupation with control, it is not unreasonable to conclude that the creative dynamic of the shadow system is easily impeded by the dominance of the legitimate system. This has significant implications for smart working. Creating informal learning environments, providing appropriate technologies and allowing time to experiment would have to be key characteristics of systems to support smart working. In reality, this might prove to be a real challenge for many organisations.

Shadow systems and social technologies

One of the consequences of social networking technologies is that they potentially make visible previously hidden shadow networks. This creates opportunity for social relationships to be monitored on social networking sites or by using social network analysis technologies, which allow companies to monitor information flows and manage expertise.

Connections and key themes can be extracted from information from a range of sources, including documents, email, instant messaging, wikis, blogs, RSS and other social data sources. These are then used to try to map information flows across the organisation (Puybaraud and McEwan 2008).

Laseter and Cross (2007) describe how a number of large corporations have used understanding of social network analysis to engineer social relationships. They take the view that 'real-world experience suggests that social networks should be actively managed', and managers ought to apply the same rigour, time and attention to designing human connections that they apply to capital and technological investments. They report significant business advantage from connecting people and physically relocating experts to influence cross-pollinated knowledge transfer across organisational boundaries and geographical regions.

There are ethical considerations in monitoring, mapping and influencing people's relationships. As part of the legitimate system, explicit attempts to use technology to surface connections, and influence network structures and dynamics requires a management culture characterised by trust, transparency, communication and commitment. Otherwise people will by-pass the organisation's communications platforms in favour of communicating through the technologies they carry around in their pockets.

Using social and collaboration technologies, the possibility now exists to link leaders who want to initiate change to communities of peers outside their organisations where they can find information and emotional support. The learning and support they gain within these external communities, which Hagel et al. (2010) call 'creation spaces' can then be taken back into their workplaces to change performance environments for the sake of themselves and their colleagues, and to the benefit of the business.

Concluding Remarks

This chapter has stressed that organisations are complex, dynamic, interacting systems of networks of human relationships. Value is both created and destroyed through these culturally influenced, emotionally driven social relationships. The formal systems enterprises put in place to mediate social activity tend to be rigid and resistant to change.

Widely publicised, high-profile examples of corporate and government agency failures are testament to the fact that adaptation of formal systems in response to environmental change is not easy to achieve. High-performance working practices are well-documented, but largely overlooked in practice. Instead, tried and tested good practices and first principles are overlooked in favour of a search for novelty.

The ability to anticipate and respond to developments in the external business environment, under conditions where uncertainty and turbulence have become the norm, is now a core organisational capability. The low take-up of high-performance work systems and associated low levels of employee engagement globally suggests that stable patterns of behaviour are not easily overcome.

If Bandura and Stacey are right that people can influence formal systems and their work environment through informal, shadow network activity, then this is now more possible than it has ever been. Social networking and collaboration technologies are providing people with unprecedented opportunity for self-determined and self-initiated learning through online creation spaces (Hagel et al. 2010). According to Hagel et al., creation spaces are: 'Environments that effectively integrate teams within a broader learning ecology so that performance accelerates as more participants join in … they emerge as ecosystems across institutions rather than within a single institution'.

Through cross-boundary creation spaces, people can now discover knowledge, design principles, research, insight, peers and approaches that will enable them to learn how to experiment with emergent changes to the performance environment within the part of the enterprise over which they have influence. This is not easy, but it is possible.

Creating the next wave of smart working begins with discovering relevant knowledge and then putting it into practice. The next two chapters seek to demonstrate the continuing relevance of practical insights and theoretical knowledge from first wave smart working approaches. In particular they explore the principle of requisite variety, which suggests that skills and capabilities must be significantly enhanced to counter environmental complexity, and control through improvisation within minimally prescribed principles. This is followed by a review of current global trends that are driving the need to engage in a second wave of smart working, made possible by the phenomenal knowledge-creating and sharing potential of social technologies.

3

First Wave Smart Working

Introduction

This chapter looks at what can be learned from the process control and innovation systems and methods that filtered through to Western manufacturing companies from the mid-1980s onwards, as they struggled to catch up with the competitive advantages the Japanese were achieving through work organisation and business process innovation. High-profile people and business publications are suggesting remedies and approaches to current competitive pressures and environmental turmoil that have been tried in the past. This means that a legacy of learning already exists.

Vineet Nayar, CEO of the Indian IT services company HCL, is gaining recognition for transforming the business through a radical 'Employees First, Customers Second' philosophy. He talks about the value zone being where customer value is created. He says: 'In traditional companies, the value zone is often buried deep inside the hierarchy and the people who create value work there' (Nayar 2010).

The value zone in the first wave was on the shop floor. Nayar is reported in an article in the *Financial Times* as also saying:

> *The era of employee empowerment is on us and businesses need to harness the skills of their workforce to improve productivity and meet customer needs. This is created by giving front line employees the responsibility to take action that will benefit the customer without layers of bureaucratic approval.*[1]

---

1   'Should companies measure well-being?', 1 December 2010. http://www.ft.com/cms/s/0/ffa62c28-fcea-11df-ae2d-00144feab49a.html [accessed: 27 July 2012].

There is a plethora of sources on how manufacturing enterprises designed organisational structures and support systems to create performance environments for empowered working practices. Some of these are referenced in this review of what we can learn from the first wave of knowledge-based process innovation. Similarly, Hamel and Breen (2007) propose that three of the most pressing challenges facing businesses today are:

1.   adapting to the pace of change;

2.   making innovation everyone's job;

3.   creating a highly engaging work environment that inspires employees to give the best of themselves.

Making innovation everyone's job through continuous improvement is a core requirement of lean and quality, as is creating a highly engaging work environment that inspires employees. It was recently suggested that 'substantial, scalable and sustainable gains are achievable by focusing on the "soft" side of lean, which is being linked to a "new era in management"' (Fine et al. 2008).

It is hard to see why this is news, and it is also hard to appreciate how it is possible to engage in lean practices effectively without integrating a culture of innovation and collaboration within everyone's jobs. How to make innovation everyone's job and how to create high-performance work environments are key lessons from lean, quality and agile manufacturing.

This chapter will begin by describing the global competitive pressures that led to the emergence of process control and innovation approaches, moving on to describe briefly the common characteristics that these approaches share. Drawing on a literature review and interviews from three case study enterprises, it will make an initial assessment of the legacy of learning from that time.

Particular attention will be paid to what can be learned about making innovation everyone's business, workforce empowerment, and issues involved in the adoption of lean approaches, since these topics are prominent among recommendations for what we should be doing to adapt to challenges and opportunities arising from current global competitive pressures.

Global Competitive Pressures

The external business environment for manufacturers was already highly pressured two decades ago by a series of factors, including:

- customisation

- time-based competition

- globalisation

- cost competition

- customer demands for quality (McEwan 1999)

Expectations of access to low-cost, quality products were leading to time-based competition. Designing, producing and introducing a rapidly evolving mix of easily customisable products to market before competitors had become urgent. This in turn was leading to short product life cycles (Stalk 1988, Stalk and Hout 1990, Hun and Sim 1996) and rapid diffusion of innovation through supply networks across countries. The consequence was that as new manufacturing technologies and work systems were adopted, costs were cut at each stage of the product life cycle, intensifying cost competition. Adapting to competitive pressures and creating product variety was made possible by advancements in technology and process innovation.

Globalisation of distributed manufacturing was putting additional pressure on manufacturers to achieve product variety and quality at no additional cost. Throughout the 1980s and beyond, Japanese electronics and automotive producers led the quality movement by delivering high-quality products at competitive prices (Dean and Susman 1989). The rest of the world's manufacturers had to recognise that there was no longer a trade-off between cost and quality. Building low-cost quality into products and processes that were environmentally acceptable had become compulsory.

Just-in-time, Total Quality and Agile

Manufacturers began to realign traditional organisational structures and operational processes to respond to market needs. Work philosophies and methods associated with lean, just-in-time (JIT), total quality management (TQM) and agile manufacturing were adopted to generate cross-functional process control and innovation. Although there was wide variation in the extent to which management structures and production processes were reconfigured, common features of new approaches to manufacturing included:

- reintegrating manual and mental labour, separated in traditional manufacturing;

- focusing on quality throughout all organisational systems;

- continuous innovation and active workforce participation in problem-solving;

- elimination of waste;

- inter-dependent, multi-skilled teams;

- workflow integration;

- customer focus (both internal and external);

- process simplification;

- measurement systems;

- reducing working inventory;

- increasing the skills and flexibility of the workforce;

- continuous improvement as an enterprise-wide capability (Womack et al. 1990, Kenney and Florida 1993, Cappelli and Rogovsky 1994, Rodrigues 1994, Caffyn and Bessant 1995, Hill and Wilkinson 1995, Lewis and Lytton 1997).

Case Studies

Marchington (1995) advises caution in evaluating published accounts of new ways of working. Failures are under-represented, and apparent successes may not be sustainable. Bearing this in mind, interviews from two case studies and participation in a small manufacturing firm in transition to a new performance culture provide additional insights to support the literature review, all of which constitute a legacy of learning.

CASE STUDY 1

The first enterprise is a medium-sized manufacturing facility in the UK, which makes a range of components that are supplied to other manufacturers. Its products have an excellent reputation, and the company had at that time won a number of awards. The company was structured around three product areas, each with different process characteristics: for example, continuous high-volume in one production area and batch production requiring changes of machine set-ups in another.

The company structure remained traditional, with a clear separation between management and shop floor. Unlike many manufacturing companies that embark on a transition to new ways of working, this company was not in crisis. Rather, the drive to commit to quality was in recognition that the company would not survive in world markets in the long run without it and there was a constant need to consider cost-effectiveness.

Continuous improvement in this company was not integrated into normal tasks, but in Lindberg and Berger's terminology, was parallel (Lindberg and Berger 1997). A number of process innovation teams were allocated to specific parts of the business, made up of management representatives and the team leaders. One day a week was allocated as an innovation day to consider improvement suggestions, monitor the progress of improvements in progress and generally to maintain continuous improvement momentum.

The person championing continuous improvement and quality was the production director, whose commitment to open communication was a driving force in the business. He believed that constant feedback on production issues was key to building trust between management and the shop floor. This was consistently mentioned and appreciated in conversations with operators. This culture of openness was put to the test when continuous improvement was first introduced. Management thought it had prepared well, taking management teams off-site for training well in advance. What the senior team had not anticipated was how enthusiastically the shop floor operators would respond, which they did.

The volume of suggestions received was overwhelming. The traditional functional structure created challenges for integrating improvement activities across functions. Engineering, which interfaces with production, found that it could not cope with the volume of work created by continuous improvement, and management had not put in place a process for evaluating production operator responses. The failure of the first round of factory-wide innovation activities was initially greeted by a 'What else did we expect?' reaction from the shop floor. The production director apologised and admitted management's mistake. His forthrightness won people round.

There was no increased autonomy or self-determination for production operators. What there was instead was a performance culture characterised by trust, openness, recognition, personal development and confidence-building. The production director spoke about his responsibilities for 'soft' issues, nurturing leadership among the team leaders and ensuring that people saw rewards for their efforts.

He said that middle managers can make or break a change initiative, and believed that building trust and confidence in leadership at the top and nurturing distributed leadership throughout the rest of the company was crucial. True to his belief in the philosophy of continuous improvement, he concluded that although the culture was open, there was room for improvement, and he thought that efforts to include the whole workforce were not as effective as they could be.

CASE STUDY 2

The second case study enterprise supplied high-technology equipment to a global export market. It was also medium-sized, and at the time employed around three hundred people. The industry sector had been in recession for several years, and this was causing severe problems. the sustained strength of sterling had exacerbated these difficulties. Senior management had made redundancies months prior to the interviews.

Quality, lean processes and continuous improvement were being introduced into a context where management had previously been centrally controlled and autocratic. Key aims were to reduce inventory and manufacturing lead times. The factory had been extensively restructured into zones, and each zone further divided in a cellular configuration. Team leaders of production cells reported to zone managers. The production director had a key role in co-ordinating activities among the zones. Whereas in the last example the production director was championing the change effort, it was in this case the human resources director.

Among many issues this company was facing, just three are selected for discussion: attempts to control behaviour through crude performance measures without engaging and communicating with the workforce, achieving simultaneous autonomy and centralised co-ordination, and the challenge of communication horizontally and vertically.

A number of key performance measures were prominently posted around the factory, including in reception. This was a source of contention and a focal point for operator grievances. Widespread cynicism was expressed about their value. One senior manager said that that the company had a 'terrible reputation abroad' for quality. Everyone understood what the problems were. The view was that the measures were on display for potential customers, to give the impression that this was a company committed to quality. The performance measures included a high proportion of 'soft' indicators designed to influence behaviour, which were used to assess salary reviews. These measures were included in the selection criteria for redundancy. Apart from the detrimental effect this had throughout the workforce, operators generally regarded the measures as peripheral to core activities.

Zone managers had high degrees of freedom in the manufacturing cells under their responsibility. This autonomy was creating problems for the production director, who had to integrate all production activities. The zone managers had expectations of independence, and they perceived any attempt at standardisation as a threat to their autonomy. The production director described the process of co-ordination as being like 'herding cats'.

Communication was a real problem at the factory, where the culture was one where soft skills were perceived as 'namby-pamby'. Training in technical skills was good, but education in leadership and people management was poor. This created significant frustrations in communicating through multiple levels within the organisation, in terms of both strategic policy issues and day-to-day management. Senior management was seen to be out of touch, and middle managers were not communicating upwards.

Despite the challenging conditions, there was evidence that individual managers at all levels were continually evaluating processes, learning and adapting. As one person interviewed put it, there was informal willingness to pull together 'to put things right'. Formal systems and organisational culture did not support these informal efforts.

CASE STUDY 3

The last case study concerns a small company that at the time employed fewer than thirty people, which manufactured a variety of short-run components. It had been acquired by its innovative parent company because the range of products it manufactured was complementary. The parent company was much larger, had been family-owned for more than fifty years, and the managing director and finance director had been friends since childhood. It was a stable business that was growing year on year at a time when manufacturing in general had been experiencing difficulties.

The subsidiary had inherited the sitting managing director, who was set in his ways and not running the business well. He soon parted company, which allowed the owners to employ a young engineer as the new managing director. The situation he took over was chaotic. There was no manufacturing discipline, and work was loaded onto machines at the start of the day according to which customer was creating the most fuss. The day proper typically began mid-morning, once the panic was over. The aim in working with the company was to begin the process of moving traditional manufacturing mindsets to thinking and acting in accordance with the principles of quality and just-in-time.

The main objectives were to improve on-time delivery, reduce work-in-progress, reduce inventory and eventually introduce just-in-time. Before anything could be done, the factory had to be cleared of the mess it had become. This was very satisfying, and it had a psychological effect on people. Implementing basic scheduling meant that customers were no longer creating anxiety for the operators. They could get on with the business of manufacturing, and the new managing director could get on with putting in place systems and processes.

Identifying who would become the team leaders and developing them was a crucial early step. Until then, the machine operators had never been included as part of the business, nor had they been expected to contribute. It soon became clear that several of the operators were able and willing to be nominated. One of them was particularly skilled in influencing people, which was especially useful in dealing with resistant operators. The team leaders were involved in deciding appropriate performance measures, as well as gathering, interpreting and acting on information. Regular production meetings were also initiated for the first time.

Over the two-year period of working with the company, operating costs were reduced significantly and objectives were achieved in delivering on time to customers. Equally importantly, performance became more proactive than reactive, which was set in motion by the managing director demonstrating behaviour he expected to see and by the team leaders doing the same. Together they communicated expectations, as well as influencing, involving and persuading. As in Case Study 2, performance indicators and consequences for non-compliance were in place, but it was constant engagement and discussion with operators that began the shift towards a new performance culture over time.

Legacy of Learning

The literature review and the case studies reveal a legacy of learning that falls broadly into three main themes:

1.   creating business value through continuous improvement and empowerment;

2.   factors that enable participation in continuous improvement, problem-solving and knowledge-sharing;

3.   the challenge of making the transition to new ways of working.

The rest of this chapter is devoted to an analysis of each of these themes, beginning with creating business value through continuous improvement and empowerment.

Creating Value

Much is being written about the move from industrial to knowledge-based economies, as though manufacturing is not knowledge work. The literature review and case studies confirm that technical knowledge (which is often tacit), process knowledge, social skills developed through cross-functional collaboration, and willingness to engage in problem-solving and process innovation were the foundations of knowledge-based competitive advantage.

INNOVATION AS CORE PHILOSOPHY

Continuous improvement was a core philosophy in first wave smart working. Performance effectiveness was sought through systemic, enterprise-wide and sustained incremental innovation. Improvement activities were supported by policies and systems to encourage participation.

A commitment to continuous improvement through small-step improvements translated cumulatively into organisation-wide capability (Caffyn and Bessant 1995). Operators were expected to be responsible for both performance and innovation, which involved everyone to participating in process innovation and problem-solving. This was often the first time many shop floor operators were invited to participate, since their tacit knowledge had been previously undervalued and overlooked.

Parallel continuous improvement

Continuous improvement activities were either parallel and separate from normal work, or integrated within workflows (Lindberg and Berger 1997). These types of continuous improvement activities are typically facilitated by permanent problem-solving teams, whose role it is to act as a resource to the rest of the enterprise. They deploy specialist expertise through systematic methods and help the rest of the workforce take responsibility for identifying, assessing and evaluating opportunities for innovation. This was the approach to continuous improvement in Case Study 1.

Integrated continuous improvement

Integrated continuous improvement is designed into normal work (Lindberg and Berger 1997). Operators are expected to perform their operational tasks, and simultaneously constantly seek opportunities for task and process improvement. Performance criteria would reflect expectations of participation in innovation. This was the dominant form of continuous improvement in Case Studies 2 and 3, supplemented by temporary ad hoc groups to solve extraordinary problems.

Performance indicators

Cynicism about the performance indicators in Case Study 2 was related to their perceived relevance and imposition. Dismissal of their value was widespread throughout the factory. Their acceptance in the other case studies, especially Case Study 3, was because they were used to monitor progress through regular production meetings and workforce involvement – particularly of team leaders.

Financial benefits

The value of employee contributions through continuous improvement activities can be considerable. Shapiro (1998) reported savings of $13 million over a three-year period at one plant of Caterpillar Tractors. A review of sources and articles claiming business benefits of empowered work methods found claims of $1 million–10 million within a year (McEwan 1999).

CUSTOMER FOCUS

Customer focus was a core attribute of first wave approaches, particularly in total quality management. Hill and Wilkinson (1995), for example, identify three common characteristics:

1. customer orientation

2. process orientation

3. continuous improvement

Customer focus is the common goal that drives quality. Task inputs and outputs are performed among inter-linked networks of internal customers to create value for the final customer. Each work unit within the value network needs to understand the quality contribution of the unit to the whole value-creating system, which in turn is crucially dependent on collaborative engagement across process boundaries. In a retrospective commentary on an article he had written for the *Harvard Business Review*, Herzberg (1987) suggests that work is enriched, and therefore he argues becomes more motivating, when there is:

- recognition for achievement, received through feedback;

- responsibility, for example for decision-making or self-scheduling;

- opportunity for learning.

He says that the key to enriching work is client relationships, and explains what he means by giving the example of various trades supplying services to one another in aircraft maintenance. This focus on relationships, service and cross-boundary collaboration is absent in his original article linking motivation and job content, saying that what matters is 'Who do I serve?' rather than 'Who do I report to?'

EMPOWERMENT

The lack of clarity and disagreement in the literature about what empowerment meant was widespread. Price (1993) offers an amusing view. He said that empowerment is:

> Delegation beefed up with a shot of testosterone … it may be the latest
> in a long line of cant terms from the managerial lexicon of hypocrisy …
> getting employees to do things against their inborn inclination to
> indolence has a long history.

Empowerment was seen by some as an outcome of increased autonomy in action and decision-making arising from vertical redistribution of status-enhancing management responsibilities, combined with responsibilities for achieving horizontal, integrated cross-boundary control and innovation.

Recurring theme

Calls for increased workforce empowerment continue to be a recurring theme in management literature, and can be traced back to previous management fads. Commenting on employee empowerment, Argyris (1998) said that despite empowerment's 'much touted potential', there had been no sweeping metamorphoses within the majority of workforces, for reasons which are complex.

A major limiting factor, however, is management concerns over control. Managers may say that empowerment is desirable, but be unable or unwilling to abandon the command-and-control model to which they are accustomed. This is an example of what Argyris and Schon (1978) mean by espoused theory and theory-in-use. There is more talk than action when it comes to empowerment (Weerakoon and Lai 1997), with a 'battle between autonomy and control that rages on while the potential for real empowerment is squandered' (Argyris 1998: 103).

Honold (1997) offers a multi-dimensional view of empowered work systems, and her summary aligns well with other views in the literature at that time:

- leadership that creates vision and develops common goals;

- use of teams;

- job autonomy;

- control over decisions;

- decentralised organisational structures;

- controls that are flexible enough to permit adaptation, based on checks and balances;

- reward systems contingent on performance.

Critical perspectives

Wilkinson (1998) is representative of a more critical perspective, putting forward the view that practitioners and academics used the term 'empowerment' loosely, and that the prescriptive literature:

- contained little detailed discussion of issues likely to arise on implementation;

- trivialised the conflict that exists within organisations;

- ignored the business context within which empowerment takes place;

- rarely located empowerment within its historical context.

Critics like Wilkinson and others argued against the notion of empowerment. They could see no shift in the balance of power in the employment relationship, and they perceived limited or no changes in the nature of production operators' work. They regarded new working practices as a sinister force that allowed management to control workforces through intensified work, increased surveillance and peer pressure to exert self-imposed social control (Delbridge et al. 1992, Sewell and Wilkinson 1992a, Sewell and Wilkinson 1992b, McArdle et al. 1995, Delbridge 1995, Willmott 1995a, Willmott 1995b, Mitev 1996, Jones 1997).

Middle management resistance

Fenton-O'Creevy (1996) saw middle management resistance as self-interested tendencies rooted in fear over loss of power and control. Tannenbaum's view that control and power are not zero-sum games was noted in Chapter 2. Handing over control and power to colleagues is in fact a control-enhancing action, as the shift is made from perceived control to influence.

Husband has coined the term 'wirearchy' to describe this two-way flow of power, where greater influence for one party feeds back into enhanced reputation and influence for the person who has been able to enhance power for others.[2] Davenport (2009) describes how influential and high-performing knowledge workers pass on information as a way of saying 'I know what you are interested in and I am thinking about you,' which enhances their reputations and encourages loyalty. Adopting the role of enhancer, facilitator and nurturer of networks is going to be a major mind shift for many managers, which will be further explored later in the book.

Operator resistance

Delbridge (1998) categorised varying degrees of operator resistance: surviving the system, moderating the system and beating the system.

Surviving the system entailed operators distancing themselves from the demands of management, for example by avoiding overtime and not participating in any form of discretionary behaviour. Moderating the system meant operators maintaining some control over their work effort in a way that was detrimental to management demands, including taking informal breaks, indulging in slack time-keeping or deliberately regulating the quality of their intellectual input (Kerfoot and Knights 1995). Beating the system included refusal to undertake specific tasks – normally a collective effort.

---

2   http://www.wirearchy.com/what-is-wirearchy/ [accessed: 15 April 2012].

Shop floor operators' non-compliance with new work practices by regulating their intellectual input highlights yet another view of empowerment. Operator tacit knowledge and participation in problem-solving and continuous improvement had a commercial imperative for the first time. Lack of operator compliance meant that performance improvement and business advantages from new working and managing practices would not be possible. Belasco and Stayer (1994) argued that it is holders of intellectual capital who hold power through knowledge that needs to be appropriated and applied to meet the challenge from turbulent markets. People cannot be compelled to contribute, so designing performance environments where people feel able and willing to contribute becomes essential.

There was no evidence of operator resistance in any of the case studies. All were pragmatic towards continuous improvement, displaying neither resistance nor enthusiasm. A common view in interviews in Case Study 2 was that continuous improvement was something management wanted them to do, and operators went along with it. Some even said that continuous improvement was already the attitude they took to their work before management gave it a name. One man who operated an antiquated machine demonstrated a table of machine settings developed for other operators' use in his absence.

Outcome of workplace relationships

Marchington (1995), in a critical review of new working practices, makes the point that much depends on the quality of workforce–management relationships, whether or not structures and processes are significantly reconfigured. Empowerment in first wave smart working was therefore ultimately an outcome of:

- trusted workplace relationships that valued workforce participation;

- systems of leadership and engagement that created learning, performance and collaboration environments, which enabled people to acquire, share and deploy knowledge for their own satisfaction and to the benefit of the business.

Although the view of empowerment as an outcome of decentralised responsibilities and increased autonomy was common in the literature, it was the quality of workplace relationships that was a crucial determinant of performance outcomes in all three case studies. It is particularly interesting to compare the Case Studies 1 and 2. The structure remained traditionally organised along functional lines in Case Study 1, but with a strong focus on distributed leadership, open communication and participation.

Decentralisation and greater autonomy for the manufacturing zones and within manufacturing cells was a feature of Case Study 2, which is normally positively associated with empowerment. The dominant sentiment from the operators in this case study, though, was dissatisfaction. The operators understood the context of the challenging global market in which the enterprise was operating and appreciated that redundancies were necessary. It was how redundancies were being handled and how social performance measures were being used that particularly upset them. Workplace relationships were poor, despite a decentralised structure and enhanced autonomy.

Empowerment enablers

McEwan (1999) critically reviewed literature on empowerment and high-performance work systems, and identified and collated empowerment enablers into a resource listing. A summary of these empowerment enablers is reproduced in Table 3.1.

Table 3.1   Empowerment enablers

Individual/Team Enablers	Organisational Enablers	Leadership Enablers
Authority	Communication systems	Access to resources
Commitment	Operational control	Create learning environments
Communication skills	Strategic control	Access to people
Congruence personal and organisational goals	Information systems	Lead through example, inspiration and influence
Cognitive capabilities	Performance systems	Articulate performance expectations
Decision-making skills	Governance policies	Communicate vision
Motivation	Design principles	Model expected behaviours
Responsible for innovation	Procedures	Provide feedback
Responsible for process integration	Structures	Set high expectations
Self-belief	Processes	Oversee integration
Technical skills	Values	Handle conflict
Social skills	No-blame culture	Rewards consistent with business objectives

Enabling Factors

This section reviews factors that influence the design of systems and performance environments. Management cultures, structures, operational processes and task characteristics all interact to become performance environments within which people create value.

These kaleidoscopic factors also generate a plethora of organisational contexts and diverse characteristics. For example, the larger the organisation, the more horizontal and vertical boundaries there are to communicate across. As for task flow, this can be continuous, or more intermittent. Both make different sorts of demands on people, their skills and their engagement with processes, which, in addition to the time-based characteristics, can be routine and familiar, or they can be complex, uncertain and non-routine.

AGILE SYSTEMS

High-value, complex products tend to be manufactured within distributed supply eco-systems. Gunasekaran and Cecille (1998) describe agile manufacturing extending across business processes and throughout the supply chain. Agility is 'the capability to survive in a competitive environment of continuous and unpredictable change'.

Components of agile systems include the virtual enterprise, physically distributed teams, rapid partnership formation, concurrent engineering (simultaneous design rather than sequential), rapid prototyping and integrated information systems (Gunasekaran and Cecille 1998). Agile systems have four common principles, which all sound remarkably current:

1.   Enterprises must have adaptive capability.

2.   Value skills and knowledge.

3.   Deliver value to customers.

4.   Operate within partnerships.

DIFFERENTIATED APPROACH

One of the most useful frameworks from the first wave was the Puttick Grid,[3] which shows products grouped according to product complexity and market uncertainty. The four quadrants of the framework categorise products according to fashion, consumer durables, commodities and high value. They represent a range of parameters and contingencies affecting systems and process design.

High-value, complex products have long lifecycles, typically requiring upgrading and refitting. Industries within this category include aerospace and defence. One response to complexity was to create flexibility and agility through cellular manufacturing, where machines, teams, tasks and processes are arranged modularly. Teams within the cells potentially have responsibility for all operations in a sub-process and for co-ordination across sub-processes, involving technical and problem-solving collaboration to achieve process integration.

As well as horizontal autonomy and integration, operational and strategic tasks – previously the responsibility of middle and senior management – are also typically devolved to shop floor operator in complex product manufacturing.

No substantive change

Low-complexity products competing on price and quality might elicit different process and management configurations, often making little difference to shop floor operators work tasks, but requiring their additional participation in process improvement and innovation.

Common in the academic critiques from that time were research findings suggesting little evidence of substantive changes to operator autonomy or decision-making responsibilities. Delbridge (1998) concluded that:

> There is scant evidence of the integration of innovation and production on the shop-floor and worker involvement is predicated on manual effort, not creativity and knowledge ... there is little to suggest that the new shop-floor is a hotbed of worker autonomy and knowledge creation.

---

3   http://www.docstoc.com/docs/76796576/Puttick-Grid---Welcome-to-the-University-of-Warwick [accessed: 31 March 2012].

This is consistent with Dean and Snell (1991), who found limited evidence to support the proposition that work becomes more mentally challenging. They also found limited support for increased task variety, and some support for increased levels of interdependence. Wilkinson (1998) similarly commented on limited re-distribution of management control responsibilities and changes to operator work responsibilities.

Radical restructuring

It was not always the case that low-complexity products meant little restructuring of production processes and management responsibilities. Lewis and Lytton (1997) documented Lewis's experience of transforming the performance culture in a small enterprise that manufactured small-batch and made-to-order metal products, which can be characterised as low-complexity within the commodity categorisation on the Puttick Grid.

The transition from traditional manufacturing was radical in the extent to which functional arrangements (welding, fabricating and polishing) were restructured along the modular lines more usually associated with high-value, complex products. Layers of management were eliminated in the restructuring, and functional organisation was replaced by manufacturing cells, whose members took on responsibilities for all manufacturing tasks. The cells, led by team leaders, ran like mini-businesses. The team members were responsible for their own work schedules and maintaining relationships with customers and suppliers. The teams also took ownership of cost control and did their own job costing, including materials and time estimates. They negotiated terms with customers and then made decisions on delivery, to which they had to commit.

A key feature of the new arrangement was working annualised hours (EOC 2007b). This means that within the paramount consideration of meeting customer requirements, on time and to quality, the workforce can decide their own working hours, including leaving early and taking time off. The expectation is that people will work the required hours where necessary. According to Lewis and Lytton, senior management provides resources, encouragement and vision. They also understand that ownership by the teams is crucially important. Management proposing solutions is not welcomed; the same solutions become acceptable when teams members identify them.

VALUES INFLUENCE SYSTEMS DESIGN

Enterprises at that time therefore had access to a range of structural and operational choices in designing new manufacturing production models. This is what Dennison meant by enterprises having choice in designing multiple value-creating process configurations. We saw in Chapter 2 that chief executives' cultural attitudes and core beliefs significantly influenced the design of structures, processes and systems (Pettigrew and Fenton 2000).

The influence of leaders is apparent in each of the case studies. The production director in Case Study 1 was driven by a fundamental belief in the role and power of open communication in effective quality management. The Human Resources manager in Case Study 2 believed that people could be coerced into changing behaviour through performance measures. He also said that you needed to go out onto the shop floor from time to time and 'shoot a few people'.

AUTONOMY AND CONTROL

Ongoing concerns over maintaining centralised co-ordination with the need to achieve simultaneous local autonomy were highlighted in Chapter 2. The tendency in the literature is to talk about the unwillingness of management to let go of control. That was not an issue in any of the case studies. Rather, what was an issue was the inadequacy of systems for co-ordinating local autonomy.

The autonomy of the zone managers in Case Study 2 was causing discomfort for the Production Manager, who was finding it challenging to co-ordinate their activities across the cellular manufacturing zones. Autonomy is misleading in the context of having to function within integrated systems that reach across business process boundaries. Self-management is a more accurate description of self-directed action in accordance with a set of performance expectations and standards, including setting expectations and responsibilities for integration.

How to design control and co-ordination mechanisms so that local autonomy can be optimised while retaining centralised co-ordination is among the topics explored in Chapter 4.

Making the Transition

Making the transition to new ways of working can be considered generally as a movement that has a trajectory across time, and also at the level of individual enterprise experience.

TRAJECTORY OF A MOVEMENT

The critics were commenting on what they saw in the early stages of transitions to new working practices. The strength of critical voices began to moderate as time went by. For example, some years later, Delbridge, who was a prominent critic of new working practices, co-authored a publication arising from research into 'the learning factory'. Barton and Delbridge (2006) note that: 'This paper contributes to the growing evidence of the devolvement of traditional managerial responsibilities to lower levels within increasingly lean manufacturing organisations.'

Barton and Delbridge cite 'a considerable body of research' in US and UK firms suggesting high-performance workplaces and work practices that depend on human capital. They gathered data from 18 US and UK automotive suppliers to test the concept of a learning factory, seeking to determine HR practices that support teams, problem-solving and continuous improvement.

Barton and Delbridge (2006) concluded that the majority of factories in the research were some way off being learning factories, but that a learning philosophy supported by practices, structures and expectations was in place and broadly in line with this perspective. This conclusion had come a long way from Delbridge's criticism of earlier years.

Constant and emergent

The first wave of smart working transformations tell us that successful transitions to new working practices are emergent. They are messy, challenging and take time. They proceed through conversations, working together, sharing information, failing, trying again, observing and doing differently. In the process of all this real-time experimenting, relationships among people develop, learning takes place and trust builds. Pettigrew and Fenton (2000) noted that:

> *Most crucially the time series data in our case studies have revealed the more or less continuous process of organizing and reorganizing faced*

by our eight firms … the innovation journeys were always incomplete, always in process, never quite there … organisations may be resting uneasily on a cusp between order and disorder.

INDIVIDUAL ENTERPRISE EXPERIENCE

The overwhelming impression is that the manufacturers who did make the transition from traditional management practices and structures to process-based methods generally found the transition challenging, or as Randolph (1995) put it, organisations were 'failing their way to various levels of success'.

Many others also noted the challenges involved in making the transition (Frey 1993, Heckscher 1995, Claydon and Doyle 1996, Jones 1997, Lewis and Lytton 1997, Wickisier 1997). Lewis is candid about false starts and facing up to people who will not or cannot commit to the transformation (Lewis and Lytton 1997).

ROLE OF SUPERVISORS

The role of front-line supervisors in the Barton and Delbridge (2006) study is of particular interest. It had broadened to include plant-wide concerns rather than just direct responsibility for teams. Barton and Delbridge comment that by then, much of what might be considered management fell on the shoulders of the supervisor, including responsibilities for co-ordinating and controlling production.

They say that the reason why the supervisor role is so crucial is that the strength of loyalty of team members to each other is strong on the shop floor. The pivotal role of team leaders was also highlighted in the case studies, where they played a key part in influencing and demonstrating expected behaviours.

TIME PRESSURES

Apart from the crucial role of supervisors, another key and related observation Barton and Delbridge made was the detrimental effects of time-based pressures. This was especially the case in facilities that were running at capacity, where it was a problem to find time to re-structure and assess improvements while attending to production. Lack of available time is currently proving to be problematic in attempts to introduce lean methods within the public sector in the UK.

PEOPLE ARE PRAGMATIC

The shop floor operators in all three case studies were pragmatic about going along with management's vision and intentions to adopt new work philosophy and practices. This was the case even in Case Study 2, where a considerable amount of fear and anger was present in the workforce. In all three cases there were dissenting voices, some of whom were influenced and brought along by their more accepting colleagues.

LEADERS AND INFLUENCERS

The influence of key people with vision and team leaders who take responsibility for making the vision happen in practice cannot be underestimated. Senior executives with influence, like the production director in Case Study 1 and the new owners of the metal pressings factory in Case Study 3, committed to a programme of reforms with integrity and driven by values in which they believed – quality, innovation, openness and trust. Of course, the business imperative is a strong driver for change.

UNTAPPED POTENTIAL

Neither can the willingness of people to contribute to process improvement be underestimated when management has earned their trust, as was apparent in Case Study 1 when suggestions for improvement were so forthcoming that the initial improvement effort collapsed. Individual managers found workarounds and their own solutions to problems in Case Study 2, even in the middle of post-redundancy unhappiness, poor communication and absence of effective leadership. People in general want to do a good job, and appreciate being listened to and having their contributions recognised.

VALUE-DRIVEN OR CRISIS?

A notable feature of many first wave implementations is that they were undertaken in response to a crisis. This meant that people were being asked to change the way they worked at a time when they were most fearful and vulnerable, especially where redundancies were involved. Other businesses are motivated by understanding the changing competitive environment and adapting before crisis hits, and a smaller group is motivated by a belief that there are better ways of working.

It is probable that enterprises adapting to current turbulent markets will be doing so under crisis conditions. It is always important to communicate, influence and persuade, but appreciation of the stresses and uncertainty requires particular sensitivity. This has implications for developing management skills. There are situations where uncompromising resolve is called for, and an example of this will be demonstrated in Case Study 4 in Chapter 8.

This is Now

This section completes this review of making the transition to new ways of working by coming back to an initial assessment of what is happening now and linking it to what happened in the past. It has taken a long time for first wave philosophies like lean to be considered outside manufacturing. The public sector in particular is beginning to evaluate the possibility that lean approaches can be used in the pursuit of efficiency and innovation (Hansen and Stoner 2009).

This presents a real danger if lean is regarded as a quick fix, focused on cost-cutting and eliminating waste. Of course, eliminating waste is a core objective of the lean philosophy but lean is ultimately about effectiveness rather than a narrow focus on efficiency, and is the combined outcome of workforce knowledge, skills and capabilities applied in pursuit of customer-focused performance.

COMMITTING TO A NEW PHILOSOPHY

According to Fine at al. (2008), the way to make operational improvements stick is by focusing on the soft side of lean. They say that 'mastering lean's softer side' forces everyone to commit themselves to new ways of thinking and working, which is challenging. As in the first wave, new working practices have to be seen as outcomes of a revised philosophy of work linked to a 'new era of management' (*McKinsey Quarterly* 2009), the foundation of which is valuing everyone's skills and knowledge and putting in place systems of leadership and engagement.

There is doubt over how many organisations are prepared for the commitment this will take, hampered as they are by a lack of customer focus, people currently working in silos, overworked staff, lack of awareness of strategic direction and a lack of understanding of system dynamics and process flow (Radnor et al. 2006). Radnor et al. evaluated eight lean implementations in public sector organisations.

The implementations involve both full implementation, where the approach is to embed lean as a philosophy into all aspects of day-to-day work, and approaches based on rapid-improvement events, where continuous improvement is the outcome of specific, time-bound interventions. They evaluate the benefits and disadvantages of both, concluding that lean is transferable to the public sector. It is thought to be most appropriate in high-volume contexts with repeatable tasks, which are amenable to standardisation and integration.

While reporting a range of tangible and intangible benefits, they also concluded that 'most sites had not achieved all the objectives they had hoped for'. Barriers included:

- lack of resources to make the changes;

- management and staff resistance;

- lack of management commitment and slow pace of change in the public sector.

They singled out from among a wide range of core success factors:

- readiness to change;

- management commitment to achieve a new philosophy of work;

- allocation of time and resources on top of the normal workload to the make the changes happen;

- expectation of changes within reasonable timescales.

CONTEXTS DIFFER, ISSUES REMAIN THE SAME

Much that should have been learned about making the transition to lean working approaches needs to be re-learned. A senior nurse with decades of experience in the UK National Health Service recently shared her views on the top-down imposition of a 'lean ward' intervention in the hospital where she works. This had been done without consulting the nursing staff and without their participation.

It was also skewing effort. It had been known for nurses to claim priority for specific 'lean activities' when critical incidents were taking place on the ward. Since service and customer focus are paramount in the lean philosophy, taking effort away from urgent patient needs to focus on additional 'lean activities' is, to say the least, missing the point.

Committing to a new philosophy of work, engaging the entire workforce, designing systems to support learning and participation, overcoming staff and management resistance, experimenting, experiencing, failing and trying again are all very familiar themes from the first wave of smart working. The contexts might be different, but the issues remain constant.

Concluding Remarks

The lessons learned from the first wave continue to be a differentiating source of competitive advantage. Office furniture designer Herman Miller found that its manufacturing processes had become inadequate in the face of changing customer behaviour. It changed from large-batch to agile, lean manufacturing, and in doing so achieved a range of business-saving performance improvements. According to Birchard (2010): 'Herman Miller have learned that the best run plants rely on people, not machines. Only people can solve problems to make assembly lines go faster, run cheaper, and deliver higher quality.'

The last wave of smart working was initiated by the need to respond to global competitive pressures, and the same is the case with the emerging wave of innovation and creativity. The finding that working practices can be transformed without radical transformation of organisational structures is important. Despite 'excitable accounts' of the shift to knowledge work (Brinkley et al. 2009), many jobs continue to be time-based and process-driven.

The quality of the employment relationship, open communication, and involvement and participation of the entire workforce were shown to be critical factors in achieving transformation of working practices. Internal knowledge flows generated through continuous improvement and innovation activities are now exponentially expanded by being linked to external knowledge flows and creation spaces.

What was previously continuous improvement is now potentially collective intelligence. Trust, open communication and involvement are essential if this opportunity is to be realised.

FACTORIES: ORIGINAL SOCIAL BUSINESSES

There is a widespread tendency in blogs and articles online to disparage 'the factory model', 'the industrial model' or 'the engineering model'. In doing so, there really is a danger of overlooking the abundant insights into workplace social dynamics that have accumulated over decades.

As people struggle to understand current developments, they are using different terms to describe what they see happening. As well as smart working, Enterprise 2.0 (McAfee 2009, Cook 2008) is being replaced by Social Business (IBM 2011). The trajectory towards Smart/Social Business/Enterprise 2.0 began decades ago with the shift towards 'the learning factory' model. As case studies slowly emerge, it is no surprise that the transition issues we currently see are mirrored in earlier developments. In making the transition from traditional manufacturing to the 'learning factory', relationships emerged as a key lever.

We see that the meaning of work was and continues to lie in the relationships we have with each other, the relationship we have with the organisation we work for, and in the service we give to others. Creating the initial conditions for relationships to develop that enhance our desire for recognition, self-determination, social status and learning will continue to be associated with high-performance and engaging work.

4

Design Principles from the First Wave

Introduction

This chapter makes the case for the usefulness of theory in informing practical action, focusing particularly on theory from which initial guiding principles can be drawn. The principles need to be evaluated and interpreted constantly for unique applied contexts.

Two theoretical approaches, the Viable Systems Model (VSM) and socio-technical systems, are proposed as particularly appropriate sources for informing design principles aligned to first wave smart working practices. It is proposed that these principles remain valid as contexts change. Design principles identified here will be reviewed later in the book to examine their relevance for current contexts.

The argument so far is that two different types of systems interact to create customer value. Highly dynamic, complex and networked systems of social interactions are influenced but not determined by the formal systems that are designed to mediate, support, co-ordinate and control these dynamics. At the core of the theme of creating the next wave is the contention that people participate in adapting and evolving the designed systems through 'reciprocal determinism', which involves people constantly shifting, mutually adapting and dynamically engaging with each other and their environments.

There is an opposing force to participating in adapting operating environments. Many people are not comfortable with change, so enterprises as organised entities are not good at adapting. They become stable, certainty-seeking and resistant to change. Senge (1993) proposes that surfacing, testing and improving our mental models is an essential core discipline for adaptive organisational learning. He attaches such strong importance to mental models because our deeply engrained mental pictures of how we believe the world to be affects what we do in practice and they hinder adaptation in a changing world. Schein (2009) talks about how we need to unlearn, like letting go of some deeply engrained attitudes and beliefs about people and management. The design principles outlined in this chapter provide insight for those taking the first steps in letting go.

Nothing as Practical

Kurt Lewin proposed that nothing is as practical as a good theory (Lewin 1951). In my experience, practical and action-focused people tend to be uneasy with theory. Being too theoretical is frequently thought of as impractical abstraction, when in fact a theory – a general proposition for making perspectives explicit and articulating relationship between elements or events (Robson 1993) – can be a tool for thinking about a problem. Having a theory allows understanding to emerge, through evaluating, comparing, testing and reflecting on what we think we are seeing in reality. Theories, like models, make perceptions of reality visible, explicit and testable by others (Pidd 1996).

They also provide the basis for designing analytical and diagnostic tools, or using them as they are to create dialogue to reveal, critically evaluate, challenge and develop alternative perspectives. After all, the value lies in how theoretical frameworks help thinking and doing. Examples in later chapters will show how senior executives have used a range of theories in practice to do exactly this. This chapter is concerned with theoretical principles and perspectives that could inform practical action to implement smart working practices. Four core design principles are proposed at this stage, drawing on insights and observations from the literature review and case studies of first wave smart working.

Designing for Adaptability

A major design consideration is designing for adaptability. Designing for adaptation in the face of complexity is such an issue because path dependency strongly biases businesses to remain committed to decisions made in the past, especially where time, money and resources have been invested. Concentrating on core products and services, 'sticking to the knitting' (Peters and Waterman 2004), without simultaneously sensing and responding to environmental change creates opportunity for disruptive innovators opportunistically to take advantage of these developments under the noses of the inflexible dinosaur companies heading for crisis (Christensen 2003).

Designing for Autonomy

A second design consideration is designing to enable simultaneous autonomy and control. It has already been noted that there have been calls for greater employee autonomy and less intensive management in response to current workplace trends (CIPD 2008a, CIPD 2008b, The Work Foundation in association with BT 2009). None of these sources mention the fact that the autonomy-control-empowerment issue has been of interest to management thinkers for at least a decade (Argyris 1998). Repeating the desirability of self-determined, empowered individuals is not necessarily going to make it happen. Research and experience tell us that there are considerable barriers to be overcome.

Designing for Integration

A third and related design consideration is designing for integration and co-ordination. It seems that autonomy is not only problematic in that it is resisted within 'command and control' cultures of centralised control, but is also problematic if undisciplined autonomy occurs. Even at the small scale of the factory in Case Study 2 in Chapter 3, the production director found that the zone managers' expectations of autonomy meant that the experience of managing their activities was like 'herding cats'.

Designing for Knowledge-sharing

A fourth consideration is designing to facilitate cross-boundary knowledge and information flows. First wave approaches to process innovation and control were founded on people working within and across discrete internal and external processes, collaborating to solve problems together to achieve customer-focused value-creation.

Fundamental Concepts

The management activist Gary Hamel is championing the cause of management reinvention (Hamel and Breen, 2007). It is striking that much of what he proposes can be traced back to first wave smart working. For example, in a blog post entitled 'Empowering individuals and empowering institutions', he suggest that organisations need to be developed around the following principles:

- Decentralise wherever possible.

- Break big units into small units.

- Ensure transparency in decision-making.

- Make leaders more accountable to the led.

- Align rewards with contribution, rather than with power and position.

- Substitute peer review for top-down review.

- Steadily enlarge the scope of self-determination.[1]

The Viable Systems Model encompasses principles and mechanisms that address some of Hamel's principles, especially decentralising where possible, breaking bigger units into smaller ones, and transparency and accountability. The model provides ways of thinking about these and other key characteristics of smart working.

McEwan (1999) explored how the VSM might be applied to resolve the localised autonomy and centralised co-ordination tension for manufacturers making the transition to first wave working practices. The model has a fractal, recursive structure that is ideal for modelling and diagnosing linked systems and sub-systems, for example autonomous teams on manufacturing shop floors. The VSM's principles:

- illustrate the fundamental requirement of sensing and adapting to internal and external threats and opportunities;

---

1   http://blogs.wsj.com/management/2010/04/20/empowered-individuals-and-empowering-institutions/ [accessed: 15 April 2012].

- illustrate the dynamics underpinning viability;

- require cross-boundary knowledge-sharing;

- enable distributed performance;

- facilitate integration and co-ordination;

- balance centralised control with localised autonomy.

We will explore Ashby's law of requisite variety (Ashby 1956) before examining the Viable Systems Model in greater detail. This is because it underpins the model. The theoretical dynamics of the model would not be possible without understanding what requisite variety is and why it matters.

REQUISITE VARIETY

Thirty-five of 'the world's most progressive thinkers on management and organisation' gathered to explore reinventing the future of management. They came up with a list of 25 stretch goals for management – Management Moon Shots – ten of which were regarded as crucial.[2] One of the ten was:

> *Reinventing strategy making as an emergent process ... in a turbulent world, strategy making can no longer be a top down activity. What is required instead is a strategy process that reflects the biological principles of variety, selection, and retention.*

So what is variety, and why did the conference of management thinkers single it out as a critical issue? Ashby (1956) describes variety as a measure of the occurrence of distinct elements from among a set of elements. In practice, variety is a heuristic indicator of complexity, based as it is on observer perception and judgement of events a system confronts and experiences.

Variety exists externally throughout a system's wider operating environment, and also internally within the system itself. Ashby's law of requisite variety states that only variety can absorb variety. This implies that in responding to their external environments – for example, organisations trying to survive within increasingly turbulent operating environments – systems must have

2   http://blogs.wsj.com/management/2009/03/02/management-moonshots-part-ii/ [accessed: 15 April 2012].

the capacity to deal with the complexity they face. Hoverstadt (2008) explains: 'The more complex the situation (the more possible states the system can be in), the more response capacity needed to remain stable.'

Requisite variety can be achieved in two ways: by trying to attenuate variety, and by amplifying responses to the variety after attenuation has taken place. Attenuating actions try to filter the variety a system has to engage with from the external environment. Attenuating filtering also takes place within a system: for example, operating standards and simplified work routines might be seen as attenuating tactics.

According to Weick (1979), organisations have to be 'preoccupied with keeping sufficient diversity inside the organisation to sense accurately the variety present in ecological changes outside it'. Amplifying tactics increase the variety of responses to external, environmental variety. Recognising, eliciting, valuing and deploying latent capability within an enterprise's workforce, including partners and stakeholders, would be an amplifying strategy. Continuous improvement and problem-solving activities, for example, are amplifying responses to operational and environmental variety. Amplifying tactics also create diverse perspectives that promote constant questioning and examining of assumptions to reveal options for future action.

The review of control in Chapter 2 showed that the dominant business response to organisational complexity over time has largely been misplaced attenuation, focused in the wrong direction towards controlling people and their behaviour – the very people whose tacit knowledge, latent potential and collective intelligence are so essential for robust competitive fitness. More than that, enterprises, in their attempts to regulate and control people, add additional management layers that create top-heavy organisations.

Tannenbaum's comment about 'circumscribing idiosyncratic behaviours and keeping them conformant to the rational plan of the organisation' is a reminder that businesses are not comfortable with the diversity of opinions and perspectives that are the outcomes of interactions among people. The proliferation of organisational layers imposed to control 'idiosyncratic behaviour' can instead create crippling bureaucracy, adding significantly to management overheads, stifling diversity and creating dysfunction.

Echoing Stacey's contention that creativity lies at the edge of chaos (Stacey 1996), Nonaka et al. (2000) propose that requisite variety 'helps a knowledge-creating organisation to maintain the balance between order and chaos'. They equate requisite variety with timely access to appropriate information and knowledge.

The Viable Systems Model

The Viable Systems Model is a framework for understanding the inter-relationships among the social, organisational and information systems that enable organisations to deal with the complexities arising from increasingly distributed, complex and uncertain operating environments. The model is based on self-regulation, information flows, feedback, communication, co-ordination, integration, adaptation and control (Beer 1989, Beer 1994). A system is viable if it:

- can maintain a separate existence;

- has problem-solving capabilities;

- can withstand trauma inflicted on it from its wider operating environment (Jackson 1986, Espejo 1989, Espejo et al. 1996).

The VSM conceptualises organisations as distributed, connected and fractal, with viable systems consisting of nested sub-systems of viable systems. The nested sub-systems are dynamically linked through social interactions. These are Weick's 'double interacts', described in Chapter 2, which you may remember are reciprocally adaptive units of behaviour that become the building blocks of dynamic processes.

A viable system can be an economy, an eco-system of enterprises in alliance, an individual enterprise, a business unit, a team or a single person. To remain viable, all systems within the overall structure must comply with the law of requisite variety and continually sense, communicate and mutually adapt to ensure that complexity is balanced and distributed throughout the system as a whole. Each viable system has five management functions. These are explained in Table 4.1.

Table 4.1   A viable system's management functions

Five Management Functions	What They Do
Operations	Implements a viable system's primary activities
Co-ordination	Co-ordinates through mutual adjustment
Control	Engages with Co-ordination to support operations. Also works closely with Intelligence to influence Policy
Intelligence	Looks outwards to the external environment to scan for opportunities and threats
Policy	Oversee strategic decisions, following significant filtering from Intelligence and Control (Espejo et al. 1996)

Figure 4.1 shows recursion of viable systems at two levels. The overall system has three separate, autonomous units that carry out primary activities. Each unit is itself a viable system. The control, co-ordination, intelligence and policy functions taken together constitute a system's meta-management. Interaction is two-way between the higher-level meta-management and the meta-management of the three lower-level systems. Their joint actions support operations, or prime activities in the language of the model.

What the five management functions in each viable system look like and how they are achieved in practice are not prescribed. They are interpreted and applied at the level of each viable system and in relation to its environment, according to specific business context and in pursuit of strategic objectives. In practice, the management functions within each viable system are not necessarily distinct roles performed by different people.

This dash through the basics of the Viable Systems Model is very simplified. Readers wishing to learn more are directed to the writings of Stafford Beer, who developed the model, as well as to Hoverstadt (2008), Espejo and Harnden (1989) and Flood and Jackson (1991).

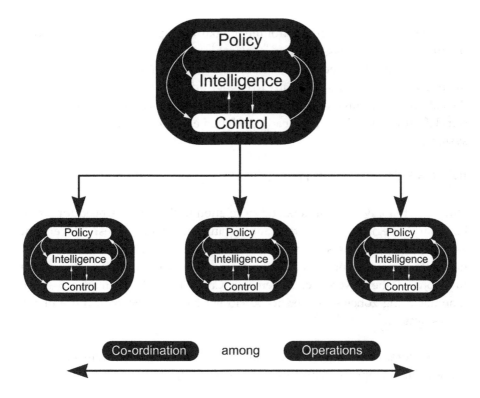

Figure 4.1   Two levels of recursion

Performing and Integrating

Control maintains internal stability for each viable system (Flood and Jackson 1991). It ensures that policy is implemented, and focuses on performance management and resource allocation (Hoverstadt 2008). Control and co-ordination work together to make sure that things get done in the best way possible and in accordance with the principle of requisite variety. The co-ordination functions of the three viable systems adjust among themselves and engage with higher-level co-ordination. The more active co-ordination, the less need there is for control to intervene in operations, which it will do where there is failure of co-ordination through, in Hoverstadt's words, 'turf wars between departments or conflicting messages to customers (internal or external)'.

Devolving responsibility for autonomous decision-making and action to lower-level viable systems is crucial to comply with the principle of requisite variety. If higher-level systems are not to be overwhelmed by the complexity absorbed from the wider environment, like champagne trickling down a pyramid of drinking glasses, lower-level viable systems must absorb complexity from higher-level systems. Any temptation of the higher-level systems to micro-manage decreases the ability to engage effectively with complexity from the external environment, threatening viability. Moreover, micro-managing is self-defeating behaviour, and leads to the emergence of destructive shadow systems.

INTEGRATED AUTONOMY

How is autonomy to be understood in relation to the obvious need for cross-boundary integration in pursuit of organisational objectives? Hoverstadt explains autonomy as self-regulation within the context and constraints of negotiated systems purpose. For example, the control and co-ordination functions of the lower-level systems in Case Study 2 in Chapter 3 – the manufacturing zones – needed to be closely co-ordinated with those of the higher system.

Therefore, autonomy does not imply unconstrained freedom to pursue individually independent purposes. As Beer (1989) says:

> The optimal degree of autonomy (given that we have the measure called 'variety' to deploy) is in principle a computable function of the system's purpose in relation to its environment. If that conclusion appears outrageously to delimit freedom for those within any organisation, then so be it.

If Beer is interpreted as outrageously delimiting freedom, he is not the only one. Hansen (2009) says that in decentralised management, 'predictably, managers focus on reaching their targets', which 'risks turning a company into a loose collection of units, which become fiefdoms or silos'. He recommends 'disciplined collaboration'.

INTEGRATING IN PRACTICE

One of the key planks of first wave approaches to smart working was the focus on process innovation and integration. It has already been noted from Case Study 2 in Chapter 3 that the autonomy of the manufacturing zones was causing problems as zone managers sought to protect the identities of their own cells to the detriment of integrated effort. The challenges posed by co-ordination in

Case Study 1 in Chapter 3 were different, being a mismatch between demands created by the needs of engineering and other functions rather than an issue of turf-defending.

The nursing profession provides a different example. As if nursing isn't challenging enough, current pressures include nurses feeling that they are being held accountable for systemic failures. Interviews with nurses reveal that some of the pressures they experience arise from support functions behaving as though they exist for their own benefit, attempting to pass on their responsibilities to already over-stretched nursing staff.

The absence of a senior administrator taking responsibility for co-ordinating policies, many of which conflict, is problematic. One nurse gave the example of having to comply with health and safety and infection control requirements. A new fire door on a pantry, which housed a fridge to be kept at a minimum temperature and a dishwasher, was causing the fridge to overheat. The nurses were not consulted about the proposed door. They would have immediately known there would be a problem. When the problem was reported, the solution offered was to jam open the door, which defeated the purpose of the fire door.

This might seem a trivial issue, but it is not. Besides creating a problem in complying with competing policy requirements, the new door had no observation panel and created the danger of assaults on nurses. These are 'not infrequent' occurrences in a geographical area that experiences high levels of social problems arising from alcohol and drug dependency.

Achieving effective cross-boundary co-ordination within and across organisations has always been challenging. Co-ordination is assuming crucial significance as enterprises become more globally fragmented and mobilise for speed and flexibility (IBM 2010b). Effective systems designed to encourage co-ordination within and beyond boundaries must be dynamic, participative and negotiated.

Scanning and Adapting

The control function focuses on internal operations, scanning the internal operating environment for current issues concerning resource allocation and performance management. The intelligence function monitors external complexity. Its focus is on scanning the external environment for current and future threats, opportunities and market trends.

It used to be that the external environment for viable systems at front-line, operational levels – for example on manufacturing shop floors – would be internally focused on other production units within the business. This has changed radically now that people are globally connected through social networking technologies. The external environment at that level now additionally includes the environment outside the business. Strategic threats and opportunities to the business can now be scanned by many, rather than by only a limited number of senior executives.

In practice, the 'inside and now' and 'outside and future' perspectives are highly inter-related, and the barriers between what is considered inside and outside are weakening. Control and intelligence therefore work very work closely together to evaluate and filter strategic issues before bringing residual matters to policy for consideration. This is an example of attenuation so that policy is not overwhelmed by complexity.

Policy has several roles, one of which is governance. Hoverstadt describes the role of governance as 'ensuring that the organisation has all the mechanisms that it needs to ensure both its internal cohesion and efficiency and also its ongoing fit with its environment'. It was noted in Chapter 1 that differences in governance accounted for the fact that not all banks got into difficulty in the financial crisis at the end of the first decade of the twenty-first century (Walker 2009). Policy is also responsible for setting the conditions that allow culture, value-based purpose and organisational identity to emerge. Higher-level control communicates all this to the policy functions of the three lower-level systems. They in turn reciprocate to engage in two-way, continual communicating, sensing and adapting.

The Value of the Viable Systems Model

The value of the VSM is that it:

- encourages explicit and structured thinking around sensing, assessing and responding to internal and external environmental complexities;

- focuses attention on the critical issues of viability and adaptation;

- shows how responsibilities for core management functions have to be distributed throughout a system for it to remain viable;

- explains mechanisms for integration and co-ordination;

- explains how to enable simultaneous local autonomy with centralised control;

- can be used be used to inform systems design;

- can be used as a diagnostic tool to assess threats to an organisation's viability;

- can be used as a tool to facilitate dialogue and shared understanding around purpose.

As discussed in Chapter 2, Pettigrew and Fenton found that the ability to negotiate paradoxes was one of the key characteristics of innovating organisations. This is consistent with the Viable Systems Model, which requires competing conditions to be satisfied. Requisite variety, for example, demands that local autonomy is maximised. The co-ordination function, on the other hand, places restrictions on autonomy in the interests of integration and negotiated outcomes. Tensions arising from these competing requirements demand constant negotiation to achieve integrated, self-determined performance and adaptation.

The Viable Systems Model is valuable as a tool to prompt dialogue, challenge mental models, reveal differences of perception and create the sort of interpretive diversity that contributes to shared learning. This echoes Checkland's Soft System Methodology (SSM), which explicitly recognises multiple world views in attempts to frame questions and elicit different interpretations of a situation (Checkland 1981, Flood and Jackson 1991).

Criticisms of the Viable Systems Model

Criticisms of the VSM include objections to hierarchy, which is said to be implicit in recursion, and the charge that the model is inherently autocratic. It is not my intention to defend the VSM against the criticisms. Opposing perspectives are to be expected, and these are briefly summarised, beginning with hierarchy.

The hierarchical depiction of the VSM has led to claims that it is authoritarian and inappropriate for democratic management. Defenders say that this misunderstands what the VSM hierarchy implies – that it does not describe relationships of subservience, but rather management policies that apply to different purposes that materialise over different timescales. Higher-level activities are based around decisions whose effects are felt over a longer timescale than lower-level systems, whose activities take place in real time (McCarthy and Menicou 2002). Hierarchy in this interpretation is more to do with differential purpose and function, rather than status within a social structure.

There is a tendency in the management literature and in blogs to decry hierarchy. Chapter 3 showed that open communication and workforce engagement in continuous improvement can coexist within a hierarchical structure. Pettigrew and Fenton (2000) found that innovating companies are simultaneously networked and hierarchical, and that the tendency is to build stronger hierarchies during tough operating conditions such as those dominating the global business environment at the time of writing. The increasing significance of networks as organisational structures obscures the fact that hierarchy remains relevant and present in networked structures.

The second criticism levelled at the Viable Systems Model is that it is inherently autocratic. Jackson (1989) admits to valid concerns. Power relationships distort the best intentions of the VSM. He puts forward the view that autonomy and decentralisation create opportunity for the powerful to pursue their own ends. Audit, which is part of the control function, is an attribute of the VSM that might be particularly perceived as autocratic. Hoverstadt prefers to refer to audit as the monitoring function: '[Monitoring] supplants performance reporting with sporadic, in-depth checks of operations at the next level down, bypassing one level of management.'

This potentially poses anxiety, both for the operations subject to audit and the meta-management of the level above. As Hoverstadt (2008) observes: 'Done well, it builds trust between managers and the units they manage. Done badly, it can destroy trust almost faster than anything else.' Monitoring managerial and leadership effectiveness is consistent with Hamel's call to make leaders more accountable to the led. The monitoring function is also defended to eliminate the charge that senior management are out of touch with what is happening at the operational front line. Auditing actions must be transparent, widely communicated and their purpose understood by all concerned.

Jackson says that although criticisms of the VSM have to be heard, the charge that the VSM 'inevitably serves the purpose of narrow, elite groups is ... seriously misplaced'. Espejo and Harnden (1989) conclude that the VSM, used effectively, does not constrain the world to fit it; rather, it is 'a pointer for understanding and action ... the model has been presented as an instrument to focus debates about the social nature of human activity'. Used in this way, the VSM's principles and mechanisms facilitate 'the effective contribution of all members in constituting on-going, dynamic structures that realise the viability of the particular social system in real time' (Espejo and Harnden 1989: 458). Attention therefore needs to be paid to how cultural values and strategic purpose are socially constructed, through dialogue and shared practice.

The Viable Systems Model as Heterarchy

Having defended contextually appropriate hierarchy, perhaps it is now time to reconceptualise the VSM as heterarchical, which can be understood as: 'Networks of elements in which each element shares the same 'horizontal' position of power and authority, each playing a theoretically equal role.[3]

Heterarchy is simultaneously horizontal and vertical. Although the VSM has always consisted of horizontally and vertically distributed flows of information and connected business processes, the horizontal dimension is seldom stressed. Surplus requisite variety is usually depicted as being absorbed through vertical recursion. In the network age, with more emphasis on peer-to-peer management processes, requisite variety is increasingly taken up horizontally as well as vertically. This aspect of design principles for smart working is re-visited when reviewing the VSM's relevance for the emerging second wave of smart working.

One final point on viability, although already mentioned in several places, is that threats to system viability obviously do not only come from the external environment. Beer (1989: 27) has said that monoliths such as universities and hospitals, 'creaking and choking like the valetudinarian organisations that they are', operate at the edge of viability.

---

3   http://en.wikipedia.org/wiki/Heterarchy [accessed: 15 April 2012].

The arrival of social technologies is creating further external pressures on universities, as online learning environments and technologies change how people are engaging with learning, using abundantly available quality learning resources and learning from each other. Universities are not going to disappear, but they are going to have to change fundamentally. They are likely to operate even further towards the edge of viability if they do not change their structures and working practices, especially once the consequences of cuts to publicly funded services begin to affect operations and service provision.

Connectedness, as well as creating expanded opportunity for requisite variety, is paradoxically also a threat to viability. The financial crisis shows that threats to the globally linked financial system had their origins within investment banks and financial institutions. The fall-out from the consequences of the failure of credit default swaps and collateralised debt obligations spread out beyond the walls of institutions and into the global financial systems. It continues as the creditworthiness of some European countries is questioned, systemic weaknesses exposed and national economies are affected.

Developing skills and capabilities to diagnose and assess the viability of systems, sub-systems and networks in the face of environmental complexity and uncertainty is now a core business imperative. The Viable Systems Model is proposed as an aid for assessing viability through dialogue, joint reflection and action throughout fractal, distributed and connected systems and sub-systems.

Socio-technical Systems

The next theory to consider in evaluating smart working organising principles is socio-technical systems theory. Socio-technical systems theory emerged in the 1950s when psychologists sought to understand group behaviour and how application of this knowledge might overcome the de-humanisation of work. The aim was to increase productivity and improve the experience of work. Socio-technical systems theory says that human work systems, how people are organised to work together and technical systems are mutually influential. Their joint impact must be carefully considered and optimised.

FAILED EXPERIMENTS?

Experiments in developing production systems based on a humanistic, socio-technical philosophy in the automotive industry were most famously associated with the Volvo plants at Kalmar and Uddevalla (Rehder 1992). Redher comments that the Uddevalla system required a high commitment and upfront cost in selection, retention and training. The Uddevalla plant closed in 1993, and Kalmar in 1994 (Sandberg 2007).

Although there were reports of problems in the first year of operation, with high turnover and high rates of absenteeism, productivity is reported to have improved significantly as learning became embedded. In a preface to the digital edition of *Enriching Production*, Sandberg maintains that the factories were closed prematurely. He says that 'ideas of competitive and human-centred forms of industrial production are still alive and practiced in various sectors'.

THEN CAME LEAN

Lean was beginning to demonstrate another way of combining social and technical systems. In the socio-technical perspective, long work cycles and work group autonomy are seen as motivating and productive. In the lean approach, the emphasis is on short cycles, standardised work procedures applied to the whole organisation, and worker involvement in process innovation and control (Sandberg 2007: 24). In stressing autonomy over process discipline and integration, the socio-technical systems approach requires buffers in the form of work-in-progress, whereas lean requires their removal (Klein 1991).

The relative merits of lean and the socio-technical approaches are hotly disputed (Adler and Cole 1993, Berggren 1993, Berggren 1994, Dankbaar 1997). Heckscher (1995) is scathing about autonomous work groups that eventually build walls around themselves, worsening bureaucracy and increasing organisational politics. Significant criticisms of lean systems were reviewed in Chapter 3. Sandeberg (2007) admits that 'lean production is not monolithic' and that tendencies towards humanisation of lean approaches were emerging.

RENEWED SIGNIFICANCE

The socio-technical philosophy acquires new significance with the explosion of social networking and collaboration technologies that is bringing the mutual influence of social and technological systems back into sharp focus. Business processes are not only increasingly abstract, they are distributed across time, place and multiple organisational boundaries. All this implies significant degrees of technologically enabled social interaction. Re-examination of some of the developmental thinking around the socio-technical systems approach is timely, especially the work of Cherns (1976, 1987) and Clegg (2000).

Socio-technical Principles

Cherns proposed a set of principles for participative socio-technical systems design. The principles are particularly appropriate for designing smart working practices, especially since they pay particular attention to the design of social support systems for knowledge-sharing and learning, and autonomy in deciding how work is to be performed. The intention here is not to reproduce each of the principles, but to draw attention to the fact that they support smart working practices and reflect the reality of social dynamics.

MINIMUM CRITICAL SPECIFICATION

According to Cherns, we must 'realise that design is an arena for conflict' and that how conflict is managed sets the conditions for emergent participative design, which continually adapts through constant evaluation. This means that the design teams must 'work to their own process and principles of operation', principles of operation that must comply with 'minimum critical specification'. This requires that just enough essential design criteria are articulated, leaving ample latitude for interpretation and application. What has to be done must be stated clearly, but how is left unspecified and decided by those doing the work.

The musician Brian Eno, who is an enthusiast of Stafford Beer's work, believes in improvising within rules and principles that are interpreted according to context:

> Cybernetician Stafford Beer had a great phrase that I lived by for years: Instead of trying to specify the system in full detail, specify it only somewhat. You then ride on the dynamics of the system in the direction you want to go. He was talking about heuristics, as opposed to algorithms. Algorithms are a precise set of instructions, such as take the first on the left, walk 121 yards, take the second on the right ... a heuristic, on the other hand, is a general and vague set of instructions.[4]

---

4   http://www.wired.com/wired/archive/3.05/eno_pr.html [accessed: 15 April 2012].

Socio-technical principles and the principles embedded within the Viable Systems Model – the five management functions with which each viable system must comply – facilitate the emergence of dynamic, improvised action.

SUPPORT CONGRUENCE

Another of Cherns's principles is support congruence, where systems of social support should be appropriate for local operational objectives and desired behaviours. Information and social support are crucial for those closest to value-creating performance. The principles of support congruence and local action are highly consistent with the VSM.

BOUNDARY LOCATION

Another of Cherns's principles that is highly relevant for smart working practices is boundary location and design. Boundaries should be drawn so that they facilitate learning, information-sharing and knowledge-sharing, which he says is the 'essential feature' of this principle. This is similar to the integrated, cross-boundary focus of the co-ordination function in the VSM.

MULTI-FUNCTIONAL

The multi-functional, multi-skilling principle is about creating flexibility and redundancy within work systems through expanding skills, knowledge and capabilities. This is equivalent to requisite variety in the VSM, where skills, knowledge and capabilities are crucial for engaging with complexity and ensuring viability.

CHERNS'S PRINCIPLES UPDATED

Clegg (2000) subsequently expanded on Cherns's principles, updating them to reflect the fact that the business environment had changed significantly in the intervening years. The revised and expanded principles are intended to:

- provoke questions and provide a framework for the design of work systems;

- propose a participative approach to process articulation and choice of technologies.

Specifying the management practices and process control techniques associated with first wave smart working – like team-working, JIT, TQM, supply-chain partnering and cell-based production – Clegg comments that these new management and working practices were accompanied by the introduction of new technologies. He observes that many technical innovations at that time were less effective than intended, and that management practices were not adapting to enable technological innovations to be realised to their full extent. Clegg (2000) organises his revised socio-technical principles for systems design into three groups:

1.   meta-principles intended to capture social values, contingent factors, cultural dimensions and stakeholder needs;

2.   content principles, including issues around core processes and their integration, task design, allocation of performance responsibilities and performance criteria, design for flexibility, and problems to be tackled at source;

3.   principles concerned with the process of participative design (which he stresses is political), including resourcing and supporting the design process.

Clegg says that, like Cherns's earlier work, he is offering his own work as ideas and to promote debate and to encourage action.

Concluding Remarks

The Viable Systems Model and the social technical systems theories are underpinned by common themes, including the need for maximised local autonomy and resolving challenges at the point where people have practical knowledge. This means recognising latent capability distributed throughout the organisation, particularly those people at the front line of operations whose skills and knowledge may have been previously overlooked.

Despite criticisms of both theoretical approaches, the Viable Systems Model can be used to 'focus debates about the social nature of human activity' (Espejo and Harnden 1989), and since the ideas behind the socio-technical systems design principles are contested: 'Such ideas are worth making explicit; in this way they can be debated and challenged, but also defended and approved' (Clegg 2000).

The aim of this chapter was to make the case for the usefulness of theory to inform systems design. The need to design for adaptation, autonomy, integration and cross-boundary knowledge-sharing was identified from the review of first wave smart working.

The VSM and socio-technical systems perspectives provide design principles concerning adaptability, autonomy, integration and knowledge-sharing that can be built into tools and frameworks for people to use as they act together to create adaptive social structures in real time. Both theoretical approaches facilitate adaptation and integrated autonomy through environmental scanning, performing and integrating at the point where value is created. Allocating resources and social support systems for action as problems arise sets the conditions for adaptive learning, and possibilities for co-evolving technical and social systems through a process of reciprocal determinism.

PART II
All Change

5

What is Happening?

Introduction

Combined global workplace trends are generating rapid continuous change on many fronts, which pose constant challenges and escalating levels of complexity and uncertainty for businesses. Mobile technologies, cloud computing and social technologies, are playing a key role in how work and organisations reconfigure in response to these global workplace trends. This chapter explores a number of global trends and summarises their implications for people, processes, performance environments and knowledge.

Social Technologies

The effect of people connecting, conversing and creating content online has led to the fundamental re-structuring of entire industries. Traditional broadcast media and the music industries are the first to have felt the consequences. According to one source (Charron et al. 2006):

> The avalanche of high quality videos, photos and emailed news material from citizens following the July 7 bombings in London marked a turning point for the BBC ... evolving from being a broadcaster to facilitator of news. Richard Sambrook (Director, BBC Global News Division) likened the increasing use of user-generated content to a sports game; the crowd was not only invading the field but also seeking to participate in the game, fundamentally changing the sport.

CONNECT AND INTERACT

The social networking phenomenon is spontaneous and self-organised. Social technologies outside enterprises are being adopted without permission.

They are connecting people within and across networks and communities, enabling relationships among people to flourish. The influence of time and distance is now irrelevant. Network ties and conversations are energised and made visible. danah boyd, an ethnographer of digital culture, expands on the core properties of social networking sites. Particularly speaking about young people, she says that social networking technologies:

- let people create personal profiles, which can be seen as a 'digital body' where people write about themselves and 'write themselves into being';

- let people identify others as friends, who then comprise an imagined audience and a self-defined social group;

- contain comment structures that allow public interactions and where relationships with others are displayed (boyd 2007).

DISCOVER, CREATE, DISTRIBUTE

As well as giving us a voice and opportunity to publish, the social communication technologies we have at our disposal create endless opportunities to discover other people, and to discover, create and distribute content. Mobile devices allow us to 'capture information at the point of inspiration' (Jaokar and Fish 2006), and this is then shared throughout personal and business networks. Om Malik, a well-known blogger, echoes Jaokar and Fish's insight when he says: 'Today most of us walk around with newfangled smartphones that are nothing short of multitasking computers, essentially content creation points. And they're networked, which means creating and sharing content is becoming absurdly simple to do' (Malik 2009).

Of course, connections among people that inspire discovery and creativity are nothing new, as Cees Noteboom (1998) observes on his travels through Spain. In the museum attached to the cathedral in El Burgo de Osma, he sees a map of what people thought the world looked like in 1086 and notes Carolingian influence in the colours used, Arab influence in its geometric patterns, Lombardian influence in the use of animal motifs, Irish spiralled braiding and so on. He says: 'But we know how profound the pollinating influence in those days was, that the world was already a world, that people communicated and saw each other's art, that artists and craftsmen travelled and inspired one another.'

Like the medieval artists who travelled, discovered and were inspired by each other, we now have amazing tools and technologies that let us do the same. Only now, we do not have to travel long distances to foreign lands, pleasurable though that is. We can carry the world's people and the things they know, think about and create around in our pockets.

BEYOND ENTERTAINMENT

Entertainment is a major reason why people use social technologies, but they also fuel creativity and social learning on a massive scale. They allow the ability to co-create, be inspired and learn together across organisational boundaries, therefore expanding learning horizons through exposure to the pollinating influence of different working practices and cultural influences.

Co-creation, discovering, sharing, inspiring and learning are the source of so many possibilities for second wave smart working. They are also changing the balance of power towards communities of customers (Ahonen and Moore 2005).

Social Technologies at Work

Behind corporate walls, though, the story is frequently different. Workforce use of social technologies is resisted, and the reflex reaction of many companies has been to ban access to social networking sites through fear of time-wasting and loss of confidentiality (White et al. 2011).

Where they have been taken up for business use, early enterprise adoption was initially driven by a desire to communicate externally with customers or to find and engage with potential new recruits, and in some cases 'crowd-sourcing' intelligence to solve technical problems.

Innovating enterprises are beginning to extend their use of social and collaborative technologies internally, and across their organisational boundaries. Some examples of how social technologies are being used to achieve a range of business purposes will be summarised throughout this chapter.

What do these technologies allow people to do? Why, despite suspicion of them and resistance to them within organisations, do they have such disruptive and high-performance potential? The analyses of four thought leaders in the field of the digitally connected enterprise shed light on social technologies and their capabilities.

THE POWER OF RELATIONSHIPS

McAfee (2009) is recognised for having coined the term 'Enterprise 2.0' to describe the enterprise use of social technologies to pursue business goals. Together with supporting organisational and management processes, the technologies are being deployed to create business value in a number of ways. McAfee stresses that Enterprise 2.0 is not primarily a technological phenomenon, and identifies six things that 'emergent social software platforms', as he calls the range of technologies, enable:

1.   co-creating and editing of centrally stored artefacts;

2.   sharing and commenting on content;

3.   asking for information on discussion forums or micro-blogging platforms;

4.   connecting and making relationships with others visible;

5.   seeking responses from a dispersed group;

6.   self-organisation.

McAfee draws attention to different strengths of relationships among people, citing Granovetter (1973) on the strength of weak ties. Granovetter's classic paper is gaining new significance and widespread attention with the appearance of social technologies. Relationship ties are strong among people who know each other well. Groups of these strong relationships form nodes of a potential network of relationships. Each person within the node has weaker ties to acquaintances outside the strong group. These weak ties turn out to be crucial in making links between network nodes. Like Noteboom's medieval artists, they are sources of new ideas, information and knowledge.

CONNECT, COLLABORATE, COMMUNICATE

Cook (2008) provides a useful four-category framework that he calls 'the 4Cs Social Software Technology Framework', as shown in Figure 5.1, which positions technologies according to whether they predominantly enable people to communicate, co-operate, collaborate or connect.

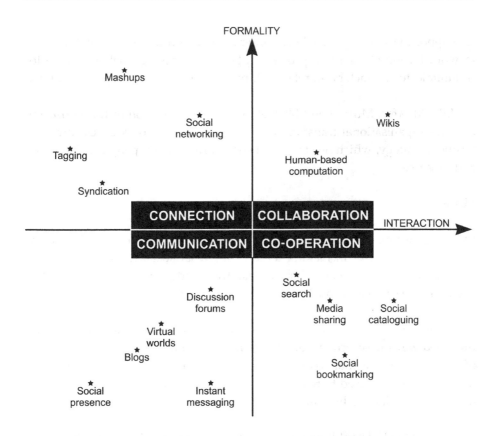

FORMALITY

Mashups

Social networking

Wikis

Tagging

Human-based computation

Syndication

| CONNECTION | COLLABORATION |
| COMMUNICATION | CO-OPERATION |

INTERACTION

Social search

Discussion forums

Media sharing

Social cataloguing

Virtual worlds

Blogs

Social bookmarking

Social presence

Instant messaging

Figure 5.1   Cook's 4Cs Social Software Technology Framework
© Niall Cook, 2008

Cook differentiates between co-operation and collaboration. Co-operation involves informal interactions that are not dictated by pre-defined goals. Individuals keep authority and ownership of their contributions. Collaboration, on the other hand, is where effort is co-ordinated in pursuit of shared goals and problem-solving. He explains how different technologies are used under each category. For example, for the communication category he describes discussion forums at the BBC, how they were introduced, and how people use them to find others, to get answers to queries and to let off steam.

PEOPLE, BEHAVIOURS, PROCESSES

Murray and Shah (2010) prefer to use the more inclusive term 'social computing' rather than 'social networking'. They summarise the role of social computing as 'supporting the way people can interact and to frame the steps for them to work on loosely defined problems'. Social computing enables people to communicate, interact, build relationships, decide collectively and collaborate.

Like McAfee, Murray and Shah stress that the adoption of Enterprise 2.0 involves organisational transformation of operational processes, culture and business strategy, which needs to be focused primarily on people, behaviours and processes.

SEARCH

J.P. Rangaswami, in a keynote address to a conference in London, adopted an economic perspective in making the case for what social technologies allow us to do, which in his view is predominantly to reduce transaction costs.[1] He spoke about search as a core business activity.

Stating that the firm of today is not the firm of tomorrow, Rangaswami proposed viewing search through the framework of transaction costs. The nub of his argument was that according to classical economics, firms exist because they are the best placed to reduce transaction costs through a superior ability to access financial and human capital.

Firms need to adapt if they are to survive as entities offering the best way to minimise transaction costs. Social tools create the opportunity to do exactly that. Recommendation is a powerful use of social networks for discovering people and information. No one can know everything, but everyone can nurture reputations for specific capabilities. We promote our reputations and others find us, applying filters to choose according to who knows what. Rangaswami spoke about the value of serendipity, of dipping into flows of information on micro-blogging sites like Twitter.

Fulfilment cycle

Rangaswami points out that none of this is new, and that what he calls the fulfilment cycle is standard business behaviour. The fulfilment cycle is: search, subscribe (ask for information such as regular status reports), have conversations and execute for a purpose. The key point now is that social networking technologies reduce transaction costs associated with search, allowing us to do what we have always done more cost-effectively.

---

1   SOMESSO/Headshift Social Business Summit, 18 March 2010.

CREATING CUSTOMER-FOCUSED VALUE

Transaction costs are also reduced when value is created. Seddon reminds us that transaction costs are reduced at the point where the organisation meets the customer.[2] The people in the organisation most involved with the customer have typically been in the front line. These people are crucial and often under-appreciated sources of customer-focused value-creation.

Social technologies potentially vastly increase the number of points where the organisation meets the customer, since all employees are now exposed to the customer through social networks and become ambassadors for the business. They also create the potential for hard-pressed front-line workforces to access social and emotional support, through communities of peers who learn and share experience among themselves.

Enabling unrealised potential

Framing organisational design issues from a transaction cost perspective is an alternative to framing in terms of value-creation through unrealised capabilities. Putting people's ingenuity to work with the aim of reducing transaction costs would be a good start.

This is exactly what the first wave of smart working was all about, and it continues to be an objective in this new wave. If continuous improvement was integral to the first wave of smart working, then the phenomenal potential of connected creativity and intelligence, which is energised and accessed through social technologies, leads to the collaborative, collective intelligence of the second wave. As Lee (2008) says:

> Many of us who push the concepts of social computing are often referred to as evangelists … what you're evangelising isn't about a bunch of technology. It never has been. It's about human potential, about a more efficient and effective way to collaborate. Collaboration is the entire reason a company exists.

BARRIERS TO ADOPTION

The potential of these new technologies, which present us with unprecedented possibilities for unleashing human potential, is hindered by entrenched

---

2   http://vimeo.com/10278907 [accessed: 31 March 2012].

mindsets and limiting formal organisational structures. The promise of new technologies is further limited by existing organisational cultures, which are fixated on control, micro-managing and avoiding risk.

Nevertheless, case studies are beginning to appear of performance cultures being transformed by focusing on business processes and deploying social technologies in bringing people together to collaborate on process innovation and control (EMC^2 2008, Shah 2010). The account of how EMC Corporation set out to transform business processes by inculcating social media proficiency throughout its globally distributed and fragmented organisation is highly recommended (EMC^2 2008).

The report's author is careful to stress that the focus is not on the technologies, but on how collaborative, sharing behaviours are developed through applying and using social technologies in pursuit of effective business processes. This is resulting in a fundamental transformation of the company, including its ecosystem of stakeholders, and leading to 'substantial and compelling results throughout our business'. Examples of how social technologies are being applied to business processes will be referred to throughout this chapter.

Blurring Boundaries

Multiple boundaries within and across organisations are currently being breached. This is resulting in complex and constantly shifting sets of interacting organisational parameters that are not easy to untangle. Like patterns in a kaleidoscope, emergent organisational configurations are made up of fragmented and distributed entities that operate across multiple workplaces, time zones and cultures.

GLOBALLY INTEGRATED ENTERPRISES

Palmisano (2006) refers to globally integrated enterprises, which are locating design and production activities anywhere in the world to take advantage of new sources of skills and knowledge. He talks about the numbers of Western companies establishing factories in China and India. The trend is not just one-way. Indian and Chinese multi-nationals, and those of other emerging economies, are increasingly buying foreign companies (PWC 2010).

Globally integrated enterprises are enabled and supported by a diversity of employment relationships, collaboration agreements and contractual arrangements that are associated with emerging business models. Boundaries are being blurred with respect to functions, knowledge disciplines, organisational cultures, demographic groups, organisations, regions and nations.

Organisational Boundaries

Instances of enterprises extending beyond their own boundaries to co-operate within geographically based regional networks are well documented. Pettigrew and Fenton (2000) discuss socially embedded enterprises in the context of inter-organisational joint ventures, and partnerships and alliances. They point out that long-established geographically located industrial clusters – for example those in Northern Italy – are influenced by political and social institutions such as family relationships that strongly determine contractual and co-operative behaviours.

The trend towards partnering and forging alliances is accelerating in recent years, reaching out globally and beyond geographical boundaries as 'companies in emerging markets will continue aggressively moving beyond their own borders and become fierce competitors on the world stage' (IBM 2010b).

PARTNERSHIPS AND ALLIANCES

Why are partnerships and alliances becoming such prevalent business models? After all, making contractual partnerships and voluntary alliances succeed can be challenging (Hirsch et al. 2005).

One reason is that collaboration is a way of sharing expertise and costs of innovation. For others, collaboration is a strategic choice to mitigate shared risks, despite the fact that 'determining whether to invest in mitigation of events beyond an organisation's internal processes' involves complex negotiations (PWC 2009). It would appear that the difficulties of complex negotiations and management challenges of partnerships are offset by superior performance outcomes.

The 2008 IBM Global CEO Study reported 'pervasive' partnering among survey respondents, with outperformers '20 per cent more likely to partner extensively than underperformers', reinforcing findings from the previous Global CEO Study. The report notes that the main business benefit is strategic access to knowledge and skills (IBM 2008). Yet others are engaging in joint ventures to gain access to capital that would otherwise be unobtainable within the current financial climate (CBI 2009).

It is obviously not just large, complex companies that operate in globally distributed partnerships. The technologies permit low-barrier entry for start-ups taking advantage of cost-effective tools to discover, engage and link globally distributed talent. It is now easy for agile, small businesses to collaborate to punch above their weight in global markets.

IMPLICATIONS FOR MANAGING

The implications for working and managing practices are profound. The increasing incidence and diversity of partnership arrangements means that organisations are beginning to look and behave like social networks.[3] A major consequence of this is that partners in business alliances cannot be commanded in the same controlling way employees have traditionally been managed.

A new type of job therefore emerges, it is argued, which concerns the management of networks of external relationships. The exercise of persuasion, influencing, negotiating and dialogue becomes critical for effective outcomes.

Cultural Boundaries

Negotiating the multiple cultural boundaries (personal, organisational and professional) experienced within joint ventures can present significant operational overheads. Mergers, acquisitions and conglomerates are complex undertakings, where conditions for merger success have to be recognised, considered and met (Epstein 2005).

Although Epstein includes 'management of human resources, technical operations and customer relationships' as one of six keys to merger success, he makes no specific reference to culture. Cross-boundary cultural considerations

---

3   This observation was made in an online article entitled 'Of Whales and Suckerfish', which is no longer available. It was previously available at http://www.microsoft.com/uk/business/peopleready/resources/economist.mspx.

are crucial, though (Very et al. 1996, Vaara et al. 2003, Epstein 2005, Zhu and Huang 2007), with DaimlerChrysler serving as a high-profile example of cultural mismatch between merging organisations contributing significantly to the failure of the merger (Badrtalei and Bates 2007).

Cultural boundaries are not only breached in joint ventures like mergers, acquisitions and consolidations. Cultural dispersion across time and place, enabled by communication technologies, and migration of the creative classes to places they find attractive (Florida 2004, Florida 2007) means that cultural diversity is increasingly the norm. Case Study 4 in the following section shows how NSN used discussion forums as one component of a post-merger strategy to influence social dynamics in pursuit of an emergent new culture over time.

CASE STUDY 4: EMERGENT CULTURE AND DIALOGUE

The following example shows how discussion forums were used as just one component among of a set of interventions in a long-term engagement between senior management and a globally distributed workforce of 60,000 people. This began the process of creating a new emergent culture at the company NSN (Nokia Siemens Networks), which was formed as a result of a merger between Nokia's Networks Business Group and the carrier-related businesses of Siemens Communications.

This brief summary is from a presentation Alistair Moffat gave to the Johnson Controls Global Mobility Network in 2009, and is recounted here with grateful permission from both Alistair and Dr Marie Puybaraud of Johnson Controls. A more detailed and authoritative account is available in Moffat and McLean (2010), who write from the perspective of 'intense involvement during the first eighteen months of rich, deep and sometimes painful learning'. The authors were instrumental in influencing the environment that created the conditions for conversations and actions to unfold. The view taken of culture at NSN is that it is socially constructed and that it emerges in time from the struggle for shared meaning, achieved through participation and dialogue throughout the workforce.

Mergers are fraught with emotional uncertainty, and this merger was no different. Underpinning the process of creating the conditions for a new culture to emerge, cultural emergence was a long-term commitment. The first stage of the process was an exploration of legacy cultures, outcomes of which were presented to senior management to determine which features to focus on.

The next crucial step was to engage the rest of the global workforce in dialogue about the tentative cultural indicators. Social networking technologies in the form of discussion forums provided the opportunity to create an online place, 'The Culture Square', where company-wide conversations could take place. People were encouraged to talk freely and anonymously. There were initial worries about being monitored, but when the CEO promised that no one would be fired for saying what they believed, participation began to build. Contributions to conversations were often difficult as people voiced their feelings about the merger.

This case shows how the discussion forum technology was an enabler in the emergent culture-creation process. The values and attitudes of the CEO and his desire to nurture an organisational culture consistent with adult-to-adult relationships, where people could disagree without being disagreeable, were core to how the conversations unfolded.

It was not easy for senior management to listen to a deluge of criticism, even if it was considered legitimate. Despite the difficulties, it was felt that these conversations would be taking place privately anyway. 'The Culture Square' provided a safe outlet for people to let off steam. It came to represent trust and inclusion, revealing issues that people were concerned about.

Professional Boundaries

As well as cultural differences between organisations, internal cultural diversity among professional and functional groups can be problematic. In conversation at a conference with the CEO of a pharmaceutical company that makes generic drugs, he revealed that one of his biggest problems was trying to get scientists within his company to communicate outside their professional and specialist knowledge areas.

The example of how the pharmaceutical company GSK restructured its organisation, using the physical workplace to support the restructuring, to encourage cross-boundary knowledge-sharing will be discussed in Chapter 6.

In another Global Mobility Network meeting, we heard an example of how an innovative legal company was proposing to position publicly accessible communication technologies within the workplace to encourage serendipitous meetings among people from different groups and functions who might not otherwise find reasons to talk to one another. Using tools that needed no technical expertise, it was suggested that people would create videos and other content, which would then made available on screens strategically positioned to increase incidental communication across functional boundaries.

The legal profession is highly dependent on knowledge-sharing. One of the fears about social tools is that people will waste time chatting. This example shows a different attitude to conversations and serendipitous bumping into people, ideas and information, considering them as primary conduits for connecting to technical knowledge, social knowledge and social resources (Erickson and Kellogg 2003). Hagel et al. (2010) expand on the significance of serendipity for discovering people and information. They stress that serendipity is more than 'happy accident', where discovery is an end in itself. Rather, they see serendipity as: 'The beginning of, rather than an end to, a discovery process … it becomes the crucial means of access to rich flows of tacit knowledge both now and in the future.'

Anytime, Anywhere?

Boundaries of time and place are blurring, and people are apparently demanding a 'new reality' from work (Equal Opportunities Commission 2007a), particularly the new generation of workers keen to work in businesses that offer them more flexible approaches to working.

FLEXIBLE WORKING

Flexibility can apply to time, place and employment contract – for example, full-time, part-time or freelance. Examples of flexible working practices might include compressed hours, annualised hours, job-sharing, flexitime, working from home and career breaks.[4]

Combinations of flexible working practices are restricted for specific groups of employees by the jobs they do, ranging from being completely location-dependent and having some limited flexibility of time, through shift-working, through to having full discretion over where, when and how work is performed (Orange Future Enterprise Coalition 2007).

---

4   http://www.cipd.co.uk/hr-resources/factsheets/flexible-working.aspx [accessed: 9 March 2012].

Five years ago, it was reported that flexible working practices in the UK were increasing (CBI 2008, KPMG/CIPD 2008) and becoming 'the norm' (Hayward et al. 2007), with evidence of 'clear interest amongst businesses in a real diversity of practices, dispelling the myth that small businesses are inflexible' (British Chamber of Commerce 2007).

The evidence appears contradictory. It is widely supposed that knowledge workers are in the vanguard of a shift away from traditional patterns of work, exercising significant autonomy over how, when and where work is carried out. According to the Work Foundation, this is not happening. Brinkley et al. (2009) report that:

> *Knowledge workers are not spear-heading radical changes in the way we work ... less than 60 per cent of knowledge workers said they have some flexibility in their work schedule, and only a very small minority said they can freely determine their own hours.*

The Johnson Controls Flexible Working Survey of 2010 found that flexible workers are spending a lot of time working on the move, even more than in the office. The office is consequently being regarded as the place to be seen, to meet others and to engage in collaborative work (Puybaraud 2010).

Workplace remains vital

Recent conversations with executives in two large, well-known global enterprises reveal an interesting counter-force to home-working. In both cases, these knowledge-intensive companies are widely recognised as innovative employers. One of the companies does not permit its software engineers to work from home, believing that they need to be co-located to collaborate effectively.

The other permits working from home, but does not encourage it. Moreover, it is the company's young workforce who demonstrate a preference for coming in to the office because they do not want to miss out on events and want to feel involved in what is happening. In both cases, considerable effort goes into the office design to make it attractive and the first choice in preference to alternatives, through facilitating creativity and collaboration. We will address this topic in greater detail in Chapter 6.

This is consistent with the Johnson Controls Flexible Working Survey, which found that people needed to be visible as economic conditions worsened. An 'urge to return to the office' was detected. Flexibility becomes more of a cultural indicator of agility, rather than new ways of working (Puybaraud 2010). It is interesting to note that younger people were found to be more dependent on the physical environment, with older workers in the 41–45 age group more comfortable in using cafes and hotels for meetings.

SUPPORTING DISTRIBUTED WORKING

Many practical issues are involved in the shift from desk-bound to mobile, distributed working. Learning points from case studies of businesses that have made the transition to remote and mobile working include:

- It is important to prepare when introducing new ways of working.

- The senior executive/board level support is critical for success.

- Senior management affect behaviour by their actions.

- There is a need for consistent and constant communication.

- Customer-focused outputs need to be understood and managed.

- People become accustomed over time to different ways of working.

- Robust technology and swift support when technology does fail are important.

- The nature of the work being performed influences the type of support needed.

- Social support is crucial.

- The needs of different sub-cultures have to be considered.

- Small irritations can be aggravated through isolation.

- There is a need for a phased, structured process to facilitate the transition to new ways of working (Ennals and McEwan 2004).

These learning points are not comprehensive. Resources on how to make the transition to flexible, distributed working and the issues involved are plentiful (Orange Future Enterprise Coalition 2007, Equal Opportunities Commission 2007a, Toshiba and flexibility.co.uk 2012).

Shrinking social distance

People have a strong preference for workplaces where strong working relationships are characterised by loyalty and mutual trust (The Work Foundation in association with BT 2009). Being separated from strong social bonds in the workplace can become problematic, resulting in social isolation and a feeling of being out of the loop.

It used to be more of a frustration for people to be working away from the nerve centre of the office than it currently is. Collaboration and communication technologies can enable a sense of social presence and restore social cohesion for people separated across diverse global business operations, shrinking social distances in workplace relationships (Puybaraud and McEwan 2009a).

Smartphones and tablets strengthen social connectedness since these technologies are carried around with us all the time and effectively become an extension of who we are. The mobile Web accessed on the go is rapidly replacing the fixed Internet accessed from desk-bound computers. In an IBM report, *Go Mobile, Grow*, Seider et al. (2008) say:

> *On the fixed Internet, social media are quickly taking off. While consumers may still manage their social networks on the PC, they will likely use their mobile to upload short videos or photos, get alerts when somebody posts a comment and get RSS feeds on selected topics sent to them while on the go.*

Communication technologies that are accessed on the go from tablets and smartphones have become a powerful way to shrink social distance in distributed, mobile working. Accessing social networks through tools like Twitter can be very effective.

An example

In a presentation he gave to the Johnson Controls Global Mobility Network as far back as 2008, Joshua March used a case study to explain why Twitter can be so effective in overcoming social distance and in strengthening ties among globally distributed work colleagues.

He explained that Twitter started out as a small group tool, and emerged into a conversation tool to learn about breaking news, to hear a new story, to get access to information, to tap into an event, to use as a personal recommendation tool and to look for people. Joshua demonstrated the business value of Twitter through a case study of a start-up of 46 people dispersed over seven US cities and a team in London.

One of the disadvantages of using email and instant messaging was that duplicate information cluttered up in-boxes and no central record of conversations was kept with instant messaging. An alternative was to set up secure Twitter accounts for everyone, which could be accessed from computers or mobiles. This created an always-on conversation that kept everyone in constant touch to communicate project status updates and as a source of support if anyone needed to ask for information or assistance. If those online were unable to help, a record of conversations was maintained that allowed those coming online later to pick and respond to requests for help.

Joshua noted that instant messaging is insistent, and that this is a disadvantage. The expectation of an instant response to an instant message is not there with Twitter; it is acceptable for people to respond in their own time. Another advantage is that in these 'attention-bankrupt' times, the limitation to 140 characters for a message forces people to make their messages concise. He reflected that ambient communication through technologies like Twitter can be a double-edged sword. On the positive side, they can create social cohesion among teams dispersed across time zones and different locations. In addition, innovation comes from incidental conversations and structured randomness. Downsides in an enterprise context include reputation and risk management, the need for privacy controls and possible dangers of the informal being made permanent.

BARRIERS TO DISTRIBUTED WORKING

'Presenteeism' is still a strong feature in management, where the time people spend in the workplace is monitored. The tendency to focus on time with insufficient regard to how people are spending that time is problematic.

In an interview with a senior executive who was talking about implementing a policy of encouraging people to work from home, she said that a major sticking point had been the attitude and skills of some line managers. They had to learn to put the customer at the centre of decision-making, and also had to comply with staff-driven flexible working. As long as customer needs were met, staff determined among themselves how and when to deliver the work. Many managers at first often found it difficult to scope and reward outputs.

Demographics

Two aspects of current global demographic shifts are impinging on business operations:

1. Populations in Western economies are ageing and retiring, taking with them years of accumulated knowledge and experience. This is in contrast to the emerging economies, which have large numbers of young people in their populations, although China's is ageing as a consequence of the one child policy.

2. The arrival of the next generation into the workplace is stimulating comment in management literature. Much of what is written is anecdotal, contradictory and contested. Research data are beginning to emerge, which are providing a clearer picture of the new generation's expectations and preferences.

AGEING WORKFORCES

The challenges of ageing populations for businesses are 'epochal' and will reshape societies, economies and markets throughout the next century (Hori et al. 2010). A United Nations report on ageing populations throughout the world in general proposes that ageing is: 'Without parallel in human history – and the twenty-first century will witness even more rapid ageing than did the century just past' (United Nations 2002).

According to this report, there were three countries whose populations included more than 10 million people aged 60 or older (India, China and the USA). By 2000, the number of countries had increased to 12 and the total over 60 had risen from 205 million to 606 million. The number is projected to rise to 2 billion by 2050. The report concludes that the older population is growing faster than the total population 'in practically all regions of the world – and the difference in growth rates is increasing'.

In an update the 2002 report and subsequent report in 2007, a United Nations working paper ranked countries by percentage of population aged 60 or over in 2009. The top ranking went to Japan, followed by Italy, Germany and Sweden. Greece, Portugal, Belgium, Denmark, the UK and France are all in the top 20, along with Switzerland, Austria, Estonia, Latvia and Bulgaria. The USA ranks 42nd and Russia 44th (United Nations 2009).

When the working-age populations of India and China are compared, China's growth prospects will be constrained by a declining working population due the combined effects of ageing and the one child policy. India has the advantage of a growing young population, giving it a 'demographic dividend'.[5] However, many are not yet ready for employment, and adult literacy rates may endanger growth.

This does not seem to overly worry *The Economist*. In an article titled 'India's Surprising Economic Miracle', the author notes that India's 'dependency ratio – the proportion of children and old people to working adults – is one of the best in the world and will remain so for a generation'. The article predicts that India's advantage will grow as the global economy becomes more knowledge-intensive, and that the growth of the nation's economy will outpace that of China (*The Economist* 2010a).

MULTI-GENERATIONAL WORKPLACES

Why is an ageing workforce viewed as something to be so concerned about? One problem is the loss of so much experience, organisational wisdom and memory when people do retire. Rather than retiring, though, a counter-trend is for people to continue to be economically active beyond traditional retirement age. A second consequence is an increase in generational diversity in the workplace. Rather than being a problem, opportunities for inter-generational learning, taking advantage of young people's energy and creativity, are significant.

The ageing workforce also has implications for management capabilities and workplace design. Managers have to understand and be sensitive to the

---

5   http://blog.euromonitor.com/2010/11/indias-working-age-population-growing-faster-than-chinas.html [accessed: 15 April 2012].

fact that needs and desires evolve at different life stages (Eisner 2005, Martin and Tulgan 2006, Wagner 2007). Myerson et al. (2010) examine the ageing workforce from the perspective of physical workplace design. Whereas a young workforce may appreciate sociability, he proposes that older people tend to prefer quiet and reflection.

GENERATION Y

The newest entrants to the workforce, aged roughly 18–25 and sometimes referred to collectively as Generation Y or Millennials, are said to be fundamentally different from other generations (Deloitte 2009). This is a strong claim to make. So much has been written about this new generation. It is difficult to separate poorly supported assertions from what is in fact a much more complex and culturally influenced picture.

According to Deloitte (2007): 'They [Generation Y] communicate differently, they socialise differently and most importantly they expect to work differently than previous generations. They are used to an age of instant gratification – be it media, music or work.' This comment, left online in response to an online article on Generation Y (Heskett 2007), supports the supposed characteristic of quick gratification – as well as receptiveness to global networking:

> So it's actually a global phenomenon. Out here in India, we have been seeing this generation which requires 'quick gratification'; the feeling is that this generation has grown up in a comparative era of plenty, not the era of scarcity, and this has fuelled this attitude. This generation is productive in ways that the earlier generation has not been and is possibly far more alive to global networking concepts.

What are they like?

It is, of course, not possible to label a whole generation of young people. Bearing this in mind, and at the risk of stereotyping, the following brief review of Generation Y's apparent characteristics comes from diverse and publicly available sources. They have been called, by themselves and others, arrogant, self-absorbed and self-confident. They have high expectations of themselves, are not deferential and are ambitious. They have been called demanding 'workplace divas'.[6] They are social, networked and connected. Although they

---

6   http://www.changeboard.com/content/1499/how-to-manage-gen-y-expectations/ [accessed: 15 April 2012].

are highly collaborative, they also struggle in teams not of their own choosing. Research from the London Business School (2009) also notes a tendency for instant gratification.

Among the research reports beginning to provide data on different aspects of Generation Y is research from Ashridge Business School about learning preferences.[7] This concludes that the current education system is failing this generation in preparation for work. In a strongly target-driven school system, exploratory learning is challenged. A perceived need to find a 'right' answer and associated lack of curiosity feeds through to university. In common with other research,[8] the Ashridge research notes Generation Y's ability to graze large amounts of data and their desire for immediacy, resulting in fears that deeper understanding is jeopardised.

Respondents across all generations in the Ashridge research, not just Generation Y, indicated their preference for hands-on, interactive and collaborative learning, which is consistent with how informal, customised learning is developing through social networking and collaborative technologies.

Networked sociability

The sociologist Manuel Castells and his colleagues (2007) support the view that this new generation might be different. They see the emergence of a new trend in global youth culture, which they call 'networked sociability'. Digitally connected or face-to-face, networked sociability drives Generation Y to form peer groups that become the context for their individual and collective behaviour. Having grown up in the Internet age, Generation Y are furiously innovative in their use of communication technologies, establishing ways of behaving that in time diffuse across different generations. How they use communication technologies creates both challenges and opportunities in the workplace.

However, young people are not having things all their own way. Early clues that Generation Y's communication and collaboration habits will not be seamlessly absorbed within organisations are available in the large numbers of businesses banning access to social networking sites behind company firewalls. It may be that some of these businesses will relent as they understand more

---

7   http://www.ashridge.org.uk/Website/Content.nsf/FileLibrary/284E3C63840CCC3C802578DF0
    04B5C10/$file/ABSGenYReport2009.pdf [accessed: 31 March 2012].
8   Mobile Work Futures for Microsoft, conducted by the futurelaboratory, January 2007.

about designing, implementing and monitoring policies for safe use of social technologies.

Generation Y as consumers

Generation Y as consumers, especially in the huge and expanding emergent markets, are a force that should be driving Western workforces to smarter ways of working and managing. Vineet Nayar, CEO of HCL Technologies, has said:

> Growth is going to come from emerging markets like China, India, and others. The consumption patterns, demographics, and cultures of the people who are going to consume your products will change ... 50 percent of the population of the world is under 25 and Generation Y is dominating the consumption, and they are looking at more collaboration to make buying decisions.[9]

Three things jump out from that statement. One is that there are opportunities for Western companies in these growing markets. The second is that the largely Generation Y consumers in the emerging markets are demanding. The third is that young consumers in the emerging markets are collaborating in making buying decisions, which links back to Rangaswami's observation of the power of recommendation.

Businesses that want to compete in markets where young customers are dominant, discriminating, highly connected and cost-conscious need to engage the energies and capabilities of their entire workforces to have a chance of meeting the expectations of these demanding consumers, which *The Economist* (2010b) links to a new wave of disruptive management innovation.

Generation Y as gamers

One aspect of youth culture and online behaviour that is particularly notable and that sets Generation Y apart is their involvement in multi-player games. These are large-scale and global, with hundreds of thousands of people playing under self-organised, distributed leadership.

Players demonstrate multi-tasking, learn how to make agile decisions, evaluate risks, manage dilemmas and are persistent in the face of adversity

---

9   http://unstructurearchives.com/globalmeet2010/opening-address-by-vineet-nayar-ceo-hcl-technologies/ [accessed: 9 March 2012].

(IBM 2007). If these skills are transferable into the workplace – and there is no reason to suppose why they should not be – they are exactly the sort of inter-personal and leadership skills that needed for complex, rapidly changing, distributed and connected business environments.

Generation Y as drivers of change

Economies are currently struggling to emerge from the consequences of a major global financial crisis. It will be interesting to see how Generation Y respond to, for them, unprecedented economic turmoil. The Deloitte (2009) source characterises Generation Y as 'confident at a time of high insecurity'.

However they respond, young people are unlikely to abandon their desire for access to social technologies. When the up-turn comes, employers of choice will be those that provide social tools, collaborative work with opportunities for learning and development, and discretion over how, when and where Generation Y are allowed to work (Twentyman 2009).

Unless their collaborative ways change as they take on more management responsibilities, their collective trait of networked sociability, as members of workforces and as consumers, is likely to influence the design of organisational structures, working habits and workplace design in the future.

Evolving Economic Landscapes

Industrial decline in the USA and Europe, and the subsequent rise of knowledge and creative economies, are viewed by some as the biggest global economic shift since the Industrial Revolution.

Florida (2007) maintains that changes taking place in the nature of work and associated developments in the workplace constitute a step change in the transformation of economic and social systems that happens once in a century or even over a longer period. He describes the shift from predominantly industrial societies to creative economies and societies as being 'bigger than the shift from an agrarian to industrial society … bigger than the rise of the knowledge economy'.

Brinkley (2008) traces the structural shift in UK employment over the past thirty years. He says:

> *In 1978 more people worked as employees in manufacturing (just under 30 per cent) than in the industries subsequently classified by the OECD as 'knowledge intensive services' (just over 25 per cent). By 2007 just over 10 per cent of employees worked in manufacturing and over 40 per cent worked in knowledge intensive services.*

He then links this shift to globalisation and the rise of knowledge-based services. Despite the decline in manufacturing, he notes that manufacturing firms contribute significantly to knowledge-based services 'as new business models emerge that break down the traditional sectoral boundaries'.

Networked Economy

In view of the significance of knowledge-intensive services in achieving competitive advantage, this section explores what is happening to knowledge as a result of blurring boundaries and networked connectedness. It also considers how effectively knowledge and skills are being mobilised in the face of the urgent need to achieve and maintain competitiveness.

The case has already been made for organisations being complex, social and networked. It follows that knowledge is similarly co-created, social, dynamic, flowing and networked. This was always the case, but is now more apparent as a consequence of boundary-spanning, connected, dynamic and distributed processes. Cantrell et al. (2005) summarise what this means for knowledge workers:

- They are dispersed across organisations, countries, cultures, professions, physical locations and time zones.

- They are required to collaborate because their work is complex, emergent are rarely amenable to repetition and therefore standardisation.

- Their specialist knowledge is constantly changing and needs updating.

Networked Knowledge

Knowledge work ranges along a continuum from routine and well-formulated to messy and ill-defined.[10] The view is that as routine knowledge work can be codified, captured and automated, it is the tacit and unformulated type of knowledge that we need to pay attention to and nurture.

Creative knowledge that is messy and novel draws on tacit knowledge, which to Polanyi (2009) is what we know but cannot say how we know. As he puts it: 'we know more than we can tell'. Tacit knowledge is surfaced and made sense of through exploration and discovery, requiring personal judgement to be exercised in assessing an external reality.

Although tacit knowledge is deeply embedded within each of us, it is made explicit and given meaning through interactions with others. Social and collaborative technologies present great opportunities for an explosion of shared tacit knowledge, since they create the possibility of 'the extension and augmentation of the body and mind' within networks of interactions that have global reach (Castells 2004).

DISTRIBUTED COGNITIVE SYSTEMS

Heerwagen (2004) reminds us that knowledge dynamics are situated within distributed cognitive systems. She says: 'We can think of ourselves, our tools, our colleagues, our toys, our stories, our Post-it notes, and our piles of files as a distributed cognitive system that helps us remember and organize our thoughts.'

Distributed cognition is an important concept. As Figure 5.2 shows, interacting systems are required to support it.

Heerwagen's insight strongly implies that the physical workplace has a core role in visualising collective cognition and in providing congenial social spaces for tacit knowledge to be revealed, shared and co-created. The role of distributed place and space in mediating distributed cognition will be more fully explored in Chapter 6.

---

10   J. Myerson, 'The Importance of Contemplation'. Keynote speech delivered at Worktech North Conference, Salford Quays, 24 July 2008.

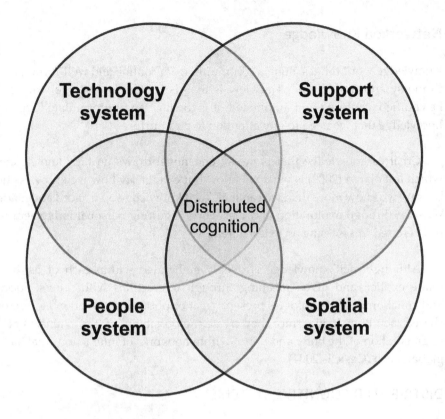

Figure 5.2   Supporting systems for distributed cognition

CREATIVE CONFLICT

Since making sense of culturally determined tacit knowledge is increasingly social, it is also inherently diverse and full of potential for conflict (Westley et al. 2007). This is especially true as conversations begin to take place across traditional discipline-based knowledge boundaries to generate reflexive, socially mediated shared responses to practical challenges (Gibbons et al. 1994).

New methodologies for changing mindsets are vital to uncover and make sense of share tacit knowledge, which is no longer constrained by physical location and is made sense of collectively. This links back to and reinforces the need to make deliberate efforts to blur persistently rigid boundaries across knowledge silos and organisational functions.

Knowledge embedded in different disciplines has to be uncovered and re-integrated within a systematic perspective. The new methodologies must therefore enable people to develop their specialist knowledge, while allowing them to integrate it with that of other disciplines and be able to facilitate fluid knowledge in dynamic situations.

SOCIALLY COMPLEX

Using an array of task attributes, Brinkley et al. (2009) compiled seven categories of knowledge-intensity and concluded that just over 10 per cent of the respondents in their study could be assessed as being in the highest segment of knowledge-intensity, leading them to say that 'these high-knowledge intensive jobs are, we suspect, what some of the more excitable accounts of knowledge work have in mind'.

Even if high-intensity, messy and creative knowledge work is not the majority of knowledge work, the blurring of multiple boundaries and emergence of partnerships as a dominant business model indicate that the ability to collaborate and navigate complex human relationships is likely to be increasingly crucial even in more routine and well-defined types of knowledge work.

COLLECTIVE INTELLIGENCE

Bollier (2007), reflecting on the deliberations of a group of business leaders who met to explore the practical implications of the rise of collective intelligence, said:

> We have become accustomed to expect creativity, innovation, and problem solving from individuals. In the new millennium, however, spurred by the ability of individuals to connect in time and place to virtually anyone, anywhere, an old mode of thinking – collectively – has taken a new turn.

Bollier gives several examples of enterprises accessing collective knowledge and intelligence as the basis of open innovation from customers, suppliers and researchers outside the business. These typically involve obtaining feedback on customer preferences and customer participation in product design. Similarly, Taylor and LaBarre (2006) cite Proctor & Gamble as an example of a business with 'celebrated research labs' looking outside the business beyond its own talented scientists to take advantage of equally talented people who do not work for the company.

Seely-Brown and Hagel see open innovation as transactional; engagement with outside people tends to end once the transaction is complete.[11] They believe this is limiting because it fails to create opportunities to build long-term relationships among participants missing the opportunity to create the trusted conditions needed for tacit knowledge to emerge and be shaped. The sort of collective intelligence that leads to co-creation, on the other hand, takes place within communities of people who share purpose and values, and who learn to trust each other and work together according to self-determined rules that influence their collective behaviour.

Barriers to collective intelligence

Technologies disseminate to the extent that they resonate with pre-existing social structures and cultural values (Castells et al. 2007). This is where the challenges begin for many enterprises. The report on mobile work futures for Microsoft referenced earlier in the chapter claimed that:

> *Organisational and behavioural structures in the workplace are only now adapting to the digital infrastructure on which so much of modern life depends ... improving on this is critical for businesses seeking to compete internationally, and it requires a new type of relationship between employer and employee. A new generation of workers is keen to embrace more flexible and federated approaches to working.*[12]

Sustained radical innovation will fall behind unless new systems of governance, collaboration, risk management and business financing are put in place (CBI 2009). These things all require investment in trusted relationships, which is a problem for many organisations obsessed with achieving and maintaining control. Moreover, this sort of systemic, structural change takes time.

On the evidence of research findings regarding the slowness of working practices to adapt to the performance-transforming potential of technology, and the initial dominant business reaction in banning access to social networking sites, it is not surprising that social technologies in the enterprise are not yet leveraging the sort of widespread benefits they have the potential to generate.

---

11 http://blogs.hbr.org/bigshift/2010/02/open-innovations-next-challeng.html [accessed: 1 November 2012].
12 Mobile Work Futures for Microsoft, conducted by the futurelaboratory, January 2007.

We are in a period of transition. The technologies are here, and businesses are both resisting and trying to work out how best to deploy them, learning how to design and put in place structures, practices and policies for their safe and effective use.

Nurturing high performers

Examples of collective intelligence interventions that draw widely on whole workforce's tacit knowledge, including an enterprise's extended eco-system of partnerships and alliances, are notable by their absence in the literature.

Taylor and LaBarre describe some of the talent-management strategies that the high-performance companies cited in their book *Mavericks at Work* use to attract and nurture 'star' performers (Taylor and LaBarre 2006). They conclude that businesses have to nurture high-performing individuals and create systems to support them. Taylor and LaBarre are not alone in proposing that all businesses have high-performing individuals.

Professor Colin Coulson-Thomas, speaking to a Johnson Controls Global Mobility Network meeting (Puybaraud and McEwan 2008), described his research into 'winning companies' (Coulson-Thomas 2007). He noted that although communication technologies have the capability to transform working practices and to support performance gains, the behaviours, attitudes and skills that enable high performance are on the whole not changing.

According to his research, every organisation has crucial people who are 'superstar' performers, and they are not being supported. High-performing companies need to know who these people are, and how to create systems and mechanisms to transfer their capabilities to others. Coulson-Thomas said that winning companies use technologies to exploit what they already have. He observed that many companies devote effort to things that do not make a difference.

The lack of awareness in many companies of who the high performers are, and the lack of systems to support them, is consistent with evidence from global CEOs who recognise that there are gaps in the information they need to make decisions about long-term success (PWC 2009). Despite most respondents believing that 'data about their customers (94 per cent) and their employees (88 per cent) are important or critical to long-term decision making', the situation is that 'strikingly low percentages of CEOs' say they have the comprehensive information they need.

HIDDEN POTENTIAL

While appreciating that many enterprises recognise and encourage elites, high-performing capabilities are by no means restricted to these people. Elites and high performers are not necessarily the same thing. One of the core contentions of this book is that enterprises have an abundance of undiscovered and under-utilised talent within their workforces.

Knowledge-management efforts need to be designed to include knowledgeable and talented people among the majority who lack the status, privileged connections or formal qualifications of elite groups. By definition, elites are apart from the majority. Paying attention to elite individuals is, of course, possible at the same time as designing learning environments for everyone.

If hidden talent is to be uncovered, it is crucial that businesses understand where value is being created, as Coulson-Thomas (2007) suggests, and who is creating it. This goes hand in hand with getting the learning and performance environment right – one where public conversation and shared learning are encouraged and made easy. Many more 'star performers' will emerge under those conditions.

One of the benefits of social networking technologies is that they make visible individual contributions and previously hidden connections along which knowledge flows are distributed. The hidden talent available to businesses extends beyond the workforces they employ directly. Each person who works for a company has access to a personal network of contacts outside the company, which can be accessed for connections and information – extending and augmenting individual and joint capabilities.

For example, my company at one time employed the services of a young animator. It quickly became clear that he was distributing work-in-progress to his animator colleagues for comment before presenting it for my consideration. In effect, my company reaped the benefit of their collective talents as well as his.

INFORMAL NETWORKS

Social technologies provide the opportunity for enterprises to discover and nurture the connected, collective intelligence that flourishes within hidden informal networks. The Global Mobility Network set out to explore how enterprise social networking might influence knowledge-management. Participants were asked to define enterprise social networking. Responses included (Puybaraud and McEwan 2008):

1. 'informal communities reaching across the formal structure of an organisation and supply chain, generating value, ideas and community spirit';

2. 'the enablement of loosely coupled, informal networks to promote the growth, knowledge sharing, knowledge management, and collaboration that drives effectiveness and competitive advantage';

3. 'self-managing democratic communities of common interests based on values and trust'.

Much of the discussion was about the design of formal systems to support and facilitate informal networks, with a major focus on guiding principles for explicit expectations for behaviours, organisational structure and technology. Together these contribute to creating operating environments that encourage sharing, collaboration and transparent, purposeful interactions.

A new type of peer leadership emerges within informal networks, where leadership is based on ideas and influence as well as personal qualities. Informal distributed peer leadership is not a function of allocated roles, changes according to context, and is based on knowledge, experience and what needs to be done.

Technologies that support learning through informal networks must be intuitively easy to use. People need to be able to choose which technologies work for them and to have secure access. The value of technologies lies in enabling people to do what they need to do with and through others. Table 5.1 lists the main barriers and benefits in using enterprise social networking technologies to enable knowledge co-creation within informal networks.

Table 5.1   Enterprise social networking: Enablers and barriers

Enablers	Barriers
Find who knows what through people	IT infrastructure and network capacity
Find others with shared values and interests	Fear of the consequences of a loss of control
Workplace design to encourage interaction and break the anonymity of sterile offices	Risk of time wasting
Organisational structures and processes that disseminate knowledge efficiently	Lack of trust
Workplace and work practices that satisfy the need to belong	'Knowledge is power' attitude limits sharing
Innovation often comes from mavericks so find out who they are and support them	Information validity, security and fear of loss of confidentiality
Chance encounters create new ideas so design for serendipity	Fear of loss of personal privacy

Concluding Remarks

This chapter has covered a lot of ground. It has tried to summarise a number of current global workplace trends and their likely effects on people, processes, performance environments and knowledge. A re-ordering of economic power was already under way before the financial crisis, with the shift eastwards of economic power linked to growing domestic markets and consumers in the emerging economies, along with large and young workforces that are hungry for opportunity.

The gap in economic power is set to widen if we do not urgently invest in innovation and smarter ways of working that make use of all talents and capabilities, not just knowledge elites. Businesses will have to make creating effective learning and performance environments a priority if they are to remain competitive because:

- As in the first wave of smart working, engaging workforce capabilities for innovation and creativity is crucial to remain globally competitive.

- Work that creates opportunities for learning and development is engaging.

- Increasing complexities arising from boundary blurring, networked relationships, conversations and collaborations demand sophisticated social skills and approaches to management that differ from traditional 'command and control'.

- Complexities arising from increasingly abstract work require creative and critical thinking skills.

- Despite widespread banning in the workplace, social technologies have enormous potential in linking internal and external knowledge flows. Young people in particular expect to be able to access these technologies at work. Incorporating the knowledge-augmenting potential of social technologies into value-creating business processes is a source of competitive advantage.

6

Space, Place and Knowledge Flows

Introduction

The CIPD/Cap Gemini four-pillar model of smart working includes the physical work environment as one of its core elements. As they and others note (Davenport 2005, Ennals and McEwan 2005, CIPD 2008a), a move to new premises is a popular catalyst for flexible and smarter working practices. The immediate driver is usually to make savings in property overheads, but a change in space usage becomes the ideal opportunity to combine this objective with introducing new approaches to work. While cost savings can be significant, new and largely unexplored opportunities exist for value-creation through using the physical workplace as the focal point for developing community and high-performance creativity. The CIPD report notes this potential and provides 'deep-dive' case studies to illustrate.

This short chapter specifically assesses the role of physical and virtual workspaces in dynamic, social knowledge-creation. Businesses are social organisations that have organisational and spatial dimensions. The organisational dimensions were explored in Chapter 2. This review of the spatial dimensions complements the organisational dimensions. It begins with a reminder that buildings are designed with social interaction and evolution in mind. The chapter draws heavily on exchanges from the Johnson Controls Global Mobility Network conversations.

Effective Spatial Design

Architect Frank Duffy,[1] in a talk to the Johnson Controls Global Mobility Network (Puybaraud and McEwan 2009b), proposed that opportunities now exist for new relationships between space, society and ideas to emerge.

He explained buildings as 'theatres of decision-making' designed in replaceable, interdependent layers of longevity which enable them to evolve and change over time. The layers encompass site, structure, services, scenery, sets and stuff (desks, chairs, filing cabinets and so on). People plant meaning into buildings and transform them into social constructions through three interacting design systems that influence how information is passed around:

1.   leadership

2.   data and information flows

3.   user involvement

Effective spatial design choreographs social interactions and information flows, creating opportunities for networking and for probabilistic chance meetings.

SYMBOLIC MANAGEMENT

Duffy says that the physical workplace can act as symbolic representation of memory, meaning and social learning. Symbolic management can also communicate company values. A colleague commented when visiting a workplace designed with knowledge workers in mind that although he was not keen on the stark, concrete walls, he did appreciate the obvious thoughtfulness and consideration being communicated through the interior design and facilities provided.

How the office is designed and furniture displayed within it conveys a hidden language and desire to communicate identity through symbolic representation. Workplace design can also powerfully convey negative messages, the accumulation of which can result in the degradation of people's identity. This was captured in a French book, *L'Open Space m'a Tuer*.[2]

---

1   http://en.wikipedia.org/wiki/Frank_Duffy_(architect) [accessed: 9 March 2012].
2   http://www.lopenspacematuer.com/ [accessed: 27 July 2012].

Degradation of identity particularly offends in France because happiness is regarded as a right.

COLLABORATION

Kristensen (Puybaraud and McEwan 2009b) observes that since technologies make it possible to work effectively and more productively outside office boundaries, choice to do so means that 'in essence people are saying that for many processes, the office is actually limiting rather than boosting productivity'.

He proposes that a really good workplace is one that enables people to do things they cannot do anywhere else. Such workplaces are characterised by the provision of appropriate collaboration spaces, enabling technologies and supporting operating principles. They are created around 'physual design', which combines physical space and virtual tools within a visual, collaborative environment.

Kristensen believes that the costs of equipping knowledge-friendly workplaces, compared to alternative solutions, are offset by the performance gains of workplace-enabled collaboration and interaction. The office will only survive in the long term if it enables new levels of knowledge worker effectiveness. This is achieved through performance environments that balance between providing space and time for solitary, noise-free reflection as well as spaces to interact with others (Heerwagen et al. 2004). Heerwagen et al. warn of 'the central conflict of collaboration'. Lack of space for thinking is particularly problematic for complex and abstract knowledge. At the same time, though, tacit and abstract knowledge requires conversation to enable individual thoughts to be surfaced, shared and shaped.

PLACE AND SPACE

In their assessment of the role of place and space in collaborative systems, Harrison and Dourish (1996) explain space as 'the three-dimensional environment in which objects and events occur, and in which they have relative position and direction'. The properties of physical space apply everywhere. As they comment, up is up for everyone.

They say that space becomes place when it is invested with meaning and expectations – for example, how people are expected to behave within a place. These expectations are culturally influenced. Place arises out of the space we occupy and emerges over time, so that 'a space is always what it is, but a place is how it is used', and this can be different at different times or simultaneously different for multiple groups. For space to become a place, self-determined opportunity to participate and adapt has to exist.

According to Harrison and Dourish, a sense of place is essentially a cultural phenomenon involving 'a communally-held sense of appropriate behaviour, and a context for engaging in and interpreting action'. This is a crucial point. It is a community that determines how a sense of place develops over a time. Since places have social meaning constructed by place users themselves, workplace designers can 'design *for*' but it cannot be 'designed *in*'.

CULTURE AND SPACE

Effective spatial design is culturally appropriate. The Global Mobility Network conversations returned repeatedly to the topic of national, organisational and professional cultures. Recurring themes were cross-boundary collaboration and design for creating and sharing knowledge. One particular session explored cultural traits as expressed in workplace design case studies from Japan, Germany and France.

Common business language has different connotations within different cultures. In France, for example, and under the influence of history, 'collaboration' conveys working with the enemy. The meanings of other commonly used business words – 'team', for example – are not obvious. How do personal relationships and bonds form? In cultures like France's, food and wine are important. In Scandinavia, collegiality may be more likely to be forged through the sauna. How different national cultures see the world, and what is accepted as normal, is influenced by historical, religious and other factors.

Francoise Bronner, who is an expert in the cultural aspects of workplace design, pointed out that while Japan and Germany are both obsessed by quality and building knowledge-creating companies, workplace design reveals different cultural approaches (Puybaraud and McEwan 2010). She explained that the Japanese use left-brain, tacit approaches to communicating and acting, which is linked to cultural history and is subject to relativity. This has culminated in an urge to consensus in the creation of competence, values and skills. She illustrated this through the example of a Japanese company who used a symbolic 'boxing ring' space where people from different functions came together to 'box' through the dynamic processes of revealing collective tacit knowledge.

The architecture of the BMW innovation centre is by contrast very transparent and explicit. A central project space, the project house, is a point of convergence where social psychologists, artists, semiotic experts and engineers come together in a central space and then disband through a dissolution process back to their own departments to review learning. Commitment to quality and knowledge-creation is built into the fabric of the building in the openness and transparency through large expanses of glass, which enables collective visual knowledge-management. Prototypes and the highly social visible interactions from which they emergence are on display.

DEMOGRAPHICS

The workplace matters very much for young people, according to a Johnson Controls survey that explored their workplace preferences (Johnson Controls 2010). Data collected from the USA, China, India, UK and Germany included demographic groups other than the target 18–25 group for comparison. Young people want to work for companies that are committed to environmental sustainability. They are also looking for workplaces that reflect their personal lifestyles. Since work life and home life are merging, they expect the office to look like home and be a 'city crash pad'.

The picture of young people that emerges from the survey confirms the impression given in the literature of their being highly collaborative: 18–25-year-olds see the workplace as a space where they socialise, learn and gain a sense of well-being. They expect access to dedicated team spaces and breakout spaces to support their social interactions. In excess of 70 per cent favour informal breakout spaces and ad hoc meeting spaces rather formal meeting rooms for collaboration.

Given that their relation to space is visible and open, it is perhaps surprising to see the extent to which young people are individually territorial: 70 per cent of 18–25-year-olds in the survey wanted to have their own desk, and less than a quarter were open to sharing. The report concludes that this lack of flexibility implies a human need to find identity within the workplace, and indicates the need to better understand human psycho-social attachment to personal work environments.

Aging workforce

Myerson et al. (2010) have explored the impact of the ageing workforce in the knowledge economy in the UK, Japan and Australia. This is an increasingly important issue, as older workers are likely to continue working in response to the pension crisis, and as businesses seek to retain their skills and knowledge.

Myerson et al. say that the emphasis on collaboration has gone too far, leading to the relative neglect of over-concentration and contemplation. This is not only an issue for older generations in the workplace; a young executive in a global corporation recently confessed in conversation that he enjoys solitary concentration, and that he feels a pressure to be seen to be collaborating.

Knowledge-creating Environments

Knowledge-creating processes are dynamic and emerge from interactions among people, or between people and their environments. Nonaka et al. (2000) propose that tacit knowledge is deeply rooted in action, procedures, routines, commitments, ideals, values and emotions, which is consistent with Weick's linking of knowledge-creation and 'chaotic action'. This section looks at characteristics of both physical and online environments that support dynamic knowledge-creation.

Groves (2010) identified four types of spaces for knowledge-creation in her review of innovating companies. These are spaces for stimulation, reflection, collaboration and play. Others note the need for facilities to support knowledge-creation through socialising, sharing, learning and connecting (Gensler 2008).

SOCIALLY CONSTRUCTED KNOWLEDGE

In a BBC podcast, the broadcaster Peter Day told the story of how the pharmaceutical company GlaxoSmithKline set about dismantling its large, siloed and ineffective 'temple to R&D'.[3]

This is a good example of how physical and organisational structures have to be co-designed to enable human-scale collaboration and socially constructed knowledge. The business was restructured into business units in an attempt to emulate the inter-linked ecosystem of small companies in the bio-tech industry.

---

3   http://www.bbc.co.uk/programmes/b00wdjyg [accessed: 8 March 2012].

At the same time, specialists who were previously organised within functions were allocated to inter-disciplinary teams so that problems were sorted out in real time.

The podcast explored the complexity of discovery, co-locating experts for knowledge creation and real-time problem-solving, the symbolism of the CEO moving his office to ground level and in among the action, breaking down silos, inter-disciplinary conversation, shared learning and serendipity. The point was made very clearly that drug development happens at scale, and drug discovery happens at the level of the individual. Drug discovery is highly human and inter-personal. Serendipity and chance occurrences play a significant role in discovery, which confirms Hagel et al.'s view of the importance of designing for serendipity (Hagel et al. 2010).

Playspace

Complex knowledge like that required in drug discovery is increasingly the outcome of technologies and abstract working knowledge that exist deep inside people's heads (Weick 2001). The realisation that technologies and abstract working knowledge are inextricably linked inside our minds is profound. So much of what we know is tacit and hidden. Weick concludes that more of the organisation has therefore to be 'imagined, visualised and filled in from cryptic clues'.

Mindsets have to change, as well as physical design and organisational structures. Meyer (2010) cites Weick in stating her belief in the need to reconceptualise the workplace as playspace. This requires:

> *A shift from a mindset that conceives of work as separate from dynamic engagement to one where the workplace is a playspace for new ideas, perspectives and possibilities. To make this shift, we must embrace our organisations as living, breathing, ever-changing systems.*

Meyer admits that there is a challenge in taking play seriously within the context of work, since play – individual and collective activity that is not necessarily purposeful – is seen as not creating value. In Meyer's view, the opposite is true. Value is created through play, which has to be reclaimed as 'an important dynamic of learning, innovation and changing'. She is not alone in valuing play. Kane, author of *The Play Ethic* (2004), says:

First of all, don't take 'play' to mean anything idle, wasteful or frivolous.
The trivialisation of play was the work ethic's most lasting, and most
regrettable achievement. This is 'play' as the great philosophers
understood it: the experience of being an active, creative and fully
autonomous person.[4]

Meyer similarly equates the concept of playspace coming to life 'when the
whole person is engaged and engages with awareness'. The current vogue
for 'gamification' is a particular example of the application of play. Large
enterprises are 'deploying reward and competitive tactics commonly found in
the gaming world to make tasks such as management training, data entry and
brainstorming seem less like work'. Points are awarded as incentives and to
'encourage friendly competition and motivate performance'.[5]

Online communities

What are some of the issues associated with designing for user participation
in creating and sharing knowledge online? As in physical work environments,
knowledge is socially constructed through relationships and conversations
characterised by trust, obligation, commitment and accountability (Erickson
and Kellogg 2003). In common with Rangaswami,[6] they propose that knowledge
and information are best discovered through people.

    Erickson and Kellogg describe what they call social knowledge and social
resources, which are only accessible through talking to people. They point out
that social knowledge is not written down, because it is too politically sensitive
or thought to be too trivial. Social resources are contacts, recommendations
or referrals. They propose that socially translucent systems, the three core
properties of which are visibility, awareness and accountability, are the
foundation of social interaction. Online knowledge communities need to be
safe and trusted places, where people can join in 'unguarded discussion among
people who know one another'. They conclude that designing knowledge-
sharing environments as trusted places is challenging. Balancing the need for
safety and trust with the organisational imperative to share information is not
easy.

---

4   http://www.theplayethic.com/what-is-the-play-ethic.html [accessed: 12 April 2012].
5   http://online.wsj.com/article/SB10001424052970204294504576615371783795248.html [accessed:
    12 April 2012].
6   SOMESSO/Headshift Social Business Summit, 18 March 2010.

CONTEXT IN MOTION

Nonaka et al. (2000), in writing about the emergent processes involved in transforming tacit to explicit knowledge, describe the Japanese concept of *ba*, the energy created by a group of people in a particular space and at a specific time. *Ba* is a dynamic, always-changing, complex 'here and now' concept.

According to Nonaka et al., *ba* is the 'shared context in motion' that creates space for emerging relationships. Multiple minds and spaces, including physical space, virtual space and mental space (shared ideals), converge at a specific point in time to create the mind, and emotional energy that converts tacit into explicit knowledge. This energy, they say, enriches both the individual and the collective.

Shared and co-created energy is apparent in the following example of a spontaneous conversation on the micro-blogging platform Twitter, which emerged over a day one weekend when I made a comment about *ba*. The result was a conversation involving about six people from the USA, UK and Germany. One of the conversation participants, Greg Lloyd, has used a tool which 'remixes tweets, status messages, and Web pages' and creates a record that can be accessed by others in the future.[7] He says at the beginning of the summary:

> *Searching for Ba – in the Google and other sense. Ba (equivalent to 'place' in English) is a shared space for emerging relationships. It can be a physical, virtual, or mental space. Knowledge, in contrast to information, cannot be separated from the context – it is embedded in ba.*

Contributions to the conversation included thoughts, links and responses to resources discovered and shared. As the conversation drew to a close, one of the participants said: 'Thanks to you all! Demonstrates #Ba is not limited to a physical place.' (The hash symbol is how entries are tagged. Any tweet containing a hashtag can be retrieved; it is a highly effective way of following who is saying what about a specific topic.)

As this Twitter example shows, a sense of place for shared energy can be created online as well in physical environments. In-the-moment cognitive, cultural and emotional energies coming together within physical and virtual places, the sense of which is determined through community behaviour and

---

7   http://keepstream.com/roundtrip/finding-ba [accessed: 12 April 2012].

values, all create dynamic context for performance and relationships to emerge over time.

CONGENIAL OR EDGY ENVIRONMENTS?

Contemporary philosopher Yves Michaud notes that artistic creativity thrives in provisional spaces, and within contexts of creative destruction, which in many cases are disorganised and disjointed. He claims that spaces due for destruction and that are abandoned provide fertile grounds for the emergence of creativity. Michaud argues that we should leave time and opportunity for disorganisation – a space for something to happen, for the creativity to emerge. Of course, his approach is based on understanding how artists work. This is in complete contrast to the majority of orchestrated, organised, structured, restricted and ordered corporate environments.

There is a tension between a desire for certainty and the turbulent, external operating environments that currently exist, which are more akin to the conditions under which artistic creativity is said to take place. While recognising a possible link between mess and creativity, a balancing with more calming influences might be beneficial. People tend to like certainty and stability in workplace surroundings. This is especially so if their personal lives are in turmoil, which might be the case where people are coping with divorce and relationship break-ups.

The desire for familiarity is deeply engrained for many people. A member of the Global Mobility Network told the story of his experience working in a company following a merger. In rationalising working conditions, who sat together was deemed to be more important than scrapping the right to a company car. People like to belong, and being physically co-located enhances the sense of identification with a group.

Heerwagen argues for creating congenial workplace atmospheres by emulating nature. She has come to the conclusion that 'more time and creativity has gone into designing natural habitats for zoo animals than in creating comfortable office spaces for humans', and she proposes that workplaces need to be congenial and socially engaging. What do socially engaging workplaces feel like?

She concludes that congenial environments are those that reflect our natural ways of relating to each other, socially, cognitively and emotionally.

She emphasises that work is about people and relationships, and that creativity and thinking are social processes. Too little interaction leads to isolation and stagnation; too much leads to distractions and stress. Congenial environments are free from irritants, distractions and threats (Rock 2009).

A report on workplace nomads (*The Economist* 2008) sounds a warning on ad hoc working spaces being uncongenial, observing that 'it is becoming commonplace for a cafe to be full of people … more engaged with their in-box than with the people touching their elbows. These places are physically inhabited but psychologically evacuated.' This is a potential danger for all workplaces.

Distributed Workplaces

There are many other possible places other than the office for doing what we do with others. Duffy warns about adopting too narrow an interpretation of a singular workplace. Saying that cities are 'layers of leaky networks' and 'brilliant inventions of interactivity', he notes that Samuel Pepys's diaries record him as a peripatetic worker, and that the scientists and men of learning who frequented the coffee shops and clubs of London in the seventeenth and eighteenth centuries regarded the whole of the city as their workplace (Duffy 2008).

There is an abundance of EU-funded research on mobile and distributed working. As just one example, the output from a consortium of universities and European companies culminated in the report *The Future Workspace* (Schaffers et al. 2006). The aim of the research project was to 'accelerate innovation in the mobile and collaborative workplace' in recognition that technologically enabled collaboration across boundaries has become commonplace, resulting in 'place' becoming a mix of virtual and physical workspaces.

One of the individual research reports contributing to the publication reviewed issues emerging from distributed processes in three industrial sectors: aerospace, automotive and construction (Schaffers et al. 2004). Of aerospace, the authors say that it is a truly distributed virtual organisation where diverse knowledge specialists are brought together, virtually or co-located, for joint project activities. In reviewing the technological and social enablers of distributed work, Schaffers et al. conclude: 'The challenge is that it is still difficult to truly collaborate in a virtual environment and many design engineers still travel to take advantage of the rich communication environment offered by face-to-face meetings.'

AUDIO-VISUAL TECHNOLOGIES

In a research report for the UK Work Organisation, Heath et al. (2000) assessed the shortcomings of audio-visual connectivity, even in the most sophisticated media environments. When people work together, their activities are mediated through social objects such as documents or diagrams.

They argue that audio-visual technologies focus on face-to-face interactions, and therefore support inter-personal communication rather than collaboration. The distinction between inter-personal communication and collaboration blurs as knowledge becomes increasingly tacit and abstract. Conversation becomes collaboration, which only makes Heath et al.'s observation all the more pertinent: 'Once we begin to recognise how practical action is embedded in, and inseparable from, the objects and artefacts in the environment in which it occurs then the attempt to support distributed, collaborative activities becomes increasingly complex.'

This is aligned with Heerwagen's description of distributed cognitive systems (see Chapter 5), where she says that cognition is not only in our heads, but is also embedded within the technologies that we use, displayed in our drawings and on whiteboards, in the notes we make and the stories we exchange.

Audio-visual technology has moved on since Heath et al. were writing over a decade ago and digital social objects are becoming embedded within 'physual' collaboration environments. Nevertheless, early insights into the vital importance of how knowledge is embedded within and distributed throughout the physical environment as well as through networks of people remain valuable.

Video technologies will no doubt continue to improve. Nevertheless, and as Schaffer et al., Heath et al. and Heerwagen all note, face-to-face interactions take place within environments where cognition is distributed and embedded within physical objects and artefacts.

The Campus Workplace

Several significant trends are now converging that make possible – and in fact mandate – reconceptualising the workplace as the learning workplace, or alternatively the campus workplace. This extends Senge's concept of the learning organisation to include a central role for the physical workplace.

Bearing in mind Duffy's warning about 'the workplace' in fact being networks of inter-linked places, the campus workplace spans multiple physical and online places where people meet to work and learn. The concept became apparent recently when visiting the premises of an international architecture practice in London. The person showing a group of us around the London head office said that the average age was just over 30 and there were around forty nationalities represented in the building, which he described as a campus.

In their *Campus of the Future* report,[8] Arup's Foresight group, in partnership with universities, explored a number of scenarios of how the future campus might look. They included a blend of physical and digital attributes, with a focus on immersive and experiential learning. The scenario in which the campus is envisaged as learning hubs distributed throughout cities implies workplaces as part of these distributed learning hubs. The sense remains, though, of campus and work being separate. I am proposing that the workplace becomes a campus, where play, learning and work are inseparable.

Concluding Remarks

Florida notes that the more we engage online, the more we need to meet face-to-face. He says that that the world is not flat, as Friedman contends; it is spiky (Florida 2007). Creative and knowledge workers migrate to be physically co-located. Florida traces the growth of global mega-regions of economic activity. The same dynamics happen in the workplace, both physical and online, where people are drawn together to meet, work, talk, learn together, co-create and share knowledge.

Knowledge flows and creative potential are situated within our knowledge networks, which are themselves networks of distributed and interlinked social, spatial, organisational and technical elements. The physical workplace is becoming particularly crucial for enabling and visualising the emergent, dynamic outcomes of the sum of our collective, distributed intelligence.

---

8   http://www.driversofchange.com/make/research/campus-of-the-future/ [accessed: 9 March 2012].

People connect emotionally within their physical environments and gain a sense of belonging from them. There is therefore also the additional issue of designing for workforce well-being. High-profile cases of suicides because of work[9] are reminders that people can experience work and the workplace as extremely stressful (Marmot 2006, Rock 2009).

Finding as many ways as possible to overcome boundaries and walls – physical and organisational – that emotionally isolate and separate people in organisations is essential to meet the psycho-social needs of a healthy, creative workforce. This includes the physical, organisational and online elements of performance environments.

---

9   http://www.guardian.co.uk/world/2011/apr/26/france-telecom-worker-kills-himself [accessed: 9 March 2012].

7

Patterns and Parallels

Introduction

This chapter takes stock of key observations from the review of smart working and high-performance work systems in previous chapters, and compares patterns and parallels between the process-based organising approaches from the first wave and current second wave contexts. The emerging contexts are characterised by increasingly complex inter-personal, relationship and network dynamics. The comparison reveals that design principles identified earlier remain highly relevant in setting the conditions for performing, innovating and adapting in the face of currently turbulent global operating conditions.

Developing organisational capabilities for uncertain, emergent conditions means paying attention to whole systems of learning and leadership, which underpin the emergence of contextually appropriate, socially and culturally determined, adaptive performance environments.

How systems and working environments that support people's desire for learning are designed and implemented cannot be prescribed. They depend on assessment of what is most appropriate in specific contexts and are highly subjective, based as they are on judgements, perceptions and values. There are no best practices to replicate and slavishly roll out. Rather, there are theoretical insights, design principles and high-performance work practices which provide guidance for action.

Smart Working Re-visited

As a reminder, the CIPD view of smart working (CIPD 2008a) is linked to high-performance work systems and work environments that generate and release collective energy to drive the business. Particularly crucial in their interpretation is high-trust management values underpinning everything and people being regarded as crucial to the success of the business.

IBM defines smart working in terms of developing the capabilities and behaviours that are essential for effective performance within connected, integrated workplaces and to generate dynamic, distributed knowledge flows (Pearson et al. 2010). Multiple boundaries within and across organisations are being breached, resulting in complex and constantly shifting sets of interacting organisational parameters that are not easy to untangle. Like patterns in a kaleidoscope, emergent organisational configurations are made up of fragmented and distributed entities that operate across multiple workplaces, time zones and cultures.

First wave smart working and the emerging wave are similar in that they are both knowledge-based and driven by the need to recognise, nurture and deploy workforce value-creating capabilities. Requirements for boundary-spanning, problem-solving and collaborative behaviours were features of the first wave, and remain crucially relevant for current business conditions.

The contexts within which these practices and behaviours are playing out, however, have become significantly more complex and challenging. The opportunity for innovation and value-creation is also phenomenal. Internal knowledge flows associated with continuous improvement and process innovation in the first wave are now potentially linked to external knowledge networks. What was continuous improvement has now become collective intelligence.

Having examined the characteristics of first wave smart working and the global trends driving a new wave of disruption to management practices, smart working can finally be confirmed as combining attributes of the CIPD and IBM perspectives. Smart working is an outcome of designing social performance environments that are adaptable and developed around value-creating workforce knowledge, skills and potential for learning. The dynamic elements of smart working include:

- performing

- innovating

- adapting

- leading

- co-ordinating

- collaborating

- monitoring

- integrating

- connecting

- sharing

- learning

- thinking

Since people's desire for learning and opportunity to be engaged in meaningful work is so consistently affirmed through many research sources, it turns out that what is crucial for high performance is also good for people. The ideal would be to develop enterprise-wide capabilities in these smart working elements through whole systems of learning in which the entire workforce participates. Where senior leadership fails in vision and implementation to do this, local leaders now have the opportunity to influence their own work environments.

Patterns

There are five patterns which are themes recurring through time:

1.   complexity of social systems;

2.   the tendency of formal organisational systems to be resistant to adaptation;

3.   the challenge of making the transition to new ways of working;

4.   the enduring influence of outdated Taylorist influences;

5.   social co-creation of knowledge.

COMPLEX SOCIAL SYSTEMS

Dynamic organising is profoundly social, and value is created through how people relate to their work, performance environments and to each other. Social systems have always been complex, but the evidence of considerable management effort expended in trying to control behaviour and achieve predictability over the decades suggests that the inherently complex nature of organising is not widely appreciated in practice. People are not and never were predictable. Nor were they ever compliant.

It is clear that environmental turbulence was already building before the financial crisis, due to the convergence of Web-based communication and collaboration technologies, demographic trends, economic shifts and the breaking up of enterprises into globally distributed ecosystems. Large companies are fragmenting into ecosystems of alliances and partnerships, and smaller companies are coalescing into distributed networks. Enterprises are beginning to look and behave like social networks, and fragmentation is adding significantly to integration and co-ordination overheads.

In addition, the increase and rate of change in complexity and uncertainty accelerates as work becomes more abstract, which make significant demands on social skills in appreciating different personal and organisational agendas, in cracking the codes of cultural diversity, in integrating across multiple boundaries and collaborating to co-create new knowledge, co-operating in the 'here and now' to sense and respond to environmental threats and opportunities.

Take the following as an example. James Balsillie, joint CEO of RIM, compared business to whitewater rafting at a conference on the future of the workplace at the University of Waterloo, Canada, in 2007. He said that business is about 'navigating cascading circumstances' and is an exercise in continuous, multiple optimisations in which you have to pay close attention to distilling, collaborating, constantly gaining feedback, monitoring and modifying. He and his colleagues know roughly the direction of the course they want to take, which he calls 'the long-wave bet'.

They aim, rather than steer, towards their desired direction. Their energies are constantly in the moment, and everyone has to pull together to keep the boat upright and heading in the right direction as quickly and safely as possible, while attempting to avoid the rock that has just come into view. The metaphor graphically conveys the speed and turbulence of operating within rapidly evolving and highly competitive global markets.

At the time of writing, RIM appears to have hit a rock and is experiencing difficulties in the highly competitive smartphone market. Poor sales of its Playbook tablet and customer fury at the service outage in October 2011 are piling up trouble for the company. One analyst has said that 'RIM's like a plane at 30,000 feet and the engines have stopped running.'[1]

RESISTANT TO ADAPTATION

Organisations are complex, and are too frequently not adaptive. Many enterprises failed to make the transition to new ways of working last time around. The story of how the CIA and other agencies were unable to adapt from Cold War mentalities and working principles had tragic consequences, as Farmer (2010) demonstrates in his analysis of what happened in the lead-up to, during and after 9/11. He writes with authority since he was senior counsel to the 9/11 Commission, led the team that reconstructed events, and also contributed to the final report. Information not available at the time has been declassified and sheds new light on events.

He presents evidence for the claim that old attitudes and ways of operating from the Cold War era prevailed within the intelligence agencies, particularly the CIA, the FBI and the Department of Defense. Unwillingness and inability to share information within and across agencies were systemic failures and outcomes of systems that were 'flawed by design'. Farmer says:

> *The boundaries between and within departments separated knowledge gained domestically from knowledge gained overseas; knowledge gained through human intelligence from knowledge gained electronically; and knowledge gained through the investigation of criminal conduct from knowledge gained for the purposes of situational awareness as general intelligence … each boundary amounted to a fault line, an opportunity for the system to fail.*

---

1   http://www.canadianbusiness.com/article/60032--rim-will-take-more-than-a-half-billion-dollar-hit-on-playbook-service-outage [accessed: 12 April 2012].

Efforts to transform the CIA were hampered because the director was not able to 'overcome his estrangement from the rank-and-file career employees of the Agency'. Farmer concludes that top-down edicts were resisted by field officers unwilling to change from the Cold War paradigm, who resisted co-operation with the FBI and who did not recognise the director's authority. His vision for change was not matched by changes to how the work of 'ground-level employees' should adapt. The FBI's 1998 strategic plan for fundamental change was equally ineffective. It made terrorism 'a priority in theory, but never in practice'.

He also reviews subsequent failed responses to Hurricane Katrina in 2005, and in an afterword to the second edition of the book, the attempted bombing of an aircraft out of Schipol Airport in Amsterdam bound for Detroit on Christmas Day 2009. With respect to Katrina, he notes 'the same estrangement of the rank-and-file bureaucracy from upper-level management' and that 'top-officials were talking largely to themselves, and passing inaccurate information'. He concludes:

> The bureaucratic unwillingness or inability to cooperate across departments crippled efforts to anticipate and respond to Katrina no less than it had crippled efforts to interdict and then respond to 9/11, preempting the possibility of a unified chain of command.

If this unwillingness to co-operate and inability to change mindsets from a previous, outdated bureaucratic era can arise in the defence of a nation and a city, it can certainly happen in the pursuit of profit. A number of other systemic failures were summarised in Chapter 1, most notably in the recent global financial system.

CHALLENGES OF MAKING THE TRANSITION

Making the transition to new ways of working last time involved challenging long-established working practices. Although resistance was sometimes found on shop floors, it was often more likely to be manifested at the level of middle management. Even where there was no resistance, making the transition to new ways of working was still challenging, and as was noted in Chapter 3, many businesses 'failed their way to success' (Randolph 1995).

Back then, the need to adapt was urgent in the face of global competitive pressures. Just because the need to adapt was urgent, many could not change.

With renewed pressures from the global environment, it is expected that something similar is likely to happen this time around. Many enterprises will struggle (*The Economist* 2010b), and this is perfectly illustrated by this quote from a blog post about overcoming risk-averse behaviours:

> *Companies often say they want to promote 'risk taking' and 'innovation' but we don't reward them for that. The truth is that we ask for this, but when we take a risk and it doesn't pay-off, the company often comes down hard on those people ... Human Resources (HR) is about what we shouldn't do. Corporate Communications is about what we shouldn't say, Finance is about what we shouldn't fund. Someone help! We are 'risk managing' ourselves to death!*[2]

The need to adapt is once more urgent, and we now have technologies that promise phenomenal performance potential. This is, however, no guarantee that transformation will happen. This is a key lesson from the first wave.

Loosening the Taylorist stranglehold

The managerial style that has dominated the majority of Western workplaces for most of the twentieth century, known as Taylorism after its originator, Frederick Winslow Taylor, is based on his method of Scientific Management in the pursuit of efficiency through specialisation and repetition.

Duffy (2008) made the fascinating observation that Taylorist offices influenced by Scientific Management, with their unremitting focus on efficiency, have resulted in unsustainable workspaces that are under-occupied and unsuitable for emerging business conditions. He calls office buildings 'misleading and obsolescent units of analysis', and wonders why self-reliant people should be constrained by them. Despite unstoppable and converging forces in the external business environment, management practices and attitudes, also significantly influenced by a century of Taylorist approaches to management, remain similarly stubbornly resistant to change. The parallel between under-utilised workspaces and under-utilised human capability and creativity is striking. Process innovation approaches of the first wave began to restore the separation of thinking and doing in traditional manufacturing. Nevertheless, managers thinking and controlling while everyone else is supposed to do what they are told persists.

---

2   http://rexsthoughtspot.blogspot.com/2008/03/keeping-faith-e20-evangelist.html [accessed: 12 April 2012].

Structuring organisations along functional lines is also proving problematic and outdated for collaborative knowledge-creation and sharing. The pharmaceutical company GlaxoSmithKline, for example, decided to 'dismantle its industrial-scale temple to R&D' in favour of structuring around a network of autonomous Centres of Excellence for Drug Discovery and a move towards an entrepreneurial culture. The restructuring took place because at the time its large state-of-the-art R&D facility was failing in drug discovery.

Taylorist attitudes have also been influencing IT deployment in the UK. Although take-up of information technologies in the UK is high, one of the publications from the Future of Work, a six-year research project involving 22 universities, drew attention to the fact that enterprises have the choice of using communication technology as an enabler, in combination with high-performance human resources measures, or as a monitoring tool to control workforces. White et al. (2004) commented that the trend of the time towards control without workforce participation was 'deeply disquieting'. In their view, there was a substantial risk that low-cost, automatically generated monitoring and control information, not shared with those being monitored, would be likely to become damaging and divisive.

SOCIAL WORKPLACES

As well as talking about smart working practices (Pearson at al. 2010), IBM is also promoting 'social business' as a concept (IBM 2011): 'Today's enterprises face the dawn of a new era – the era of the social business. Just as the Internet changed the marketplace forever, the integration of social computing into enterprise design represents another enormous shift in the landscape.'

The white paper goes on to say that social business is a people-centric approach to business that draws on the skills and capabilities of mobile, globally connected workforces and work that 'empowers people and empowers problem-solving'.

This sounds very familiar. Factories are highly social places. It may be surprising to many who speak disparagingly of 'the factory model' to learn that factory shop floors are no different, and in fact they are explicitly social. Team members' allegiance to each other is strong. The social influence they can exert is one reason why front-line supervisors are so crucial to the successful functioning of process innovation approaches.

Despite empowerment characterised by decentralisation, control over decisions and job autonomy (Honold 1997), this form of empowerment was the exception. Common in the academic critiques from that time were research findings suggesting little evidence of substantive changes to operator autonomy or decision-making responsibilities. Empowerment in first wave smart working was therefore ultimately an outcome of trusted workplace relationships that valued workforce participation in a holistic workplace philosophy based on appropriating tacit knowledge, inclusion, and participation in problem-solving and continuous improvement.

There is an interesting parallel between what is happening now in the social business movement and the previous 'enormous shift in the landscape'. Brinkley et al. (2009) investigated the extent to which knowledge work exists and what forms it took. They found that high-intensity knowledge work, characterised as high-level cognitive activity with high-level management tasks, represented 11 per cent of the workforce. They said:

> These high knowledge intensive jobs are, we suspect, what some of the more excitable accounts of knowledge work we have in mind. The reality is that even after 40 years uninterrupted growth in knowledge based industries and occupations, such jobs account for only one in ten of those in work today.

As the GSK example in the previous section illustrates, organisational restructuring to break down functional silos that impede knowledge-creation and sharing is essential. For many more people, the majority of Brinkley et al.'s findings are accurate; their knowledge is not of the complex, uncertain and always-changing nature (Cantrell et al. 2005). Moreover, work remains process- and time-constrained for many. What the last big shift in managing and working practices suggests is that performance cultures can be transformed even in the most process-driven contexts. The early academic criticism of new working practices in time gave way to a tentative recognition of 'the learning factory' (Barton and Delbridge 2006).

As in the first wave, there are critical perspectives of the social business movement:

> The kinds of management and structures you need in order to make these ideas work in a sustainable manner is almost non-existent. Command, control, power and status have a huge part in this. And no

*amount of putting lipstick on those organisational pigs will change
the fundamentals.*[3]

Parallels and Differences

Comparison of parallels between then and now reveals points of similarity and
divergence. The most immediate similarity is the need to mobilise and nurture
knowledge in the face of threats from global competitors. The impetus for the
process innovation and agile manufacturing approaches of the first wave was
the need to respond to the competitive advantages gained by the Japanese
automotive and electronics industries. The second wave is an outcome of the
competitive opportunities and threats as a consequence of the shift in economic
power to the emerging economies.

VISIBLE AND INVISIBLE

In the first wave, process innovation and control were applied to processes that
were mainly tangible and visible. Although manufacturing was distributed
across supply ecosystems, processes were largely contained within the
constrained physical environment of factories. In contemporary sectors that are
based on abstract and creative non-manufacturing knowledge work, processes
are tacit, abstract and distributed throughout networks of people on the move
across multiple physical and virtual workplaces.

INNOVATION AS EVERYONE'S JOB

Lean, quality and agile manufacturing were the last big disruptive management
innovations. Engaging people in sharing their tacit knowledge of processes and
their machines, problem-solving and continuous improvement – especially
those previously overlooked on shop floors – was core to the success of
approaches. This was about committing to a different philosophy of work,
changing attitudes (especially middle management) and new ways of doing
things. Radnor et al. (2006) comment that readiness to change and management
commitment to a new philosophy of work are core success factors in introducing
lean practices into the public sector, and of course, their absence is a barrier.

---

3   http://www.zdnet.com/blog/howlett/enterprise-20-is-beyond-a-crock-its-dead/2607 [accessed:
    12 April 2012].

The big difference between the first and second waves is that continuous improvement from the earlier era now becomes innovation and knowledge-sharing through widespread connected, collective intelligence that breaches and reaches across organisational boundaries. The entire workforce needs to be mobilised to create and deliver customer value, including suppliers, customers, employees and freelancers. Easier access to social technologies now means that each of these stakeholders is connected to a personal network of knowledgeable people, influence and contacts. What was previously localised continuous innovation is now potentially and exponentially augmented through their access to connected global knowledge networks.

BUILDING ORGANISATION-WIDE CAPABILITY

A lesson learned from last time around was that a lot of time and effort was spent preparing the entire workforce to engage in continuous improvement and putting in place systems that were designed to generate organisation-wide capability in innovation. Examples of similar current efforts are beginning to emerge. The story of how the global IT corporation EMC[2] developed 'social media proficiency' capability within a globally distributed ecosystem of customers, employees, suppliers and partners is highly recommended.

The approach taken was to frame the capability-building effort as a cross-functional business strategy. The white paper documenting the transformation journey tells a familiar story of effort, engaging passionate people, overcoming conservatism, and experimentation. The result was 'substantial and compelling results throughout our business'.[4]

Building organisation-wide smart working capabilities, like last time around, will be challenging for many. Fine et al. (2008) say that 'mastering lean's softer side' – for example, leadership that provides people with all technical capabilities and inter-personal skills they need to perform – is difficult because it challenges existing ways of thinking and doing. The 'soft side' of lean has now become more complex as processes become invisible, abstract and distributed across boundaries and time zones.

ENTERPRISE-WIDE ADAPTATION

Enterprise-wide, systemic transformation in the first wave was initiated and sustained by support at chief executive and director level, for example

---

4   http://chucksblog.emc.com/content/social_media_at_EMC_draft.pdf [accessed: 12 April 2012].

production directors or human resources directors. Despite the possibility for local leaders to initiate limited transformation within the part of the organisation over which they have influence, the evidence is that top-down initiation of fundamental strategic transformation will continue to be influenced and supported from senior levels.

In the example of the NSN post-merger culture initiative described in Chapter 5, the CEO influence was crucial in creating safe conditions for candid opinions to be expressed. It may be remembered that he made a commitment to 'honouring shadow' conversations, which at times were overwhelmingly negative. The 2.0 Adoption Council is a network of large corporations that are transforming working practices and integrating social technologies into distributed business processes. The conclusion from the recent poll of members is that 'social business is serious business and merits primarily six-figure, Director-level oversight'.[5]

LOCALLY INSTIGATED ADAPTATION

It may be remembered that Pettigrew and Fenton (2000) found that one of the characteristics of innovating organisations is their ability to accommodate what they call dualities: 'Simultaneously building hierarchies *and* networks; seeking greater performance accountability upward *and* greater horizontal integration sideways; and attempting to centralise *and* decentralise operations'.

Adaptation and transformation can happen as result of enterprise-wide, top-down leadership, and it is now feasible at a local level, instigated by local leadership distributed throughout the enterprise. Another possible duality is therefore top-down *and* local adaptation.

Design Principles Re-visited

The design principles linked to first wave smart working approaches were designing for:

- autonomy

- adaptability

---

5   http://itsinsider.com/2011/05/12/news-flash-social-in-the-enterprise-is-not-for-amateurs/ [accessed: 10 September 2012].

- integration

- collaboration

It is hopefully clear from the review of patterns that emerge over time and parallels between the two eras that balancing autonomy and co-ordination, adaptability, integration and cross-boundary knowledge-sharing remain pressing issues. Having reviewed current global trends impacting on workplaces, what additional principles ought to be emphasised?

In the emerging second wave, business processes are not only increasingly abstract and cognitive, they are now distributed across time, place and multiple organisational boundaries. Ubiquitous connectivity increases the pace and reach of change. Business processes are no longer contained and constrained; they are manifested in personally networked, physically distributed, hidden tacit knowledge flows that need to be surfaced, visualised and shared. Additional design principles that take account of these factors include designing for:

- 'wirearchy'

- networked viability

- distributed diversity

- social learning

WIREARCHY

Wirearchy is a design principle that is a consequence of abundant information, ubiquitous connectivity and a shift in the source of knowledge as power. Husband has been developing the organisational principle of wirearchy, which links 'networks that carry out the full range of human activities that include work, research, business, entertainment, gossip and news'. He defines wirearchy as: 'A dynamic, two-way flow of power and authority based on information, knowledge, trust and credibility, enabled by interconnected people and technology'.[6]

Central to wirearchy is the changing nature of knowledge as power, since the Web-enabled operating environments that wirearchy creates provide

---

6   http://www.wirearchy.com/what-is-wirearchy/ [accessed: 12 April 2012].

'the conditions for a dramatic re-making of power relationships built on information and knowledge'. Knowledge as power has traditionally been associated with creating scarcity and hoarding. This type of power came from being the person with intelligence, which conferred advantages over those without access to it. Husband argues that sharing knowledge is the new source of power. Rather than secrecy, now in the Internet age of abundant information, this new source of power is transparent.

This might seem counter-intuitive to people used to the 'power as scarcity and influence' perspective. The new power source begins to make sense when we refer back to Rangaswami's analysis of the value of social technologies as lying in their ability to reduce transaction costs through search and discovery. Universal connectedness means that those who were previously unrecognised can be discovered and recognised as the people to go to for specific information and expert knowledge. For those already in positions of formal and recognised authority, universal connectedness potentially extends the scope and immediacy of their influence, rather than what they want to communicate being filtered and possibly distorted through hierarchical management levels.

Network viability

As businesses form partnerships and alliances to share risks (CBI 2009) and begin to look and behave like social networks,[7] they form meshes of horizontally linked entities linked across geographical location and organisational boundaries. The Viable Systems Model depicts vertical absorption of requisite variety, but the fragmenting of organisational structures into integrated networks implies a greater emphasis on horizontally absorbing requisite variety. Shaw et al. (2004) explored how complexity might be absorbed within networks through what they call 'smart business networks'.

They sought to understand how smart business networks help businesses to survive longer as environments become more interdependent, and as the speed and reach of interdependencies increase. They applied the Viable Systems Model to an analysis of how the UK electricity market copes with large and unpredictable volumes of user registrations and de-registrations. The context of their analysis is a market that is subject to regulation and where two networks interact: the electricity network and the network that controls

---

7   Microsoft, 'Of whales and suckerfish' [online, September 2007]. Previously available at: http://
     www.microsoft.com/uk/business/peopleready/resources/economist.mspx.

the electricity network, circulating data among the supply ecosystem that links producers, suppliers and consumers.

The additional concepts Shaw et al. introduce – network viability and 'smartness' – are interesting. They say: 'Smartness is operationalised as a capability and the distinction is that if the network is smart then all elements within the network have access to this capability.'

Network smartness has three key properties, which in Shaw et al.'s terminology are:

- functional locality

- response capability

- distributed coordination

Functional locality is having a sensor near to an event that requires a response, which might be a person or a technology. The respondent then has to be able to decide what to do, and how. Having acted independently in response to local requirements, 'networked actors also act in parallel in response to signals from other network members'.

Shaw et al. talk about the detrimental effects of increasing search costs. Relying on distributed capabilities and networked action in responding to local events is consistent with Rangaswami's view that transaction costs are minimised by making use of social networks to rapidly locate the most knowledgeable and capable people. The network becomes the source of knowledge and capability that improves individual chances of business survival.

DISTRIBUTED DIVERSITY

Emerging contexts characterised by increasingly complex inter-personal, relationship and network dynamics have significant practical implications for culturally diverse social interactions. Performance environments have to be designed to take account of cross-boundary, distributed diversity, which includes flexibility that facilitates local interpretation, co-creation and appropriation of minimally specified critical design principles.

SOCIAL LEARNING

The increased complexity in external operating environments and a commensurate increase in operational complexity arising from the need for cross-boundary conversations, the increase in partnering among enterprises signifying a shift in management communication from 'command and control' to influence and persuasion, and the shift to tacit knowledge-intensive work all imply significant challenges to operational skills and capabilities.

It was interesting to discover, serendipitously, a resource from the CIA (Fishbein and Treverton 2004) offering an 'invitation to dialogue, debate and further research' on an 'alternative analysis' approach to extreme complexity. This is particularly interesting in the light of Farmer's analysis of systemic failures. Fishbein and Treverton suggest that concepts like mindfulness, sense-making and intuitive thinking, taken together, can promote enterprise-wide continuous wariness as an outcome of 'institutionalised, sustained collaborative efforts'.

They conclude that constantly deploying critical and creative thought as habit, questioning judgements and assumptions, will require fundamental transformation of cultures and business processes. It will also mean equipping people with the ability to think critically and creatively.

Work contexts are highly dynamic, flowing, social, sensual, emotional and experiential. Juxtaposed against the prevailing Taylorist orthodoxy of standardisation, division, separation and control in the pursuit of efficiency, the mismatch between what is and what ought to be is apparent. We already know what humanising, high-performance working practices and systems look like. Too many enterprises remain locked into old patterns of thought and habit. The 'tools for getting things done, like business processes, people and support systems are too rigid and static' (Pearson et al. 2010).

OVERCOMING ORGANISATIONAL INERTIA

The pull of organisational inertia is strong, and much existing know-how is overlooked in practice. In that case, does inertia thwart smart working and learning? No, not necessarily. Peer support and opportunities for learning and development – the things that people value highly – are no longer available solely through the enterprise.

As noted earlier, transformation can happen as an outcome of deliberate organisational intention, or it can happen informally within creative shadow systems, through chaotic action and determined local leaders taking control of their own working lives to the benefit of themselves, their colleagues and the business. This is obviously not easy, but is now more possible than it ever was.

People can now freely discover, create and share content outside the confines of their workplaces. Many corporate research reports are freely available, and top-ranking business schools like MIT[8] make content accessible through the Creative Commons.[9] Not only is quality content freely available, it is now possible to regard people beyond organisational boundaries as peers who share similar problems within different contexts.

As people begin to realise that social networking technologies are useful for more than entertainment, the possibility opens up for online learning networks to discover content, act on it and reflect on it together, sharing resources, insights and emotional support.

With access to all these resources and community support, determined local leaders within organisations can act like 'Trojan mice', bringing learning from outside back into the organisation. Fryer, the originator of the Trojan mice metaphor, says:

> *But if we are able to view our organisations as evolving systems, we can see them for what they really are – vibrant communities and we can set about releasing a powerful force; the imagination and ingenuity of our people, which is the true competitive advantage.*[10]

Hagel et al. (2010) talk about people accessing and attracting knowledge resources, which they then use to achieve some performance objective within 'creation spaces'. These are collaborative, problem-solving networks that are characterised by trusting, open and supporting relationships, which are used to find innovative solutions to 'vexing problems'. Chapter 9 will describe a creation space for learning about how to make the transition to smarter working practices.

---

8   http://ocw.mit.edu/index.htm [accessed: 12 April 2012].
9   http://creativecommons.org/ [accessed: 12 April 2012].
10 http://www.trojanmice.com/index.htm [accessed: 12 April 2012].

Concluding Remarks

Undoing the stranglehold of over a century of industrial structures, methods and mindsets that are no longer appropriate presents a challenge. A start was made almost thirty years ago when lean and quality approaches to manufacturing began to be adopted in response to global competitive pressures. Much of this learning appears to have been lost with the decline of manufacturing.

Lean is now being re-discovered and aligned with 'a new era in management'. Principles associated with designing for autonomy, adaptability, integration and collaboration from the first wave of smart working remain relevant. They obviously have to be interpreted and applied to current contexts, but that was always the case.

The trajectory of dismantling inappropriate structures and designing systems and performance environments that enable workforce participation in innovation, knowledge-sharing and problem-solving continues into a new phase, which I have been calling 'the next wave of smart working'. Social technologies now present a golden opportunity to rediscover sound performance and systems design principles from the earlier era of organising for innovation and knowledge-sharing.

Speed of change, ubiquitous connected networks and intensified complexity arising from increasingly abstract, distributed knowledge flows are key features of the emerging wave of smart working. In addition, design principles for performance environments need to address the changing nature of knowledge as power, network viability, mobility and social learning. As well as providing opportunities for discovering old knowledge and knowledgeable people, social technologies also turbo-charge performance potential when they are combined with the re-discovered principles and application of emerging principles. Continuous improvement from the first wave now has the potential to become the collective intelligence of the second wave.

The pull of the status quo remains strong despite warp-speed economic and technological changes, and pressures linked to demographic, energy and sustainability developments. The disparity between what is known about good practice and what happens in reality is deep-rooted and long-standing. Barriers exist at all levels, from the individual to operating environments. The emphasis in smart working has to be on action, reflection, discovery and experimentation that result in customer value. This can happen as an outcome of deliberate organisational intention, or it can happen informally and outside enterprise boundaries.

With access to resources and social support outside their working environments, determined people can now apply to their work what they learn for their own satisfaction, and to the benefit of their colleagues and the business. Part III of the book, which begins with the next chapter, will focus on how smart working practices can be initiated informally and formally through 'chaotic action'.

PART III
Creating the Next Wave

8

Do Better or Do Differently

Introduction

The analysis so far has shown that there is an abundance of existing know-how about high-performance work systems and working practices, design principles and performance environments. Discovering existing insights is only the first step. Discovery has no performance benefit until those insights are interpreted, translated for context and put into practice.

This chapter will focus on the examples of two leaders who had the courage to take the initiative and act as catalysts for doing things better or doing things differently, influencing the performance climate and performance environments for new ways of working to emerge.

One did it through experimenting, persevering and muddling through, and the other through a more formalised and structured approach. In both cases, the approaches they adopted were consistent with the value-creating customer focus of lean philosophies.

Whereas the manufacturing examples in Chapter 3 were from small and medium-sized manufacturing enterprises, the examples in this chapter are both from large public sector institutions. A comparison reveals similarities with each other and consistencies with the manufacturing cases.

The chapter will then consider formal and informal learning approaches to developing leaders, to equip them in their role of catalysing, creating and sustaining second wave smart working.

Do Better or Do Differently

Hagel et al. (2010) contend that small moves, smartly made, can set big things in motion. The examples in this chapter illustrate the approaches that two very different leaders took to setting things in motion to transform performance cultures and behaviours within the organisations, and parts of organisations, for which they were responsible.

What the examples have in common is that the efforts to initiate transition to new performance cultures were the outcomes of the actions of two individuals with vision, passion and determination. As well as reviewing the approaches they both took, the analysis assesses the support they received.

This is a vital consideration since these people were so pivotal in establishing conditions for new performance cultures, which often meets resistance and creates stress for those initiating change as much as it does for the people who are affected by the changes.

CREATIVE LEADERSHIP

Respondents to a global survey of CEOs selected creativity as 'the most important leadership attribute' necessary for coping with complexity (IBM 2010a). According to the report's authors:

> *Creative leaders invite disruptive innovation, encourage others to drop outdated approaches and take balanced risks. They are open-minded and inventive in expanding their management and communication styles, particularly to engage with a new generation of employees, partners and customers.*

Disruptive innovation involves challenge. The neuroscientist Susan Greenfield also associates creativity with challenge. She says that creating new insight begins with challenging dogma, which means challenging existing neural connections. Challenge and deconstruction combine to bring together unusual elements, 'seeing one thing in terms of something else'. 'Aha!' moments that arise from the creative process are where new neural connections are made.[1]

---

1   Speaking at the Flamingo Big Ideas Breakfast, 8 November 2010. http://www.flamingo-international.com/events.php#!/past&&event=future-of-work [accessed: 12 April 2012].

CHAOTIC ACTION

Payne and Keep (2003) observe that paralysis can be the result of looking into the abyss at the apparently overwhelming challenge of change. It can take courage to challenge and initiate change in the face of complexity and resistance. Doing things better or differently involves creative leaders engaging in 'chaotic action', and enabling others to do the same, to challenge the status quo and overcome paralysis: 'Once people begin to act, they generate tangible outcomes in some context and this helps them to discover what is occurring, what needs to be explained, and what should be done next' (Weick 2001).

Weick's focus on action is about providing tangible outcomes that help people to make sense of what they think is happening within a particular context. He says that meaning lies in the path of action, and proposes that chaotic action is preferable to orderly inaction (Weick 1979).

Performance becomes more effective as people struggle to make sense of shared meaning through their collective actions. Chaotic action also has psychological benefits as people feel that by acting they have more control if they are able to act to change a situation in which they otherwise might feel overwhelmed.

The two leaders considered and compared in the following sections demonstrated abilities to challenge and engage in chaotic action – in one case, considerably more chaotic than the other.

Operational, Localised, Informal

The first example concerns a senior nurse in charge of a hospital ward. She is responsible for 40 people who provide 24-hour care across day and night shifts to patients, many of whom have multiple medical and social problems. She has little power, but a lot of experience and determination.

The hospital is embedded within the UK's monolithic National Health Service, and is located in a geographical area that is still feeling the effects of catastrophic industrial decline more than thirty years ago. Medical staff routinely cope with health effects within a population that has high incidences of alcohol, drug misuse and other illnesses associated with social deprivation. The work environment is particularly challenging.

At the time the change in performance culture was initiated, the nurse had newly taken charge of a ward which was disorganised. She describes her early feelings of anxiety as she struggled to create order out of the chaos that faced her. Following several weeks of this anxiety, she decided to take action and not to allow herself to be a victim of the poor systems and performance culture she had inherited.

She is careful to attribute no blame to her predecessor, who although having a more *laissez-faire* attitude to management than her own, was nevertheless operating within a wider management system that failed to set expectations and which has recently been undergoing fundamental transformation.

As well as commenting on the systems she inherited, the nurse reflected on her own perception of her capabilities. Despite her experience, she did not feel prepared for the role she had 'fallen into'. She understood that she was capable of planning her own workload, but she had received no formal education on workload planning for the staff for whom she was responsible, and was managing people instinctively.

STRUCTURAL CHANGES

A crucial element in the narrative is that simultaneous structural changes were at that time taking place within the regional health authority, which meant that a new nurse manager was appointed as the senior nurse came into post. The excellent relationship that developed between the two was vital. Although the intention and energy exerted in sustaining the performance culture transformation was self-initiated, the encouragement the nurse received from her new manager gave her confidence and enabled her to carry on when the going got particularly tough.

SUPPORTIVE RELATIONSHIP

The relationship was pivotal in two ways. The first was that everything she was trying to do was within policy guidelines, and the wider management environment was changing in the senior nurse's favour. Her new manager was entirely behind both the structural changes and the nurse's determination to change local systems and behaviour on the hospital ward. Her manager's authority and support gave her the armour she needed to forge ahead with what she wanted to do.

The second way in which the relationship was crucial lay in how their attitudes to each other strengthened their professional interactions. From the outset, the nurse regarded her manager as 'outstanding', since she encouraged her, giving her full freedom and not interfering. The manager gave advice when she was asked, but otherwise remained in the background with the public spotlight falling on the nurse. The manager communicated confidence, and this did not waver as things became difficult.

ACTIONS TAKEN

One of the first issues the nurse decided to tackle was attendance management. There was no sickness control, resulting in 'free-for-all' attitudes to attendance. Lowering rates of absenteeism was an immediate priority. This was problematic because there were nurses on the ward who had poor attendance records and whose behaviour in this respect had gone unchallenged for years. This was her opportunity to 'tell people what I was about and that I would take no nonsense'.

What then happened was that people began to leave, and at one point the ward was 40 per cent down on resourcing levels. The shortfall had to be addressed through agency staff, which was expensive, and the quality of the nurses provided was unpredictable and variable. What the senior nurse had set out to do was to make a very public statement about the boundaries and expectations she was setting.

As she fretted about whether or not she had done the right thing, her manager reassured her that the right people were leaving, to stay resolved, and that this in time would give her the opportunity to build the team she had envisaged.

OVERCOMING RESISTANCE

These early actions met stiff resistance. Apart from challenging long-held attitudes and behaviours, the nurse had to battle against the fact that she was dealing with peers. Earning respect and being seen as someone with authority was not easy. Nevertheless, the effects of her actions were quickly noticed across the organisation.

Having secured management backing and made her intentions publicly known, the next step in the transformation was to continue building personal support. She set about nurturing deputies in whom she would demonstrate the same level of confidence as she received from her manager. This personal support team has become a close-knit unit that reinforces attitudes, values and performance expectations.

NEXT STEPS

The next step in her approach was to get others on board and to initiate a recruitment drive. She knew that she was seeking to recruit primarily on attitude, and is not shy in admitting that she was looking for nurses who would be compliant and mouldable around the values, high-performance behaviours and caring attitudes that she expects from her staff. It took her just over two years, but she has now taken the ward from the one with the worst reputation to the top-performing ward along a range of indicators, including the best record on infection control, the most co-operative ward in the hospital, and the ward with the consistently lowest absentee rates.

AND NOW

The ward still feels chaotic, and this is partly in the nature of work. As well as the work having elements of routine – for example, feeding, washing and administering medication – there are large elements of unpredictability, such as emergency admissions and sudden deterioration in patients' condition requiring immediate attention. Much of the chaotic activity is due to having to comply with inefficiencies created by the wider system, for example a target and record-keeping culture that skews where effort is expended.

There was, for instance, deep unhappiness following a widely publicised and national outcry over deaths at another hospital in the region due to an outbreak of *Clostridium difficile*. Nurses on the ward felt they would be unfairly blamed for systemic failings over which they had no control. The senior nurse feels that it is her job to influence morale when something like this happens, by modelling behaviour and maintaining positive attitudes.

The unpredictable elements of the work and the challenges posed by the constraints imposed by wider management systems create stress for the staff. The senior nurse therefore tries to create a strong ethos of caring and looking out for each other among the nurses. There is currently an issue with the nurses in her care being too conscientious in their handovers between shifts, and they are taking too long to leave the ward. At the time of writing, this is something she was looking at urgently.

Central to her approach to management are values, attitudes, emotional well-being, support and setting expectations. She constantly tries to lead by example, whether in good hygiene practices or remaining positive.

When asked whether it would have been useful if she could have had education on creating culture change, she said yes. She would have known that the conflict and resistance she was experiencing were normal. The process was emotionally challenging. She was very grateful to have had a manager who believed in her and who would have been prepared to back her up had it been necessary.

LEARNING FROM PEERS

She is now seeking to learn from other senior nurses, which she believes would be of great help in her desire to lead by example. Having experienced the personal cost of challenging the status quo, she wants now to create a learning network for other senior nurses within the hospital and beyond it. She knows that others are doing things differently, and is seeking to share experiences.

A certain amount of this is happening in the hospital at formal monthly review meetings. Additional informal forums where nurses can share informally and asynchronously, at a time that is convenient to them, would be welcomed. The National Health Service is now actively promoting lean systems and working practices.

Strategic, Systemic, Formal

The more strategic, formalised example has a much larger scope of influence and is drawn from working closely with a senior executive in Russia as he sought to introduce customer-focused working practices and values into a municipality (Markov 2008).

The city administration is responsible for delivering a range of services, including health care, education, transport and land acquisition services. Markov chose the improvement of processes associated with land acquisition to introduce 'client-oriented design'.

PROBLEM CONTEXT

Land acquisition service provision was chosen for several reasons. As he explained, land plays a critical role in human affairs the world over. The situation is particularly problematic in the region, since the territory is so vast that road networks and infrastructure are not always adequate.

Markov observed that equitable land management is extremely complex, involving as it does multiple federal and municipal departments and commercial institutions like banks. It was important to address problems presented by land management since they pose a significant barrier to the business investment climate.

PROBLEM OBJECTIVE

Drawing on his prior experience in the private sector, he knew that he wanted to initiate the process of change by implementing an IT system in which the municipality would lead the process of integration in negotiation with all participating institutions.

From the client point of view, a front desk in the city administration building removed the ambiguity and uncertainty over how to begin the process. Information would then be simultaneously distributed to back-end operations, drastically reducing lead times from the previously sequential process. This is what Markov set out to do:

- Understand and model the complex nature of problems arising from work-related tasks.

- Critically evaluate options for possible solutions, including assessment of risks and criteria for selections.

- Consider issues arising from a theoretical and best practice perspective.

- Review barriers and evaluate approaches to overcoming and mitigating their effects.

- Develop and deploy analytical tools.

- Assess outcomes and develop recommendations.

He also knew that implementing the IT system would mean tackling fundamental business processes, which would encompass deep changes to the behavioural, mindset and cultural dimensions of organisational structures, human resources strategy, operations and control processes.

THINKING CRITICALLY

Implementing the IT systems, designing supporting systems and processes, and influencing the performance culture were achieved within a formal learning programme which is described later in the chapter. This gave him the opportunity to be exposed to new ideas and to compare his instinctive and experiential knowledge against a number of theoretical perspectives. It also gave him access to senior peers from the private sector with different specific business problems but similar organisational issues.

He learned to think critically, systematically and reflectively. He used the opportunities the formal programme gave him to step outside his day-to-day responsibilities to reflect on the shape of the business problems and issues involved in designing a solution.

PROBLEM-FORMULATION

This was a particularly complex business problem, involving sets of dynamic, interacting factors that included process architecture, strategic human resources and organisational culture, client expectations and external stakeholders. He therefore spent about the first third of the two-year learning programme thinking about the nature of his business problem, having been introduced to the concept of complex adaptive systems and a meta-model devised by the programme director, Professor Robin Matthews.

The model depicts the interacting complex adaptive systems of inner dynamics, outer dynamics and their relationship to what Professor Matthews calls organisational grammar – values, rules and supporting systems (Matthews 2010). Risk assessment was also an important part of this iterative process, the output from which was the modelled solution space shown in Figure 8.1.

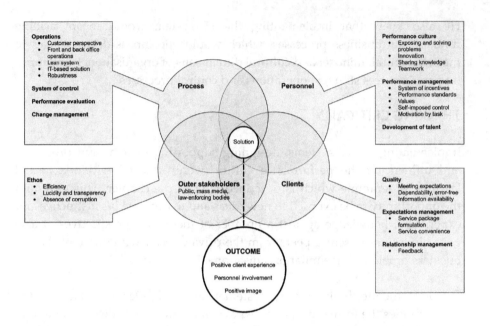

Figure 8.1   The Markov Model
© Roman Markov, 2008

The systemic, dynamic inter-relationships among the components of the model are complex: movement in one of the solution model's components has an impact on the others. Visualising both the elements of the problem and the relationships among the elements was vital for his own understanding, and to allow him to explain his thinking to his peers and colleagues.

IDENTIFYING BARRIERS

A core barrier to the proposed changes from the outset was relationships among participants in the service supply chain. Inter-departmental power struggles, territorial behaviour and building power bases to influence control over land acquisition processes among various municipal departments (land, architecture and law) had resulted in poor cross-boundary collaborative relationships. In addition, there were problems with internal communications within departments. A further issue was departments avoiding taking responsibility in difficult cases, and shifting blame to other departments.

It is against this backdrop, which may be familiar to many readers from their own experience of organisations, that the IT systems design and implementation was developed. He needed to nurture a performance culture that encouraged co-operation, willing participation and the ability to deviate from formalised responses when creative solutions were needed.

OVERCOMING BARRIERS

Complexity of individual behaviour was a significant barrier. Influencing behaviour through changes to performance measurement and reward systems was at the core of his approach, but he also recognised that people cannot be directed. Responding to the reactions of all participants in the process was the biggest uncertainty he faced, which required a combination of skilful leadership that included influencing, persuading, challenging, demonstrating and involving people.

He sees his biggest achievement as having had a measure of influence in changing mindsets and encouraging willingness to participate by involving his colleagues. The process was far from easy. For example, he had created two cross-functional teams that brought together people from different departments and allocated joint responsibilities for specific outcomes. The early stages in the teams' development were characterised by conflict, misunderstandings and rivalry. He concludes:

> *Mitigation of destructive outcome should be done mainly through such formal systems as organisational structure, job design, work organisation, physical workplace, support and control systems. But to run this 'hardware', 'software' must be developed that includes leadership, team working, communication systems and continuous improvement culture as suggested by the lean implementation framework described above.*

Comparing the Examples

The example of the hospital ward was local in scope, and focused on improving existing working practices. The much more complex cross-boundary, inter-institutional example of the Russian municipality focused on designing and implementing new businesses processes, requiring far-reaching changes to multiple systems.

A number of common themes emerge from these cases, despite their differences in scope and complexity.

VALUE-DRIVEN CHANGE

One aspect the cases have in common is the vision, determination and energy of the two leaders who wanted the performance culture of their workplaces to change. Both change initiatives were the personal visions of leaders who were dissatisfied with the existing performance cultures and the reputations of their workplaces.

As well as improving the investment climate, another of Markov's key objectives was to create value in service provision. He held an executive position at the highest level in the city administration, and was able to use his influence to pilot lean, customer-focused working practices.

The motivation for the senior nurse was initially self-preservation, because the disorganisation and lack of systems was stressful to her. Beyond that initial personal need, she had a deeply held commitment to patient care and a desire to embed her work ethos into the culture of the ward.

STRATEGIC OR OPERATIONAL

The examples show that determined leaders, wherever they are in an organisation – whether acting in a strategic capacity from the top or in an operational context – can initiate and influence change if they have authority and support.

SUPPORT FROM ALLIES

Both leaders said how important it was to have the support of people to whom they reported directly. This has already been mentioned with respect to the partnership between the senior nurse and her nursing manager, whose support was vital. There was never any sense that the nursing manager felt threatened by her colleague's initiative – indeed, she went out of her way to show the nurse that she had capabilities she did not previously realise she had. The nurse's success reflected well on the nursing manager's own reputation.

The nurse was explicit in saying that making an ally of her manager was only one element of building a network of support. She deliberately put a lot of effort into creating a team of highly supportive colleagues who shared her values and work ethos, and who themselves then modelled leadership behaviours to others.

Markov also talked about seeking out and influencing leaders distributed across the different municipal departments. It was also similarly crucial for him to secure the support of the head of the municipality, who was initially unsure about his new thinking. To his credit, the head of the municipality allowed him to continue to implement the IT system and to manage the process as he wished. The municipality head became more enthusiastic in time as he saw positive results and was involved in how decisions were made, particularly in difficult situations. Markov's success became his own success.

INTUITION

Both leaders said they acted from intuition. The senior nurse has had no formal management education. When asked whether it might have been helpful to know about organisational behaviour, lean principles and leadership, she affirmed that was the case. She would then have known that the resistance she was experiencing was not unusual, and she would have been able to compare her intuitive responses and experiences with people who had initiated similar performance culture transformations. She said it would have helped her to understand why things she was doing were effective or not, and would have given her options for alternative ways to do what she did.

It is interesting to note that Markov also acted initially from intuition and experience. He says that learning to think systematically and making use of models, frameworks and theoretical perspectives helped him to reflect on why things happened or did not happen.

This reflective process gave him principles, insights and learning that will shape his approaches to future action. Reflecting on what he perceived was happening came after he had acted, which is exactly what Weick means by 'chaotic action' – doing something, then seeing what you think happened. In his case, the reflections will feed forward into future action.

RESILIENCE

It is clear that their attempts to influence performance cultures in their respective workplaces made heavy demands on their leadership skills, which developed as they reflected on their practical experience. It also demanded personal resilience and social support that encouraged this resilience.

The nurse manager displayed sensitivity and adopted a nurturing 'servant leader' approach in helping the nurse to achieve her objectives. The nurse, on the other hand, felt that she had to demonstrate resolve in communicating her intentions to staff. She was firm in her approach, while maintaining respect and giving people the opportunity to talk about the intended changes. Demonstrating a sense of resolve while retaining a commitment to creating a humane and caring culture, characterised by mutually respectful relationships, was not easy. Remaining resolved while knowing that people were unhappy about changes was difficult for all concerned.

Markov's resolve to influence the performance culture in the land acquisition process, which was distributed across municipal and federal departments, was faced with opposition. He did not go into specific details about these challenges, although he did say explicitly that he countered resistance.

PERFORMANCE CLIMATES AND ENVIRONMENTS

Markov's comment about running the 'hardware' through the 'software' of 'leadership, team working, communication systems and continuous improvement culture' is insightful. The 'software' creates enabling performance climates, and the 'hardware' is the performance environments from which performance climates emerge.

Both leaders set out to create performance climates where performance expectations were articulated, communicated clearly, and where expected behaviours were modelled. This was particularly the case for the senior nurse, who was able to communicate and model behavioural expectations and standards, influencing the behaviour of others.

She was able to set the performance environment in a limited way, for example in declaring a new approach to absence management. It is important to note that the wider policy environment was changing in line with what she was seeking to do. She was pushing at a door that was beginning to open.

Markov had considerably more influence in determining the wider performance environment, the 'hardware' of interacting, formal support systems, for example performance indicators, measures and rewards.

NO MORE HEROES

The notion that transformational change is due to primarily to individual influence is diminished in both cases. Certainly, both leaders were pivotal in catalysing and influencing the transformation process, but it is unlikely that either would have succeeded without persuading others to support them and act in accordance with the performance expectations they set.

To gain that support, whole systems of leadership and engagement – Markov's 'hardware' – need to be in place (Towers Perrin 2007).

FIRST WAVE REFLECTIONS

It was noted in Chapter 3 that the influence of leaders throughout organisations in initiating and sustaining transformational change cannot be underestimated. This would include the management the production director in Case Study 1 and the managing director in Case Study 3, who both instigated effective, value-driven change. It also includes the team leaders and supervisors who were vital in influencing and supporting their colleagues as they participated in problem-solving and collaborative continuous improvement.

The attempt to transform working practices in Case Study 2 is notable for the absence of value-driven leadership. The impetus behind this change initiative was severe competitive pressures. Redundancies and coercive use of behavioural performance measures to select those who were to be made redundant contributed to low morale and lack of trust. The poor performance climate was exacerbated by an inadequate performance environment, particularly in terms of the lack of integration among the manufacturing zones. It may be remembered that despite this, there was willingness in the workforce 'to put things right'.

NO SINGLE BEST WAY

Although common themes emerge from both examples and share similarities with first wave workplace transformations, what leaders do and how they set about influencing others and gaining support for what they want to achieve varies according to context and culture. It also varies with the personality and management style of the person initiating the transformation. There is no single best way.

The examples just described demonstrate that lean principles have global relevance and application outside manufacturing. They also show that leaders with vision, determination and who adopt systemic and systematic approaches to transforming performance cultures play a critical role in enabling customer-focused, value-creating learning and performance to take place.

Developing Leaders

Leaders who shape performance environments have always been important. They become even more crucial in second wave smart working, as knowledge processes become abstract, non-routine, distributed and tacit. Leadership consequently becomes similarly distributed. Identifying effective local leaders, supporting them and developing their confidence and capabilities are core to creating the new wave of smart working.

'Creative leadership' is easier to talk about than to make happen in practice. The burden of expectation on leaders increases significantly as business environments become more socially and cognitively complex. The role of leader now includes:

- shaping operating environments that are consistent with high-performance, creativity, individuality and emotional well-being;

- challenging dogma and overcoming organisational inertia in making the case for new ways of working and in creating agile, adaptive responses;

- ensuring that appropriate tools and technologies are available for continual learning, adaptation and development of collective intelligence;

- displaying skills, knowledge and at least a foundation understanding of the emotional, psychological, cultural, learning and social needs of people;

- appreciating the role of the physical workspace in generating shared knowledge;

- understanding social issues arising from working together in distributed knowledge environments, including ability to manage the constructive conflict that is inherent in cross-disciplinary, culturally influenced collaboration;

- taking responsibility for surfacing knowledge, connections, mental models and processes;

- displaying and modelling emotional intelligence;

- taking responsibility for reflecting on one's own practice and that of others.

This all demands personal qualities of resilience, self-confidence, determination, experience and intuition. Challenging the status quo is not for the faint-hearted. As well as needing knowledge and capabilities in understanding and influencing performance environments, leaders need to be capable of developing creative habits and integrative, critical thinking processes in themselves and others.

Martin (2007) explains integrative thinking as the ability to look beyond the apparently obvious, adopting a systematic perspective to problem-solving that takes into account non-linear relationships among variables and tensions among available options. Leaders must therefore be able to think critically and engage in integrative, systematic thinking, conceptualising organisations as sets of living, interacting sub-systems and understanding how formal systems influence behaviour.

As if this were not enough, Stacey (1996) proposes that a key role for leaders is to contain anxiety. The senior nurse demonstrated this in attempting to maintain a positive attitude when the ward was under particular pressure. She saw this as one of her main functions, which supports Stacey's contention.

Demonstrating social, emotional and cognitive capabilities is a lot to ask of leaders, whose roles are so pivotal and who themselves are working under increasingly challenging conditions characterised by increasingly complex business processes, long hours and stress. To further require leaders to be responsible for developing creative leadership capabilities in others increases the pressures of expectation.

EXPERIENTIAL LEARNING

Supporting and preparing leaders is now, more than ever, imperative for their personal well-being, and crucial if adaptive and agile business performance is to be achieved through smart working and managing. Datar et al. (2010), in their critical assessment of the MBA in US business schools, concluded that experiential learning is the new hallmark of the MBA as it adapts to the complexities of a rapidly changing global business environment.

The following sections will examine one example of an experiential formal learning approach and one of an informal experiential learning approach to leadership development, both drawn from personal experience.

Formal Approach

The formal approach is based on my experience of helping to develop a work-based Master's degree programme together with colleagues at a university in the UK, later further developed with the same university in partnership with colleagues at an academic institute in Russia. The intention is not to describe the degree in detail; rather, it is a personal reflection on how learning through acting and reflecting, which was the basis of the degree, is highly appropriate in developing creative and resilient leaders.

LEARNING FRAMEWORKS

The formal experiential learning approach was based on learning frameworks, also known as learning contracts (Knowles 1986, Laycock and Stephenson 1993). These facilitate a reflective, active and experiential approach to executive learning. A learning framework can be compared to a set of empty boxes which is populated by customised content, tools and methods according to specific learner needs. These learning resources are used in a just-in-time way, at the point where they are needed, to prompt thinking and reflection about action.

The real value of learning frameworks lies in the opportunity they provide for thinking about how to scope and articulate desired learning outcomes and the assessment criteria against which they are evaluated. Used effectively, learning frameworks can be an invaluable tool for structured thinking, providing the starting point for dialogue between those seeking to learn and colleagues working with them to facilitate their reflections.

Learning frameworks contribute to informal learning through the conversations and peer support that emerge from the formal learning process. Used badly, learning frameworks can represent nothing more that bureaucratic hoops to be jumped through.

PROBLEM-FORMULATION

The initial stage of the formal learning process required students to examine a strategic business challenge in detail, examining internal and external relationships and inter-connections. Learning outcomes at Master's level are articulated in the context of cognitive skills, operational capabilities, and capabilities in interacting with peers to develop critical analysis and pattern-discernment skills, intended to enable students to: 'Deal with complex issues both systematically and creatively, make sound judgements in the absence of complete data, and communicate their conclusions clearly to specialist and non-specialist audiences' (QAA 2010).

THEORETICAL PERSPECTIVES

Theories are used as aids to thinking, reflecting and generating hypotheses, and as vehicles for initiating discussions with colleagues in the workplace. For the Russian executive, complex adaptive systems and lean approaches were particularly appropriate aids to thinking and acting. Through using a framework that conceptualises organisations as interacting complex adaptive systems, he saw that everything is inter-related. This was a crucial learning point for him.

Path dependency was another useful theoretical perspective for him. This is the idea that organisations, once set on a particular course of action, continue down that route even when the indications are that the action may no longer be appropriate. The more time and effort is expended, the more difficult it becomes to change. He concludes that the 'Personnel' system in his model would be the most path-dependent, and therefore where most barriers to implementing the IT system would be found.

Kurt Lewin's contention that there is nothing as practical as a good theory was mentioned in Chapter 4. Using the case of Enron as an example, Ghoshal (2005) argued that bad theory harms good management practice. Critical thinking and reflective practice therefore become vital in assessing ideological bias and vested interests.

JUST-IN-TIME CONTENT

A core curriculum of key subjects can be included in programme design. This is not necessarily the case. The starting point can be a customised set of resources initially proposed by the student, based on work experience and learning objectives, in consultation with a learning mentor. Students are also encouraged to source input from their practitioner networks, as well as from the peers with whom they are learning.

This is in addition to academic and workplace advisers, who play a crucial ongoing role in suggesting additional content that is specific to the student's business problem. Learning advisers become like brokers who propose appropriate people and information at the point where it is needed. Of course, students are also expected to find content for themselves as the learning process progresses.

SOCIAL AND EMOTIONAL SUPPORT

Critical thinking and reflective learning skills were the main objectives in the early days of developing the Master's degree programme. It soon became clear that the learning at this level of operational complexity was emotionally and cognitively challenging. Self-confidence and perception abilities influence action and learning.

Bandura (1978) says that self-expectations of personal efficacy influence coping behaviour in the face of adversity, and that the ability to persist and master an activity leads to an increased sense of self-efficacy. The opposite is also the case, and a person's belief that they are not able to do something may become self-fulfilling.

PEER SUPPORT

The emotional impact of learning at this level cannot be emphasised enough. This is especially true for experienced professionals who have learned through experience and who may have been away from formal learning for some time, or even never experienced formal university-level learning. The support team of a learning facilitator, workplace adviser and an academic adviser with appropriate subject knowledge are all crucial people (Lipscomb and McEwan 2001).

The programme administrators are equally important, since they are often the first point of contact with students and build up a rapport with them. The administrators are often the first people to pick up on difficulties students may be having – for example, assignments being late because students are working long hours.

The real support students get, though, is from each other, which corroborates long-established good practice in professional learning (Boud 1999, Boud et al. 2001). The executives understand the emotional pressures each is under, and they experience common challenges. Weekend workshops bring people together for intensive periods of learning and socialising. The camaraderie that can develop among a group of executives is a joy and privilege to observe.

Informal Learning Networks

An alternative to the formal learning programme is an informal approach to leadership development through learning networks. Taking the Johnson Controls Global Mobility Network as an example, this network is not specifically action-focused. It provides leaders with a space for talking, exchanging experience and viewpoints, and reflecting together. These sessions tend to be characterised by fun and generate a lot of energy. It is therefore unsurprising that social relationships develop.

Learning networks can differ in the extent to which they are formal or informal, and more or less directed towards practice. Whatever form they take, they are inherently social, and learning is an outcome of relationships. Much has already been written about communities of practice. Wenger (2006) describes communities of practice as: 'Groups of people who share a concern or a passion for something they do and learn how to do it better as they interact regularly'.

Communities of practice vary in the degree to which they are formally organised. Some operate as managed communities that abide by rules, while others are very fluid and informal. At Arup, the global engineering design and engineering services company, communities of practice are integral within a culture based on knowledge-creation and sharing. Another reason communities of practice are so valued within Arup is the threat of the loss of critical knowledge in an ageing population, as engineers retire and as challenges escalate in 'recruiting quality graduates as fewer choose engineering careers'.[2]

EXPLORATORY CONVERSATION

Exploratory informal networks are particularly effective for complex or unfamiliar topics that have inter-related elements. The Johnson Controls Global Mobility Network, which brings together IT, human resources and facilities management practitioners from different companies, institutions and knowledge disciplines, is a learning network that meets several times a year to explore and share information, experience and perspectives on topics related to the globally changing workscape.

Participation in the network is by invitation, and is limited to a maximum of 15 participants. Experience tells us that this number is large enough to create energy, while small enough to ensure that everyone has the opportunity to contribute in a comfortable environment. Invitation is based on our knowledge of people and their interests, so that we target those we feel might benefit from the discussion. We also seek to create a mix of people who might not otherwise talk to each other professionally. In this way, we seek to set the stage for creative insights to emerge, as thoughtful people generously contribute knowledge and insights to discussions from across a range of knowledge disciplines and organisations.

For most of the Global Mobility Network members, improving practice is a secondary consideration to the personal development that network members tell us is the main benefit they gain from attending network meetings. Energy is created through the conversation that emerges when we meet, which is helped by the 'it goes where it goes' approach to facilitating with the lightest of touches (Puybaraud and McEwan 2007). Meetings are characterised by informality and intense engagement.

Puybaraud and McEwan speculated that a spin-off from external informal learning networks might be that: 'Once senior executives have experienced personal benefits from participating in strategic workplace networks, they could champion the establishment of a similar system of networks throughout their organisations and supply chains.' They noted that feedback received from executives outside the network was not encouraging. Presenting to a

---

2   http://www.arup.com/_assets/_download/F01A0F5F-19BB-316E-40ED890DF0885EB3.pdf [accessed: 12 April 2012].

conference of knowledge managers, one said afterwards: 'That sounds great, but we would never be able to fund and support something so fluid with no measurable outcomes.' We concluded that this seemed to us a shame, given our experience of executives finding network meetings so stimulating.

FREQUENCY OF MEETINGS

The fact that the meetings occur just three times a year makes it feasible for time-pressed senior people to attend. Members are keen that dates are communicated well in advance so that they are in their diaries and fixed. They value and look forward to a rare respite away from day-to-day pressures to spend time on personal development. If busy executives value learning networks, then surely they are highly effective mechanisms for leadership development? Being able to take time to explore with peers in other departments and other companies provides the richness of perspectives that are essential for understanding connections and inter-relationships, which raise complexities that require integrated thinking (Martin 2007).

These infrequent, in-person network meetings may have to be supplemented by ongoing conversations, especially in high-risk, high-ambiguity and uncertain knowledge environments (Fishbein and Treverton 2004). Fishbein and Treverton explore the concept of 'alternative analysis' to address transnational and terrorist threats. Proposing that a culture of mindfulness of past and potential systemic failure has to recognise mental biases in sense-making and pattern recognition, they say:

> A continuous, sustained program of small to medium-sized efforts, however, would regularly explore different possible outcomes and debate assumptions, all linked to incoming information about the issue under consideration. This probably is best thought of as an ongoing conversation (both face-to-face and electronic) among interested parties, structured to encourage divergent thinking.

Making It Happen

At first sight, the arguments constructed in this and earlier chapters appear to be signalling mixed messages. On the one hand they contend that organisational inertia is strong – so strong that the defence of a nation is compromised by inability to adapt old mindsets and habits. Risk avoidance becomes institutionalised as people within functional silos seek to cover their backs, defend their territory and avoid making decisions. Confronting structural rigidities is difficult, and is not be underestimated.

The two examples summarised earlier in the chapter, both from the public sector, show that performance cultures can be transformed through the actions of determined leaders. Organisational inertia can indeed be strong, but can co-exist alongside innovation and adaptation. Emergent transformation can be instigated effectively by identifying local leaders who are impatient with the status quo and who know that things can be done better or differently.

This approach is consistent with Nayar (2010), who proposes instigating change at the point where value is created. This is with employees who are more likely to be directly in contact with customers than senior executives removed from day-to-day operations, which was revealed to be particularly problematic in Farmer's analysis of 9/11 and Hurricane Katrina (Farmer 2010).

ONLINE SUPPORT FOR LEADERS

A point forcefully made in this chapter is that leaders are carrying a heavy load of expectations, and that they need to possess personal qualities and sophisticated social and cognitive skills. Leaders only know in outline what they want to achieve at the start of an intervention (Callaghan and Drake 2008). Apart from the effort and resilience required to sustain a transformation of performance culture, the lack of clarity and confusion associated with emergent processes add to the cognitive and emotional pressure on leaders.

Fortunately, there has never been a better time to embark on developing creative leadership. According to an Economist Intelligence Unit report (2008), 'digital tools will democratise access to information', taking control out of the hands of managers and leading to greater autonomy for employees. Even if social technologies are banned, as they are in many workplaces, the Internet is easily accessed through smartphones and tablet devices.

The genie is out of the bottle, with democratisation of information meaning that people can freely discover, create and share content. Using social technologies makes conversations visible and captures dialogue, streams of thought and judgements that can be retrieved to inform continual reflection.

Legacy of learning

This means that decades of academic research, which in earlier times might have remained hidden within academic journals and accessed only by researchers in universities, is now available to anyone willing to pay. Some of the supporting references in this book, for example, are from academic papers and books already in my possession. Many more are freely available corporate research reports, and yet others are purchased academic journal articles.

Top-ranking business schools are making their content freely available through Creative Commons licences.[3] The number of innovations coming out of these business schools is growing.[4] This is ground-breaking. There is now no shortage of quality content available for anyone willing to seek it out. As Cole and Foster (2008) point out, the Massachusetts Institute of Technology makes course materials freely available because 'the value of an MIT education is not in the content, but in the interaction between students and the instructor'.

Social support

Not only is quality content freely available, it is now possible to regard people outside organisational boundaries as peers who share similar problems in different contexts. This would be the online equivalent of informal learning networks like the Johnson Controls Global Mobility Network. The close and trusting relationships that develop in person can develop online among people who have never met.

Online learning communities can be created to discover good practice research, to act on it and to reflect on it together, sharing sources and insights for mutual benefit. It is hard for those whose have never experienced this level of engagement with people they have not met in person to understand how energising the experience can be. There is nothing for it but to try it! Hagel et al. (2010) refer to this online innovation support system as 'creative spaces', which can involve networks of millions of people. They say that creative spaces are not for learning, but for performance. It is hard to see how performance and learning can be separated.

---

3   http://creativecommons.org/ [accessed: 12 April 2012].
4   http://www.nytimes.com/2012/05/04/opinion/brooks-the-campus-tsunami.html?_r=2&partner=
rssnyt&emc=rss [accessed: 4 May 2012].

The formal and informal action approaches to leadership development described in this chapter can now be instigated wholly or partially online, and can be available to people who may previously not considered that they had access to executive learning and leadership development. Digital tools create democratisation of access to learning.

Concluding Remarks

A major contention of this chapter is that doing better or doing differently can be initiated by determined local leaders from anywhere within fractal organisations. These key people need to have the personal support of colleagues and a sufficiently favourable operating environment – or one that can be made more favourable – to enable them to try to influence, persuade and engage their colleagues. They in turn shape the performance environments in which others can excel.

The review of formal and informal approaches to leadership development gave practical examples of leaders initiating transformation, and indicted how leaders' social, cognitive and emotional capabilities can be developed so that they in turn can set the conditions for learning environments to emerge, where they and their colleagues can do what they do better or differently. Social and emotional support in workplace transformations is crucial, not just for those initiating the changes, but for all involved.

Diagnosing, Designing and Learning

Introduction

This chapter shows how the formal and informal approaches to leadership development outlined in Chapter 8 can be applied specifically to making the transition to smart working, creating the opportunity for learning and developing skills from the experience. Outputs include the Smart Work Framework, and a Diagnostic Grid and Checklist. These tools help to diagnose, design and implement a learning project.

Dialogue Takes Centre Stage

These are three key learning points from the assessment of formal and informal learning approaches in the previous chapter:

1. Making the transition to new ways of working, and learning from it, can be emotionally challenging. This is because of the conflict created by disturbing the status quo, because leaders are working under time pressures and pressures arising from increasingly complex operating environments, and also because some people can lack confidence in their own abilities to engage in formal learning – even though they are highly competent.

2. In the course of engaging with formal learning, the informal conversations that people have among themselves, and the close personal relationships that can develop, become a highly effective

way of coping with the emotional and practical challenges that are typically experienced.

3.   Time-pressured executives value the conversation and relationships that developed through the Global Mobility Network to such an extent that they regard meetings as a treat not to be missed, rather than yet another demand on their time. Making space and time to reflect on workplace trends, research findings and presentations from guest speakers creates opportunities for energetic conversations.

Far from wasting time, the opportunity to engage in casual conversation and dialogue is valued, valuable and necessary for shared learning and social support.

WHAT IS DIALOGUE?

Schein (2009) describes dialogue as: 'Low-key "talking around the campfire", allowing enough time for and encouraging reflective conversation, rather than confrontational conversation, discussion or debate'.

The purpose of dialogue, he says, is to create opportunities for deeper levels of thought and to appreciate the tacit assumptions of self and others.

Smart working processes are knowledge-based, culturally influenced, cross-boundary and distributed. Second wave processes are increasingly complex, hidden and abstract. Dialogue therefore becomes pivotal in creating shared learning and in making abstract, tacit and collaborative knowledge processes explicit.

The following section describes a number of tools that pull together insights and design principles from all the previous chapters. They are intended to help scope the project plan for the learning project. They also promote dialogue and help to elicit multiple perspectives from people who come from different national, organisational and professional cultures.

Tools for Dialogue

The first tool to be described is the Smart Work Framework, which reflects current workplace trends. The purpose is to help people think about where their companies (or the part of the company for which they are responsible) ideally should be now, and where they think they ideally ought to be going into the future.

It could be used as a prelude to diagnosing and implementing a practical project to make the transition to new ways of working, or it could be used to raise awareness of high-performance working to get people thinking about where the business currently is, where it needs to be, and what heading in a new direction would imply.

The next tools described are the Diagnostic Grid and Checklist. These are used together to scope and diagnose a practical project to make the transition to smart working, which also provides the context for experiential learning. Like the Smart Work Framework, the Diagnostic Grid and Checklist are intended to be used to create dialogue among diverse participants and adapted as required for unique operating contexts.

THE SMART WORK FRAMEWORK

Figure 9.1 shows four profiles along five dimensions: structure, global reach, knowledge and learning, flexible work styles and social complexity.

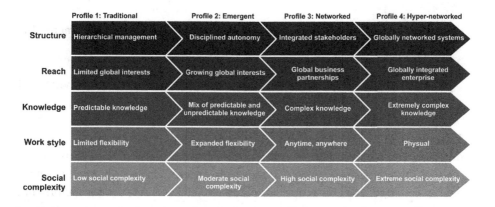

Figure 9.1   The Smart Work Framework

A fundamental difference between first and second wave smart working is the fact that everyone's knowledge is now potentially augmented by being connected to personal networks. The internal knowledge flows of the first wave, which emerge from continuous improvement and engagement in problem-solving, become exponentially expanded by being connected to external knowledge flows.

Each of the profile characteristics is explained in further detail in the following sections, including the degrees to which cognition is distributed internally and externally within each profile and what this implies for supporting systems.

Profile 1

In Profile 1, the organisational structure is traditional and hierarchical. Nevertheless, management values reflect the view that people solve problems rather than creating them. Culture is based on trusted relationships. Choice in how work is carried out is limited. Knowledge is routine, perhaps with elements of unfamiliarity. People are confined to working from specific places and to time constraints – shifts, for example.

As we saw in Chapter 3, many small manufacturers work in this way. Smart working in this profile is an outcome of:

- a positive employment relationship;

- trusted, supporting personal relationships among people;

- workforce commitment to contributing to creating customer value through listening and responding to customer feedback;

- workforce participation and engagement in problem-solving and continuous improvement.

Since work in Profile 1 remains routine and relatively unchanging, it is not unreasonable to speculate that cognition remains distributed mainly across internal functions. There is no need to access external knowledge networks for new knowledge. See the 'empowerment enablers' in Table 3.1 for factors that enable cross-functional continuous improvement and distributed cognition for this profile.

Physical space in this profile needs to be psychologically and physically safe, with 'at-the-bench' collaboration facilities supplemented by informal areas for socialising.

Profile 2

Profile 2 is similar, but now with expanded opportunities for flexibility of time, place and employment contract. Operational complexity is increasing, and varying degrees of management responsibilities are devolved to operations.

Nurses constrained by place, working in shifts and having to comply with strict policy guidelines, might come into this category. Their work is a mix of routine and unpredictable. Knowledge is becoming more complex, and senior nurses are now performing junior doctor tasks. Social dynamics are particularly put under pressure in this fast-moving and stressful occupation.

Another example could be conciliators working to prepare employment tribunal cases. They might work from home but be time-constrained – not by shift working, but by continuous time pressures. Having to prepare cases for fixed court dates adds a continuous production element to their work, which also has elements of familiarity and unpredictability.

The same positive employment relationship and trusted, supporting personal relationships apply. As technical knowledge and social relationships become more complex, a core management belief is that people are the answer to complexity, not the cause of it. Informal conversation, collaboration and networking are encouraged for social support and learning.

Cognition and knowledge flows become more distributed across space, time and organisational boundaries, which increases the complexity of social interactions. Social technologies are increasingly used to diminish social distance for distributed work, connecting people to informal social support and information.

The workplace in this profile offers a mix of formal and informal spaces. 'Sofa-style' spaces reflect the fact that people working away from the office take the opportunity to reconnect socially with colleagues when they return. Space also needs to be made available for collaboration and for solitary concentration.

Profile 3

In Profile 3, cognition and knowledge flows become distributed within and across multiple, connected workplaces. The workplace becomes an integrated learning workplace, or workplace as university campus. Human resources, facilities management and IT services must collaborate to create work environments that support technically and socially complex knowledge. Operations are becoming more global, with networks of organisations collaborating within ecosystems of international partnerships to gain access to capital, markets and talent.

Work is project-focused and carried out by teams of culturally diverse knowledge workers that kaleidoscopically form and disband. Work is also performed from multiple geographical locations, from a range of workspaces, across time zones and performed by people operating under a variety of contractual arrangements. Freelancing for knowledge workers is increasingly preferred.

Controlling, hierarchical management is no longer appropriate. Management and leading is through influence and cajoling. Leaders nurture other leaders, paying particular attention to providing technology, high-performance work systems and workplaces that enable people to get on with what they need to do as autonomously as possible. Project teams breach multiple cultural boundaries (national, professional, demographic, organisational) and collaborate across knowledge silos. Work activities need to be integrated across external and internal organisational boundaries.

Knowledge is continually and rapidly evolving. Cognition is distributed and buried within people's heads. This deeply tacit, complex knowledge emerges through conversation and is made visible through artefacts – flipcharts, whiteboards, computer files, Post-it notes and so on.

Highly connected and distributed workplaces constitute performance environments from which complex, collaborative knowledge emerges. Mobile knowledge workers choose from a range of internal and external workplace options according to specific tasks and social needs.

Workplaces are furthermore physical and virtual, with always-on, mobile and cloud-based applications giving access to knowledge networks within the business and outside it for learning, mentoring and social support.

Profile 4

Profile 4 is similar to Profile 3, but the knowledge being created is rapidly changing, particularly complex and uncertain. Culturally diverse, distributed workplaces exist across global knowledge networks, ecosystems of partners and knowledge specialists. For example, drug discovery is described as being more complex and more expensive than going to the moon in the GlaxoSmithKline example referenced in Chapter 6.[1] AstraZeneca's recent announcement of redundancies bears out the difficulties the sector is facing. Part of its solution is to create virtual laboratories, partnering with bio-tech companies and universities.[2]

Smaller, nimble bio-tech organisations are making new discoveries. GSK restructured its operations away from a silo structure – its 'temple to R&D' where knowledge specialists were isolated from each other – to a structure based on business units that try to emulate the entrepreneurial nimbleness of small bio-tech companies. In this new approach, knowledge specialists work together 'at the bench, solving problems together as they arise'.

An interesting development in this profile is that some intensive knowledge organisations are restricting the choice of locations for knowledge workers. The reason is to have people physically co-located because of the complexity of knowledge being generated. The objective for these businesses is therefore to provide the workplace of preference. Social amenities like rest and play areas, as well as cafe and restaurant facilities, are common features of these knowledge-intensive workplaces.

THE DIAGNOSTIC GRID

The Diagnostic Grid in Table 9.1 gathers together the design principles related to smart working. Information in the grid cells cross-references questions and topics summarised in the Diagnostic Checklist. In this way, a checklist for the learning project plan can be benchmarked against key design principles and characteristics of high-performance work systems.

---

1   http://www.bbc.co.uk/programmes/b00wdjyg [accessed: 12 April 2012].
2   http://www.guardian.co.uk/business/2012/feb/02/astrazeneca-cuts-7300-jobs?newsfeed=true [accessed: 12 April 2012].

Table 9.1   The Diagnostic Grid

		Viability Indicators			
Socio-technical–spatial	**Look Out**	**Look In**	**Adapt**	**Innovate**	**Integrate Collaborate**
People	*External:* Demographic trends Labour market Connected customers Risk and constraints	*Internal:* Operations Climate Risk and constraints	*Internal:* Operations Climate Risk and constraints	*Internal and External:* Operations Climate Environment Knowledge networks	*Internal and External:* Operations Climate Environment Operations
Physical Space	Distributed workplace Knowledge networks	Climate Environment	Climate Environment	Climate Environment Distributed workplace	Climate Environment Distributed workplace
Virtual Space	Technology trends Knowledge networks Distributed workplace	Environment Climate Operations	Climate Environment	Climate Environment Knowledge networks	Climate Environment Knowledge networks
Technology	Technology trends Knowledge networks Demographic trends	Climate Environment Risk and constraints	Climate Environment Risk and constraints	Climate Environment Risk and constraints	Climate Environment Risk and constraints

THE DIAGNOSTIC CHECKLIST

Learning to challenge and ask good questions is part of learning to think critically, besides which, questions and responses to them create opportunity for conversation. The questions in Tables 9.2–5 are based on the research and insights summarised throughout the book. They may not be the best questions that might be asked but they are illustrative, providing a starting point for questions that can be adapted and tailored to specific contexts. Getting stakeholder input on determining what those questions might be adapts the checklist to reflect the problem context, increases the diversity of perspectives, and increases opportunities for participation and engagement. The following sections describe the questions suggested in the Diagnostic Checklist.

Exploring external context

Unique context is created from factors within the wider external environment interacting with internal operating environments, or the part of the organisation relevant to the business problem and project. Assessing external factors is a first step.

The questions in Table 9.2 are from the perspective of the highest level of the enterprise. The external environment in this case really is outside the enterprise, which is extended to include partners and stakeholders. Taking the viable systems perspective, the 'external' environment for a lower-level viable system would include an internal dimension as well as external aspects, accessible and relevant through the connectivity of social technologies.

Table 9.2   The Diagnostic Checklist: External environment

External Environment	
Regulation	How are regulatory requirements affecting the business?
Economic trends	What impact are the emerging economies having?
Demographic trends	How are demographic trends affecting the business?
Technological trends	What impact are social technologies having?
Globalisation	Is the business becoming more globally connected?
Distributed workplace	To what extent does the workforce use external workspaces?
Knowledge networks	How is the business accessing knowledge networks?
Labour market	How much of an issue are skill shortages for the business?
Customers	How are socially connected customers affecting the business?
Threats	What are the greatest threats to the viability of the business?

Assessing what is internal and what is external becomes less clear as social technologies weaken the boundaries between inside and outside the organisation, making them much more porous.

Exploring the project context

The next step is to explore operational issues through an initial assessment of the learning project. This part of the checklist is about scoping project activities, and assessing workflow and relationship dynamics (see Table 9.3).

Table 9.3   The Diagnostic Checklist: Operations

Internal Environment: Operations
Who is involved in the project? What is to be achieved, and by when?
What are the performance objectives? How will success or failure be judged?
What are the performance criteria and indicators?
To what extent are project activities unfamiliar, uncertain and complex?
Is the project partnership distributed across time zones and workplaces? What are the consequences?
What are the possible impacts of cultural diversity?
How will cross-boundary integration be achieved?
What are the desired learning outcomes from the project? How will evidence of learning be assessed?
How might pre-existing conflicts, alliances, personal and institutional agendas etc. affect the project?
How will constructive and destructive conflict be managed?
Who inside and outside of the project partnership might act as champions for the project? Whose support would be essential to the success of the project?
How might the external environment impact on project dynamics and outcomes?

Some people undertaking a transition project are clear at this stage about what they want to achieve. Many are not. Even if problem parameters and project objectives are clear, uncertainty is typically high concerning how project objectives are to be achieved and how outcomes will emerge. There are many unknowns at this stage. Project objectives emerge through iterative dialogue.

Similarly, although relationship dynamics cannot be predicted at the outset, it is possible to think through relationship dynamics that may influence performance outcomes. Using Weick's analysis of power dynamics, alliances and cliques summarised in Chapter 2, how might relationship dynamics present barriers to implementing smart working processes and practices? What can be done to remove or overcome barriers?

Performance climate

This part of the checklist prompts the user to consider how effective governance, leadership, and support for learning, knowledge-sharing and open communication will be achieved through the project (see Table 9.4).

Table 9.4   The Diagnostic Checklist: Performance climate

Internal Environment: Performance Climate
How will mutual trust and recognition be achieved throughout the project partnership?
How will governance support decision-making autonomy?
How will design principles (especially integration and adaptation) be incorporated into project activities?
How will reward and recognition systems encourage participation and knowledge-sharing?
How will performance and monitoring information be made available to all project partners?
How will distributed control (strategic, operational and social) be approached?
How will distributed leadership be recognised and encouraged?
How will unwillingness to share knowledge and information be addressed?
How will opportunities for learning, a key enabler of engagement, be incorporated?
How will the project culture encourage open, safe and transparent communication?
How will management values be articulate to project partners?
How will leaders demonstrate leading by example, and communicating vision and purpose? How will leaders nurture other leaders?

Performance environment

Whereas creating the performance climate concerns putting in place policies and procedures that influence and enable behaviour, the performance environment encompasses the technologies that create the virtual workplace plus the physical workplace (see Table 9.5).

Table 9.5   The Diagnostic Checklist: Performance environment

Internal Environment: Performance Environment
How might social technologies to encourage behaviour consistent with values of openness and trust?
What social and IT support will be available to project partners working away from the main office?
Does the project workspace(s) have quiet places for concentration? Collaboration?
Has the cultural appropriateness of online and physical workspaces been considered?
Do collaboration spaces have facilities for displaying drawings and information?
What collaboration and social technologies will be used for project communication?
What social technologies will be used to create conversation around progress monitoring?
How will social technologies be used to encourage informal conversation and knowledge-sharing?
Where online can people co-create, collaborate, and discover people and content?
How will social technologies be used to make work activities observable?
What policies will be put in place to ensure the security of project information?
What role could social technologies play in sensing early warnings of possible problems?

Risks and constraints

The final section of the checklist invites the user to think about the risks to project outcomes and possible constraints on achieving outcomes (see Table 9.6).

Table 9.6   The Diagnostic Checklist: Risks and constraints

Risks and Constraints
How might pre-existing relationship dynamics be detrimental to project outcomes?
How will emergent politics and power bases within the project network be monitored?
What risks, from the external environment and within the project, threaten successful project outcomes?
How might those risks be minimised?
How might risk to the project team, from time pressures and complexity of collaboration, be reduced?
How might lack of appropriate skills and capabilities constrain the project? How might this be overcome?
How might distrust of social technologies be overcome?
What can be done to increase social media proficiency throughout the project partnership?
Will challenging the status quo and innovation be accepted by all project partners?
If not, how might this present a risk to project outcomes?

Induction

The tools are used within a phased approach to making the transition to smarter working practices through experiential learning; action, reflection and conversation. The approach begins with induction.

The conversation and dialogue-based elements of the formal and informal approaches to learning summarised in Chapter 8 can be unfamiliar to people whose prior experience of formal learning has been expert-led, or where the professional culture does not value so-called 'soft skills'.

An induction phase is therefore crucial, and provides the opportunity to prepare people for a new way of thinking and learning with others, introducing the social, thinking and technological skills and capabilities they will need.

SKILLS AND CAPABILITIES

Induction activities can take place in person, online or a mix of both. However it happens, this phase involves introducing people to each other, to work-based experiential learning and to core smart working concepts. People will also be introduced to the basics of leadership skills, critical thinking and reflective practice. As Figure 9.2 indicates, they will also be shown how to source information and theoretical content, critique it, interpret if for their own context, apply it and then reflect on outcomes.

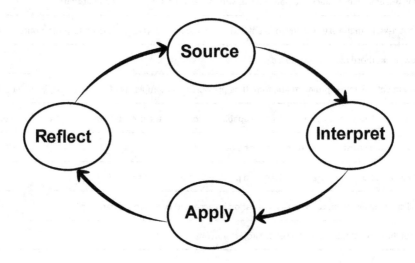

Figure 9.2   Critical and reflective skills

Like dialogue, reflective practice can seem alien to many. Exploring the value of reflection, providing examples of how it can be used and the opportunity to practise are all investments that will pay off as the transition to smart working practices progresses.

SOCIAL SUPPORT AND COMMUNITY

The induction phase is where expectations are set, laying the foundations for supportive community and social relationships to form to enable participation in shared learning. It is important to clarify boundaries. What are the rules for engaging with each other? What behaviours are unacceptable, and what happens if unacceptable behaviour does happen? Who is available to help when clarification or explanation is needed – either administrative help or learning support? How can help be accessed, and how often? These are far from trivial issues.

Apart from induction being vital to prepare people emotionally and socially for learning in complex, uncertain environments, there is evidence that effective support teams can make a significant contribution to the difference between success and failure of knowledge transfer projects (Lipscomb and McEwan 2001). Induction aligns expectations about the nature and frequency of the support offered, and makes clear how support will be managed.

FOUNDATION TOPICS

The induction phase introduces foundation topics on smart working, focusing on the themes explored in Chapter 2 concerning how organisations work and do not work, the legacy of learning on smart working from the first wave, and the nature of second wave smart working. Foundation topics also include a review of the skills and capabilities leaders need to instigate second wave smart working practices. This could include a personal review and audit of leadership capabilities to identify areas that need to be developed.

As described in Chapter 8, the induction phase makes clear that this content is used in a just-in-time manner, at the point where it is needed, critically evaluating and reflecting on its relevance.

TOOLS AND TECHNOLOGIES

The Smart Work Framework, the Diagnostic Grid and Checklist and any other tools that will be used all need to be explained as part of the induction phase. It is also important that people are familiar with the collaboration and social networking technologies they will be using in learning together, as they co-create and share knowledge.

Barriers must be removed. People need to feel comfortable with the technologies they are using, and to be given the chance to experiment with them before engaging in the diagnostic and implementation phases of the learning process. They also need to feel confident that the technology will be reliable and that support will be on hand if there are problems.

Diagnosing and Scoping

Once induction has taken place, the business project that will be the vehicle for making the transition to new ways of working is diagnosed and scoped.

This includes identifying interacting elements of the business problem, including how the external environment impacts on the internal environment. Possible risks, barriers and enablers are considered. This phase is where the Diagnostic Grid and Diagnostic Checklist can be used to produce a first iteration of what needs to be done.

Gap Analysis

The next step is to assess gaps in current knowledge, capabilities and systems. Are there topics and themes arising from the initial analysis of internal and external dynamics that need further investigation? How are these going to be addressed?

Implementation

The project scope and proposed project activities are reviewed in the light of all the analysis so far. Adjustments are made and an implementation strategy is devised, which is also a framework for guiding learning. Project activities include sourcing, interpreting and adapting information, insight, design principles and theoretical perspectives to put into practice.

Implementation proceeds through continual acting, reflecting, challenging, questioning and adjusting. Fishbein and Treverton (2004), referenced in Chapter 8, describe a process of 'alternative sense-making' and 'mindfulness of analytic failure' in fast-moving, complex context like international terrorism.

These approaches also apply in less dramatic contexts, to encourage a culture of critical thinking, creative conflict and 'daring to disagree'.[3] The iterative nature of implementation means that additional sources and insights emerge in action, discovered serendipitously and recommended by the learning community.

ASSESSING LEARNING

The implementation strategy contains all the elements of a traditional project plan, including project activities and milestones. As a learning framework, it also includes learning outcomes and the criteria by which learning is assessed.

---

3   http://www.youtube.com/watch?v=PY_kd46RfVE [accessed: 10 September 2012].

Chapter 8 showed that leaders need to be able to function in contexts where rapidly moving targets, complexity and uncertainty are normal. Rather than regarding increasing complexity as a problem, high-performing businesses are capitalising on complexity and using the opportunity to 'shake up ... old ways of working and long-held assumptions' (IBM 2010a).

The leadership skills and personal qualities needed to influence people, performance environments and performance climates that allow smart working to emerge are therefore likely to be at post-graduate level. Learning descriptors and learning outcomes for learning at this level are publicly available (QAA 2008). For example, those learning at this level should be able to:

> *Deal with complex issues both systematically and creatively, and they will show originality in tackling and solving problems. They will have the qualities needed for employment in circumstances requiring sound judgement, personal responsibility and initiative in complex and unpredictable professional environments.*

They should also 'be capable of decision-making in complex and unpredictable situations'. The transition to new ways of working takes place through iterations of action, reflection and adaptation. Post-graduate-level skills emerge through formal assessment of project progress and through informal dialogue among peers. The process of real-time distilling and adjusting happens at the same time as slower, more reflective, playful and serendipitous interactions among members of learning communities.

Learning is evaluated against learning outcomes and assessment criteria, which are specified within the context of the activities being performed and to reflect the characteristics of post-graduate-level learning. These would typically include reflecting, critically evaluating, analysing, synthesising, integrating, learning to choose from among alternatives, specifying criteria, defending decisions, assessing risks, challenging and other high-level thinking capabilities.

Pulling It All Together

The Smart Work Company learning communities are currently experimental, with various levels of access to experiential learning programmes.[4] One of

---

4   http://www.thesmartworkcompany.com [accessed: 12 April 2012].

the learning communities, the *open-learn* community, is open to all, subject to conditions. The tools developed in this chapter will be available to community members.

The objective is to build a network of people who want to explore smart working topics, through conversations on the community blogs, discussion groups and wikis, as well as seeding and facilitating conversations wherever online people choose to gather. This might be on LinkedIn groups, Google+ circles or on Twitter. It is hoped that the energy and engagement that happens in person can be emulated online by facilitating discussions on topics that are of interest and use to the community.

Participation in the *open-learn* community is mandatory for people who want to go further and participate in one of the Smart Work Company post-graduate-level learning experiences, either for their own satisfaction or to gain post-graduate accreditation from a university in the UK.

Concluding Remarks

The Smart Work Framework, the Diagnostic Grid and Checklist are contributions to ongoing conversation about how to stimulate chaotic action in making the transition to smarter ways of working. As with the last wave of process innovation in response to global competitive pressures, the need for a new wave of innovation does not mean that the transition will be easy.

The difference this time is that insights and principles from the previous era remain relevant, and there is an abundance of freely available tools to help anyone wishing to learn how to put all this information into practice. Social technologies allow us discover and experiment with this legacy of learning, creating opportunities to transform ways of working, and to do it by learning together. The final chapter will provide suggestions for additional resources and sources of help.

10

Tools, Techniques and Resources

Introduction

As knowledge becomes more distributed, conceptual and emergent, people need tools to make their thinking visible to themselves and their colleagues. People also need techniques that will enable them to have conversations about the different ways in which they see the world.

This final chapter suggests tools, techniques and resources to help you get going on creating the next wave of smart working. It points to a software tool and two approaches for making intangible business processes visible and transparent. It also makes suggestions of sources of research and places online where you can find information on topics connected with smart working. This brief review cannot possibly be comprehensive. The hope is that practitioners will want to use the sources as a starting point to discover tools, techniques and sources for themselves.

The tools and techniques evaluated in this chapter are social project planning, value network analysis and service design. Traditional project planning software was used by individual managers to monitor their own projects. Cloud-based project management tools are now making project planning and monitoring a social affair, allowing distributed networks of people to follow and contribute to project progress. Value Network Analysis and a group of techniques assembled under the collective heading of 'service design' enable value-creating activities and interactions to be visualised. Service design techniques, in particular, help to generate empathy and engagement. The process of discovery and learning is as crucial as the outputs. With their focus on customers, both internal and external, value network analysis and service design can be seen as an iteration of lean principles applied to visualising intangible service and knowledge processes rather than tangible, manufactured products.

Social Project Planning

This section describes the philosophy behind the design of a social project management tool called Milestone Planner,[1] which is designed to co-ordinate collaborative project management. Rather than being directed centrally by a project manager, the tool facilitates a different approach.

The cloud-based software tool brings people together to collaborate, negotiate and track project progress. Milestones, not detailed tasks, are specified. In this way, the starting point articulates the desired end result. What needs to be done to get there is left up to whoever is responsible for producing the output. Benjamin Ellis and Jim Anning, who jointly designed and developed the tool, say that the planning journey can be explained through a simple exercise that they ask groups of people to perform. They say:

> *Draw a square. Now draw a triangle on top of the square. On the right hand side of the triangle, just on top, draw a rectangle. Now inside the first square you drew draw four other squares – but make sure they don't touch each other, or the edges of the first square etc. ...*[2]

An alternative would be to say: 'Make a picture of a house.' Ellis and Anning point out that few people end up drawing anything like a house when they follow the detailed instructions. The alternative instruction to make a picture of a house starts with the objective and requires people to collaborate, contributing their experience and knowledge in agreeing what needs to be done to draw a house.

DESIGN PHILOSOPHY

Linking back to Chapter 4, the tool design is consistent with socio-technical principles and generates the diverse, multiple perspectives suggested by requisite variety. Not only does using the technology result in the collective knowledge, experience and self-management capabilities of many people, rather than just one manager being available to a project, the expanded knowledge and experience belongs to the people most closely involved in the work. In the past, the full extent of these talents would typically have been overlooked, since people were restricted to doing what they were told to do.

---

1   http://www.milestoneplanner.com [accessed: 12 April 2012].
2   http://socialoptic.com/2010/05/a-different-way-of-planning-milestones/ [accessed: 12 April 2012].

The outcome-based approach to negotiating milestones, inherent in the design of the software, enhances the likelihood of psychologically satisfying work, since it maximises individual and collective self-determination.

WHO IS USING IT?

Creative businesses already working within distributed contexts are early adopters. Other clients are larger corporate that operate across time and place. These two categories of clients are unsurprising, since the tool fits with their existing business processes. An interesting and growing client base is government departments, which know that they 'need to do something' and do things differently. They are using the tool to contribute to shaping long-term strategic thinking and action, experimenting and learning as they go along. Using collaboration tools therefore becomes an iterative way to visualise conversations and record joint reflections. Anning comments that traditional plans create a false sense of security. He says that the iterative, dynamic plans that emerge from using Milestone Planner are 'roughly right', but traditional plans are 'exactly wrong'.

Value Network Analysis

The first of the two process mapping approaches is Value Network Analysis, which Verna Allee defines as: 'A methodology for understanding, visualizing, and optimizing internal and external value networks and complex economic ecosystems'.[3]

Work flows are mapped in the form of tangible and intangible deliverables, which are associated with the roles people adopt in enacting business processes. Intangible deliveries are informal entities – for example, feedback, advice or ad hoc conversations – which build relationships and help formal activities to run smoothly.

Verna refers to Value Network Analysis as 'Lean Plus' because rather than imposing a standardised process model, the approach enables dynamic processes and workflows to emerge from the patterns of informal network dynamics that support formal business processes. Value networks can be

---

3   http://valuenetworks.com/public/item/207716 [accessed: 12 April 2012].

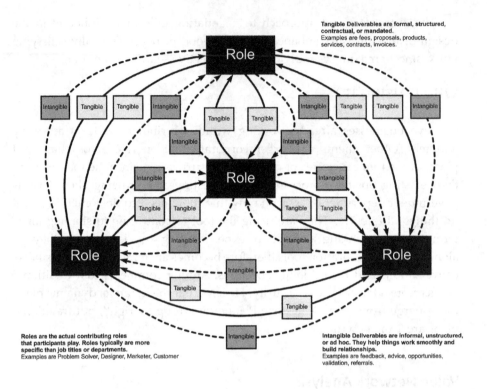

Figure 10.1   Allee's ValueNet Map

ValueNet Map™ Reproduced with permission. © ValueNetworks.com

internal or external, and like the fractal structure of the Viable Systems Model, can consist of shop floor teams or large-scale, distributed global networks.[4]

The value network approach is consistent with Weick's framing of organisational processes as inter-linked behaviours that dynamically become flows of work and knowledge. The approach is also consistent with the analysis of organisations as complex adaptive systems. Allee's conceptualising of the interaction between formal, tangible business processes and intangible interactions arising from the roles people adopt is also directly comparable to Stacey's 'murky relationship' between an organisation's legitimate system and the shadow system, where creativity and adaptation takes place.

A case study of how Boeing used value networks to visualise business activities when setting up a Test Operations Centre explains why focusing on

---

4   http://valuenetworks.com/public/item/252634 [accessed: 12 April 2012].

roles is effective.[5] All jobs encompass multiple roles. Articulating and visualising them enabled critical roles to be identified. Previously unacknowledged roles were made explicit, and also more efficient. In addition, the analysis highlighted the frequency of different roles and where they occurred within a process (Angers 2008).

Verna notes that the iterative, living systems approach of Value Network Analysis supports experimentation that leads to new insights and innovation. She stresses that although outcomes cannot be predicted, value networks are associated with increased probability of effective outcomes through their capacity for cultivating resilient, adaptive behaviours.

Service Design

Service design is a new knowledge discipline that adopts an interactive, conversation-based approach to emergent process design. From the *Guardian*:

> *Service design is a relatively new discipline that asks some fundamental questions: what should the customer experience be like? What should the employee experience be like? How does a company remain true to its brand, to its core business assets and stay relevant to customers?*[6]

The approach uses engaging, simple, graphic techniques to help people make intangible processes tangible, enabling them to communicate together to visualise connections and iteratively make sense of a bigger picture. Service design is gaining rapid recognition in the public sector as the pace of change escalates and awareness grows of having to improve customer experience.

DESIGNING FOR EXPERIENCE

The information in this section is from an interview with two young designers in Glasgow. Lauren Currie and Sarah Drummond are co-owners of a service design company that is currently gaining a reputation for innovative service design.[7] They work with a range of public and private clients to help them understand how best to meet the needs and expectations of their customers.

---

5   http://www.valuenetworksandcollaboration.com/images/FOT_V_1_.pdf [accessed: 12 April 2012]; http://www.valuenetworksandcollaboration.com/cases/theboeingcompany.html [accessed: 12 April 2012].
6   http://www.guardian.co.uk/service-design [accessed: 12 April 2012].
7   http://wearesnook.com/snook/ [accessed: 12 November 2012].

Talking to Lauren and Sarah is an energising experience. The overwhelming impression they convey is a passion for social change. Their talents as artists, designers and visual communicators come across as secondary to their desire to influence what they call 'social goodness'. They describe what they do as designing for experience, which involves 'listening emotionally' and putting people at the centre of everything they do. Their aim, they say, is to give their clients permission to be creative.

Lauren and Sarah appreciate the complexity of organisational dynamics. Their approach is nevertheless simple and direct, asking the questions that an outsider can ask: 'What is it?', 'Why is it being done?', 'Who is it for?' A colleague describes them as 'fearless' – a description which they recognise as they seek to elicit details and communicate the interaction between details and an emerging big picture.

They described 'journey mapping', just one of the techniques they use. This involves getting people responsible for delivering a service to tell the customer story, identifying touch points where the customer meets the organisation, and encouraging people to understand what that engagement might feel like for the customer. As they move service deliverers through a customer journey, putting them in the place of customers, Lauren and Sarah challenge service deliverers to check how they feel before an encounter and after an adapted process.

They use methods like interviewing, observing or shadowing to collect data for journey mapping exercises. As well as visualising customer journeys, the technique can be used to visualise service delivery from the point of view of staff, management, and even devices,[8] mapping interactions between the different service journeys from multiple perspectives.

Example 1

MissionModelsMoney (MMM) is 'a passionate network of thinkers and doers whose vision is to transform the way the arts use their resources to support the creation and experience of great art', by drawing together people, ideas and money from a network of sources. MMM carries out action research to help creative practitioners, organisations and funders to build organisational and financial resilience.[9] Lauren worked with members of MMM to explore the next phase of their activities and strategic direction.

---

8   http://tisdt.uservoice.com/forums/39924-methods-tools [accessed: 12 April 2012].
9   http://www.missionmodelsmoney.org.uk/resources/mission/ [accessed: 12 April 2012].

She began by exploring what service means, and imagined what this might look like from MMM's user perspectives. As Lauren puts it, 'the trio got colourful with cartoons and story-telling', which really helped bring the exploration to life. To help the MMM team to envisage the service journey, Lauren tasked the team members to visualise their new website from a user's viewpoint, to plan an event, and to design an information pack. This required the team to think deeply about who their users might be, what style of website would appeal, where would be a suitable venue for an event, and why. What attributes might users have that would make these design elements appropriate?

Example 2

In contrast to working with a small organisation, at the time of writing Sarah was working with Skills Development Scotland,[10] an organisation of around 1,400 people with a network of public access centres around Scotland. Skills Development Scotland is a complex organisation which includes partnerships with multiple stakeholders like local authorities, the Scottish Funding Council (SFC), colleges (through a new Colleges Forum), the NHS, schools and a wide range of industry and enterprise bodies.

The SFC was implementing systems and processes to support its strategy. Sarah helped it to do this, working with staff to visualise the journey they were on, helping to simplify complexities, revealing connections and showing everyone how they all linked together. She describes what she was doing as 'opportunity spotting'. She built capability as she taught people how to visualise relationships, and to create and embed interactive process maps. She also taught people the skills they needed to do this, including how to conduct effective interviews and create journey maps.

Sarah comments that all this capability and relationship-building, discovery and iterative big picture creation takes time. She and Lauren report that conversation-based service design techniques are highly engaging. Sarah quotes feedback she has received from people she works with, saying that they were 'skipping out the door' after having participated in her sessions.

---

10 http://www.skillsdevelopmentscotland.co.uk/ [accessed: 12 April 2012].

The Way Forward

The design philosophies underpinning service design, value network analysis and Milestone Planner are consistent with the approach adopted throughout this book, which is that people create value in organisations through complex social interactions and working relationships. The resulting knowledge flows are dynamic, negotiated and iterative, and patterns emerge over time. This was always the case in the industrial era, but has become more evident with the transition from industrial to service and knowledge-based economies.

Business processes in the first wave of smart working were mainly visible and tangible. Work-in-progress can be seen and counted. Processes in the second wave are largely hidden, intangible and distributed. Moreover, creative and tacit knowledge is embedded within distributed, networked knowledge flows within and across communities of customers, workforces, partner organisations and other stakeholders. Service design and value network analysis bring processes to life by engaging communities of people (customers, workforces, partners and other stakeholders) in dialogue to reveal and make sense of connections and experiences.

The global economic environment is changing rapidly. *Smart Working: Creating The Next Wave* has argued that there are first principles of organising, that people's psychological, social and cultural needs must be considered in creating high-performance environments, that there is a legacy of learning on making the transition to new ways of working, and that the tools and methods to do this are available in abundance. It is mindsets and attitudes that need to change.

Smart Working: Creating the Next Wave has also argued that all this evidence and existing knowledge is useless until it is experimented with and applied. We need to create our way into the next wave of smart working and managing. It is all there for the taking, and there are no excuses.

Resources

This concluding section of the chapter and the book makes suggestions of additional resources: corporate research, blogs, articles, videos, free learning materials and learning communities that can help anyone wanting to make a start on the journey to creating the next wave of smart working.

These are only suggestions, and the selection is very partial and personal. They are offered as an example in the hope that people will discover their own favourite sources. More information about tools, techniques and resources is available through The Smart Work Company learning communities.

CORPORATE RESEARCH

IBM has produced a global survey of chief executives every two years since 2004, the most recent being the 2012 report.[11] PwC produces an annual survey, the most recent, the fifteenth, produced in 2012.[12] Johnson Controls research adopts a more thematic approach, and evaluates how global business trends impact on the physical workplace,[13] as do furniture designers Hermann Miller[14] and Steelcase.[15]

BLOGS

Blogs are a rich source of information and insight. How do you know which blogs to follow? There are many ways to discover people and information. For example, start by exploring the blogs associated with an institution like The Work Foundation in the UK[16] or the Chartered Institute of Personnel Development. Another way might to follow recommendations from someone whose views you respect. An example for me is Professor Bob Sutton, whose blog posts I find pragmatic, rooted in experience and informed by academic thinking.[17]

TWITTER

The micro-blogging site Twitter can be an invaluable source of quality information, research and articles. The value comes from following knowledgeable people. There is a likelihood that these people will also be generous in sharing their insights and passing on sources they have found. Rather than keeping a look-out for specific journals and magazines, I now rely on 'planned serendipity' through Twitter. Following informed people

---

11 http://www-935.ibm.com/services/uk/en/c-suite/ceostudy2012/ [accessed: 10 September 2012].
12 http://www.pwc.com/gx/en/ceo-survey/pdf/15th-global-ceo-survey.pdf [accessed: 12 April 2012].
13 http://www.johnsoncontrols.com/publish/us/en/products/building_efficiency/gws/gwi.html [accessed: 12 April 2012].
14 http://www.hermanmiller.com/research/topics.html [accessed: 12 April 2012].
15 http://360.steelcase.com/ [accessed: 12 April 2012].
16 http://www.theworkfoundation.com/Blog [accessed: 12 April 2012].
17 http://bobsutton.typepad.com/ [accessed: 2 May 2010].

gives access to the diverse articles they share, and to people whose blogs are interesting and useful.

VIDEOS

Two sources of quality videos are TED Talks[18] and the Royal Society of Arts, particularly the RSA Animate series.[19]

FREE LEARNING MATERIALS

A further source of quality videos for learning is available through the explosion of free learning materials made available from major business schools, like the MIT OpenCourseware[20] and Udacity from Stanford University,[21] as well as from places like the Khan Academy,[22] and of course, YouTube.[23]

LEARNING COMMUNITIES

The discussion groups on LinkedIn are good for discovering niche conversations. You can also find information about the activities of specialist learning communities, for example ConnectingHR[24] and the Design Thinking Network,[25] through LinkedIn status updates.

Other sources of access to learning communities and conversations might be through Google+ Hangouts, which are video chats for up to nine people, and the many regular Twitter conversations that take place at specific times. They are organised and identified by hashtags, which are words used to categorise tweets. Searching on a hashtag gives access to all tweets identified. An example might be the hashtag #lrnchat and the associated blog, which makes available the transcripts from the conversations about all aspects of learning online.[26]

I am currently experimenting with setting up the *open-learn* community at The Smart Work Company website.[27] You are most welcome to join.

---

18   http://www.ted.com/talks [accessed: 12 April 2012].
19   http://www.youtube.com/watch?v=zDZFcDGpL4U&feature=relmfu [accessed: 12 April 2012].
20   http://ocw.mit.edu/index.htm [accessed: 12 April 2012].
21   http://www.udacity.com/ [accessed: 12 April 2012].
22   http://www.khanacademy.org/ [accessed: 12 April 2012].
23   http://www.youtube.com/ [accessed: 12 April 2012].
24   http://connectinghr.org/ [accessed: 12 April 2012].
25   http://www.designthinkingnetwork.com/ [accessed: 12 April 2012].
26   http://lrnchat.wordpress.com/ [accessed: 2 May 2010].
27   http://www.thesmartworkcompany.com [accessed: 12 April 2012].

Concluding Remarks

The multiple shifts that global businesses are experiencing are creating operating conditions where complexity and uncertainty are the new norms. When the context is so turbulent, a typical human reaction is to retreat to the familiar. This, of course, is self-defeating.

Social technologies create exponential possibilities for innovation. Since social technologies augment our capabilities, continuous improvement now becomes connected, collective intelligence distributed throughout knowledge networks. Design principles and a legacy of learning that remains relevant for current contexts, experimented with and applied through social technologies, are there for the discovery.

The next wave of smart working has to be created through action, experimentation, dialogue, reflection and agile adaptation. There are no excuses.

Postscript: Personal Reflection

One of the techniques used with the senior executives I have worked with over the years is to encourage them to engage in critical reflection on their learning, to notice how they feel about what they are doing and learning, what they think they have learned, what they have found helpful or not, and to ask questions of themselves (Schon 1991, Moon 1999).

This reflection considers the learning journey I went on while writing this book. I am not in any way suggesting that this reflection is a good example; it is a commentary on the fact that writing the book was a challenging learning journey with many surprises along the way.

Doing a Job Well

Scanning my bookshelves a while back, I noticed a marker in my copy of Primo Levi's *The Drowned and the Saved* (Levi 1989). This is what was marked:

> *Unlike the purely persecutory labour, which I have just described, work could instead become a defence. It was so for the few in the Lager, who were made to exercise their own trade: tailors, cobblers, carpenters, blacksmiths, bricklayers; such people, resuming their customary activity, recovered at the same time, to some extent, their human dignity.*

As well as describing the dignity people found in their trades, Levi describes the self-driven compulsion to do a job well. He says:

> *The ambition of a 'job well done' is so deeply rooted as to compel one 'to do well', even enemy jobs, harmful to your people and your side, so that a conscious effort is necessary to do them 'badly'.*

This is powerful affirmation of my belief that most people are eager and willing to do a good job. This is a personal conviction, and research affirms this tendency. It is astonishing to have testimony that this can happen under the most diabolical of circumstances. There is therefore a moral obligation, as well as making good business sense, to respect this human urge and to ensure that leaders are up to the task of setting the conditions that allow this desire to flourish. It is this conviction that has kept me going, especially when my self-confidence was not up to the task I set myself in writing this book.

People Never Were Subordinate

In looking back at unpublished data and stories I collected over a decade ago, what strikes me is the extent to which factories are highly social. I always knew this, but was very forcefully reminded of the fact when reviewing the sources and old interview data for Chapter 3. People never were subordinate to machines or processes. The fact that factory work may be excruciatingly dull makes the social dimension of factory work all the more significant, as people seek to find meaning in relationships. Of course, all is not sweetness and light, but people do value being consulted, heard and their participation recognised.

Rigid and outdated organisational structures, working practices and poor performance environments present barriers to people as they try to do their best. As I have tried to argue throughout the book, it is now more possible than ever for people to begin the process of change themselves.

Leadership as Influence

Another fact I think I knew but realised in a much deeper way was the powerful personal influence leaders can exert as catalysts for and drivers of change. Much of what Vineet Nayar (2010) is saying in *Employees First, Customers Second* has a strong echo in what I found in researching empowerment on manufacturing factory floors in the late 1990s. Lean, quality and agile manufacturing were founded on a work philosophy that sought to optimise the previously overlooked, hidden, value-creating tacit and process knowledge of shop floor operators. Nayar's experience of turning his company around by seeking out and supporting people who create value, who are buried 'deep inside the hierarchy', is a continuation of this philosophy.

His focus on creating trust through transparency particularly meant holding managers accountable to those who directly create value, 'unleashing the power of the many and loosening the stranglehold of the few'. Nayar's desire to replace 'zones of control' with 'spans of influence' means managers letting go of their obsession with control and re-focusing on influence. They do that by engaging in dialogue with those who are creating customer value, removing barriers to performance, and providing organisational environments that enable people to engage with their work and each other.

The ability to influence was a core capability in the stories of the two leaders in Chapter 8 as they set out to transform performance cultures within large public sector contexts in different countries. Replacing control by influence was effective for them, it was effective in first wave smart working, and it remains effective today. This is not surprising, of course. Contexts, technologies and times change; as far as I can see, people do not.

Emotional Challenge

Writing this book was challenging, which has been unexpected. Surely the task ought to have been straightforward, since I write from deep knowledge and years of experience? Putting the proposal together for the publisher was easy, as was writing the sample chapter. Sketching a thesis at a high level is not the same thing as thinking about how the separate elements inter-link across different literatures, as well as link between the past and present. Insight has been emergent. It has taken time and patience to accept the accompanying frustrations and inability to see clearly, trusting that clarification eventually occurs.

Conversations with recently published authors, and with the publisher, confirmed that my experience is far from unique. Creative thinking can be emotionally and cognitively challenging. This is relevant because it is a useful reminder that doing something new, like making the transition to new ways of working and engaging in workplace learning, can make significant emotional and cognitive demands on people. It can also take time. According to the comedian John Cleese, people need boundaries of time and space for creative thoughts to emerge.[1] This resonates a lot with my experience; writing and thinking were very time-consuming.

---

1   http://www.youtube.com/watch?v=zGt3-fxOvug [accessed: 27 July 2012].

TIME FOR REFLECTION

Emergence is messy, and therefore unsettling to some, myself included. The subconscious is amazing, though, and insights do emerge at unexpected moments. For me, insights and connections happened at the point where I was just waking from sleep but not yet fully awake. Archimedes was supposed to have shouted 'Eureka!' when he was taking a bath, although obviously neither having baths nor going for naps is practical at work.

Leaving time for reflection, rest and play is problematic in today's non-stop and stressful workplace. This is especially untenable for people in jobs that are time-driven. The nurse I wrote about in Chapter 8, for example, is resisting a move from seven-hour to twelve-hour shifts, although she recognises that this is probably inevitable. Who has time to pause and reflect on busy wards, especially on long, non-stop shifts? Time has to be made for learning, even if people have to connect in their own time and for their own well-being.

Serendipity

Apart from trusting that insight would eventually emerge from the confusion, what really helped was being connected to knowledgeable people, online and in person, who generously share resources. It is remarkable how often one would appear just at the point when I was trying to make sense of something.

As an example, a colleague who is interested in the use of narrative in change kindly told me about Callaghan and Drake's article 'Three Journeys: A Narrative Approach'.[2] This uses the story of a famous journey to open up the American West to explain various journeys taken to complete an endeavour. The first journey happens in the minds of leaders, the second involves practicing imagined skills, and the third is the actual endeavour. Callaghan and Drake say:

> *One of their biggest surprises was the scale of the Rocky Mountains,*
> *a range of peaks unlike any they had seen before. However, for every*
> *unexpected turn of events or what seemed like an impassable barrier,*
> *the expedition adapted and remained resilient.*

---

2   http://www.anecdote.com.au/papers/Anecdote3JourneystoChange_v1s.pdf [accessed: 27 July 2012].

Writing a research-based business book is hardly in the same league as crossing the Rocky Mountains, although the barriers at times felt as insurmountable. Their observations that leaders only know in outline what they want to achieve at the start, and that the landscape can change by the mere fact of setting out on the journey, apply not only to change journeys. The journey into the creative unknown, although planned and imagined in outline, felt very similar. The article helped me to see that what I was experiencing is normal.

DISTRIBUTED COGNITION SYSTEMS

Another example of how crucial insight appeared from a serendipitous discovery is stumbling across Judith Heerwagen's online article where she talks about distributed cognition systems. This is discussed in Chapter 5. So many things fell into place from that connection.

Having worked with Dr Marie Puybaraud closely for several years co-facilitating the Global Mobility Network, and having contributed to two of her major research projects, I appreciated the growing significance of the physical workplace in facilitating new ways of working. I continued, though, to see it as somewhat separate from my own specialist interest, which is making the transition to new ways of working through performance climates, organisational structures, and systems of innovation and learning.

'Distributed cognition' places the focus on a holistic view of cognition as not only residing within our heads, but also evident in the artefacts and tools that are integrated within the physical workplace. Learning systems incorporate organising principles, technologies, relationships and networks, and the physical learning environment.

Heerwagen's other insight concerns congeniality, which speaks to our need for emotional security and sociability. Work and performance are then redefined within the conceptual framework of distributed cognition, elements of which are spatial, social and technological. This led me to a much deeper understanding of how the workplace, people, enabling technologies and adaptive learning are inter-linked. The elements combine to create culturally appropriate environments for enacting connected, dynamic processes in the service of customer-focused performance. This deeper understanding emerged from the process of writing and reflecting.

Blogging

Another thing that helped me through the book-writing process was blogging. A core contention of the book is that social technologies have enormous potential to expand human creativity and productivity significantly in a second wave of smart working. I decided early in the writing process to write a blog.[3] This was useful in several ways. In the first place, it allowed me to practise writing. On reflection, this was not as useful as I had anticipated. The writing style on a blog is much less formal than in a book, so any ideas I might initially have had about cutting and pasting went by the wayside!

Writing the blog was very useful in other ways, the main one being the feedback from the community of readers. I soon began to notice the quality of people who were taking time to comment on my posts. It was immensely reassuring to appreciate that busy people of high professional and academic calibre were taking the time to read and comment. A second reason that writing the blog was useful was the conversations that developed in some of the posts, which were invaluable for gaining additional perspectives. A third reason was that it helped me to sort out my thinking, and to do it in public. A final benefit is gaining a reputation as someone who is interested in new ways of working. This ties in with what Rangaswami says about search being social and using filtering mechanisms to find out who is developing expertise in particular areas.

MICRO-BLOGGING

The micro-blogging site Twitter has been a highly effective community-building channel, which has operated in conjunction with the blog. I have the privilege of being 'followed' by interesting and influential people. To be followed means that people elect to receive all the 140-character messages I write. Many of these messages are social. If they are interested, followers can get to know me a little through the music, books and websites I find interesting.[4] The messages are also professional, in that I share research, articles and observations I think might be relevant for those who follow me. This includes links to blog posts I have written. Of course, the people I follow similarly share research, articles and websites with me.

---

3   http://www.thesmartworkcompany.com [accessed: 27 July 2012].
4   http://confusedofcalcutta.com/2010/10/10/thinking-about-social-objects/?utm_source=feedburner&utm_medium=feed&utm_campaign=Feed:+ConfusedOfCalcutta+(Confused+of+Calcutta) [accessed: 27 July 2012].

Writing the blog and publishing as widely as possible to readers who gave me feedback was an extended exercise in critical thinking and reflection, which was conducted in public.

Self-determination

Another core contention throughout the book is that people can and do assume a measure of self-determined control over their own experience of work, even in the most controlled of working environments. My initial hope for social technologies was that people would start to use them to connect to sources of help and support outside their own working environments. There came a point when I doubted this as idealistic and wondered whether these technologies would continue to be used predominantly for entertainment.

What I believe is beginning to happen is that having seen how social technologies are used to connect and share for entertainment, people are now waking up to their potential for enriching their experience of work and learning. Professional people on LinkedIn, for example, can now connect to networks of other professional people to search for information, to find people and to get news. The Groups feature of LinkedIn is potentially very useful, allowing people to gather around a specific theme or expertise. The more active groups provide access to discussion topics and constantly updated news items that the group members submit.

Specialist learning communities are springing up all over the place, the most recent addition being the knowledge-sharing circles that can be created through Google+.[5] There is no shortage of information and tools available for anyone wanting to create informal, user-led learning communities.[6] People can then choose to join these communities of peers to gain insight and support from each other. The more people in workplaces become aware of these communities and how they can help them, the more they are likely to use them to augment the face-to-face support they get at work. Online support is particularly valuable where social support is in some way lacking within the workplace.

---

5   https://plus.google.com/up/start/?continue=https://plus.google.com/&type=st&gpcaz=eale9922 [accessed: 27 July 2012].
6   http://www.feverbee.com/ [accessed: 27 July 2012].

Power of Conversation

An example is given in Chapter 5 of how social technologies were used to encourage conversation in pursuit of emergent culture creation. Conversation is how knowledge is shared and created, but the fear of conversation being an excuse for time-wasting is deep-rooted in many company cultures. Overcoming this is an essential prerequisite for knowledge-based smart working.

THREATS FROM WITHIN

My final reflection is related to the fear of conversation as time-wasting. I started out believing that events in the external operating environment presented greater risks to business in the current turmoil than threats from within. On reflection, it seems to me that major threats to viability come primarily from within. The very public mistakes and failures of iconic companies like GM, Toyota, BP and the collapse of Lehman Brothers were internally generated.

Creating the next wave is not going to happen if the existing obsessions with control and distrustful cultures of many organisations do not fundamentally change. Rigidity of mental models and management cultures are significant barriers to creating agile workplaces. Unless attitudes to conversation change, then organisations are not going to be able to gain advantage from the flows of ideas and knowledge that conversation facilitates.

Finally

My friend Tim Casswell has an approach to nurturing creativity that he uses with businesses called 'write your own book'.[7] I thought I understood what his intervention attempted to do, and I did on a superficial level. However, having actually written my own book, I can admit that I understand a lot more now of what is involved in creative thinking. Creating the second wave of smart working will not come about by reading about it. Reading this book will hopefully help you on your first journey (in your mind) and your second journey (practising the skills you imagine will be needed). The only way the new wave will be created is through chaotic action: experimenting with things and doing them better or doing them differently.

---

7   http://www.creativeconnection.co.uk/ [accessed: 27 July 2012].

References

Adler, P.S. and Cole, R.E. 1993. 'Designed for learning'. *Sloan Management Review*, Spring, 85–94.

Ahonen, T.T. and Moore, A. 2005. *Communities Dominate Brands: Business and Marketing Challenges for the 21st Century*. London: Futuretext.

Aaltonen, G. 2010. 'Experience matters'. *The Guardian* [online, 12 March]. Available at: http://www.guardian.co.uk/service-design/introduction [accessed: 12 April 2012].

Anderson, G., Boud, D., and Sampson, J. 1996. *Learning Contracts: A Practical Guide*. London: Kogan Page.

Angers, S. 2008. *Testing the Limits* [online: Boeing Frontiers]. Available at: http://valuenetworks.com/docs/Testing%20the%20Limits%20FOT&V.pdf [accessed: 12 April 2012].

Argyris, C. 1998. 'Empowerment: The emperor's new clothes'. *Harvard Business Review*, 76(3), 98–105.

Argyris, C. and Schon, D. 1978. *Organisational Learning: A Theory of Action Perspective*. Reading, MA: Addison-Wesley.

Arup Foresight 2012. *Campus of the Future* [online]. Available at: http://www. driversofchange.com/make/research/campus-of-the-future/ [accessed: 9 March 2012].

Ashby, W.R. 1956. *An Introduction to Cybernetics*. London: Chapman & Hall.

Ashforth, B.E. and Humphrey, R.H. 1995. 'Emotion in the workplace: A reappraisal'. *Human Relations*, 48(2), 97–125.

Badrtalei, J. and Bates, D.L. 2007. 'Effect of organizational cultures on mergers and acquisitions: The case of DaimlerChrysler'. *International Journal of Management*, 24(2), 303–17.

Baker, W.E. 1994. 'The paradox of empowerment'. *Chief Executive*, 93, 62–5.

Bandura, A. 1978. 'The self system in reciprocal determinism'. *American Psychologist* [online], 33(4), 344–58. Available at: http://des.emory.edu/mfp/ Bandura1978AP.pdf [accessed: 8 March 2012].

Bandura, A. 1982. 'Self-efficacy mechanism in human agency'. *American Psychologist* [online], 37(2), 122–47. Available at: http://des.emory.edu/mfp/Bandura1982AP.pdf [accessed: 8 March 2012].

Bandura, A. 1999. 'Moral disengagement in the perpetration of inhumanities'. *Personality and Social Psychology Review* [online], 3, 193–209. Available at: http://www.des.emory.edu/mfp/Bandura1999PSPR.pdf [accessed: 8 March 2012].

Barker, J.R. 1993. 'Tightening the iron cage: Concertive control in self-managing teams'. *Administrative Science Quarterly*, 38, 408–37.

Barton, H. and Delbridge, R. 2006. 'Delivering the "learning factory"? Evidence on HR roles in contemporary manufacturing'. *Journal of European Industrial Training*, 30(5), 385–95.

Beer, S. 1989. 'The Viable System Model: Its provenance, development, methodology and pathology', in *The Viable System Model: Interpretations and Applications of Stafford Beer's VSM*, ed. R. Espejo and R. Harnden. Chichester: Wiley & Sons.

Beer, S. 1994. *The Brain of the Firm*. 2nd edn, Chichester: Wiley & Sons.

Belasco, J.A. and Stayer, R.C. 1994. 'Why empowerment doesn't empower: The bankruptcy of current paradigms'. *Business Horizons*, 37(2), 29–41.

Benkler, Y. 2006. *The Wealth of Networks: How Social Production Transforms Markets and Freedoms* [online]. Available at: http://www.benkler.org/Benkler_Wealth_Of_Networks.pdf [accessed: 8 March 2012].

Benkler, Y. 2009. *The End of Universal Rationality: A Talk With Yochai Benkler* [online]. Available at: http://www.edge.org/3rd_culture/benkler09/benkler09_index.html [accessed: 8 March 2012].

Berggren, C. 1993. 'Lean production – the end of history?'. *Work, Employment & Society*, 7(2), 163–88.

Berggren, C. 1994. 'NUMMI vs. Uddevalla'. *Sloan Management Review*, Winter, 37–49.

Birchard, B. 2010. 'Herman Miller's design for growth'. *strategy + business* [online, 25 May]. Available at: http://www.strategy-business.com/article/10206?gko=9695a [accessed: 8 March 2012].

Blackler, F.H.M. and Brown, C.A. 1978. *Job Redesign and Management Control*. Farnborough: Teakfield.

Bollier, D. 2007. *The Rise of Collective Intelligence: Decentralised Co-creation of Value as a New Paradigm of Commerce and Culture* [online: Report of the Sixteenth Annual Aspen Institute Roundtable on Information Technology]. Available at: http://www.aspeninstitute.org/publications/rise-collective-intelligence-decentralized-co-creation-value-new-paradigm-commerce [accessed: 8 March 2012].

Boud, D. 1999. 'Situating academic development in professional work: Using peer learning'. *International Journal for Academic Development*, 4(1), 3–10.

Boud, D., Cohen, R. and Sampson, J. 2001. *Peer Learning in Higher Education*. London: Kogan Page.

boyd, danah 2007. 'Why youth (heart) social network sites: The role of networked publics in teenage social life'. *MacArthur Foundation Series on Digital Learning – Youth, Identity, and Digital Media Volume* (ed. David Buckingham). Cambridge, MA: MIT Press [online]. Available at: http://www.danah.org/papers/ WhyYouthHeart.pdf [accessed: 8 March 2012].

Briner, R.B. and Totterdell, P. 2002. 'The experience, expression and management of emotion at work', in *Psychology at Work*, ed. P. Warr. 5th edn, London: Penguin Books.

Brinkley, I. 2008. *Knowledge Economy and Enterprise: a Knowledge Economy Working Paper* [online: The Work Foundation]. Available at: http://www. theworkfoundation.com/DownloadPublication/Report/203_203_Knowledge %20Economy%20and%20Enterprise.pdf [accessed: 31 March 2012].

Brinkley, I., Fauth, R., Mahdon, M. and Theodoropoulou, S. 2009. *Knowledge Workers and Knowledge Work* [online: The Work Foundation]. Available at: http://www.theworkfoundation.com/assets/docs/publications/213_know_ work_survey170309.pdf [accessed: 8 March 2012].

British Chamber of Commerce 2007. *Work and Life: How Business is Striking the Right Balance* [online: British Chamber of Commerce]. Available at: http://www.britishchambers.org.uk/policy/pdf/work_and_life_report.pdf [accessed: 8 March 2012].

Brown, R. and Brown, M. 1994. *Empowered! A Practical Guide to Leadership in the Liberated Organisation*. London: Nicholas Brealey.

Burke, W.W. 1986. 'Leadership as empowering others', in *Executive Power: How Executives Influence People and Organisations*, ed. S. Srivastva. San Francisco, CA and London: Jossey-Bass.

Caffyn, S. and Bessant, J. 1995. *Continuous Improvement as a Strategic Capability: Proceedings of the first EuroCINet Conference*, Gatwick, 6 December.

Callaghan, S. and Drake, D.B. 2008. *Three Journeys: A Narrative Approach to Successful Organisational Change* [online: Anecdote whitepaper]. Available at: http://www.anecdote.com.au/whitepapers.php?wpid=17 [accessed: 8 March 2012].

Cantrell, S., Davenport, T.H. and Cross, R. 2005. *Rising Above the Crowd: How Top-Performing Knowledge Workers Distinguish Themselves* [online: Accenture Institute for High Performance Business]. Available at: http://www. accenture.com/us-en/Pages/insight-rising-above-the-crowd-research.aspx [accessed: 8 March 2012].

Cappelli, P. and Rogovsky, N. 1994. 'New work systems and skill requirements'. *International Labour Relations Review*, 133(2), 205–20.

Castells, M. 2004. 'Informationalism, networks, and the network society: A theoretical blueprint', in *The Network Society: A Cross-cultural Perspective*, ed. M. Castells. Cheltenham and Northampton, MA: Edward Elgar Publishing.

Castells, M., Fernandez-Ardevol, M., Linchuan Qiu, J. and Sey, A. 2007. *Mobile Communications and Society: A Global Perspective*. Cambridge, MA: The MIT Press.

CBI 2008. *Pulling Through*. CBI/Pertemps Employment Trends Survey [no longer online].

CBI 2009. *The Shape of Business: The Next 10 Years* [online: Confederation of British Industry]. Available at: http://www.the-mia.com/assets/20091123-cbi-shape-of-business22939.pdf [accessed: 8 March 2012].

Charron, C., Favier, J. and Li, C. 2006. *Social Computing: How Networks Erode Institutional Power, and What to Do About It*. Cambridge, MA: Forrester Research.

Checkland, P.B. 1981. *Systems Thinking, Systems Practice*. Chichester: John Wiley.

Cherns, A. 1976. 'The principles of sociotechnical design'. *Human Relations*, 29(8), 783–92.

Cherns, A. 1987. 'Principles of sociotechnical design revisited'. *Human Relations*, 4(3), 153–62.

Chrifas, A. 2011. 'France Telecom worker kills himself in office car park'. *The Guardian* [online, 27 April]. Available at: http://www.guardian.co.uk/world/2011/apr/26/france-telecom-worker-kills-himself [accessed: 9 March 2012].

Christensen, C.M. 2003. *The Innovator's Dilemma*. New York: Harper Business Essentials.

CIPD 2008a. *Smart Working: How Smart is UK PLC? Findings from Organisational Practice* [online: Chartered Institute of Personnel Development]. Referenced at: http://www.cipd.co.uk/subjects/corpstrtgy/general/_smrtwrkgd.htm [accessed: 8 March 2012].

CIPD 2008b. *Smart Working: The Impact of Work Organisation and Job Design* [online: Chartered Institute of Personnel Development]. Available at: http://www.cipd.co.uk/NR/rdonlyres/64A02358-8993-4185-BEEB-9812A9175383/0/smartworking.pdf [accessed: 8 March 2012].

CIPD 2008c. *Employee Engagement in Context: Interim Report* [online: Chartered Institute of Personnel Development]. Available at: http://www.cipd.co.uk/NR/rdonlyres/6D7D52C8-6E51-4539-A189-1E2D6EBEF01F/0/employee_engagement_context.pdf [accessed: 10 September 2012].

CIPD 2011. *Flexible Working Factsheet* [online]. Available at: http://www.cipd.co.uk/hr-resources/factsheets/flexible-working.aspx [accessed: 9 March 2012].

Claydon, T. and Doyle, M. 1996. 'Trusting me, trusting you? The ethics of employee empowerment'. *Personnel Review*, 25(6), 13–25.

Clegg, C.W. 2000. 'Sociotechnical principles for system design'. *Applied Ergonomics*, 31(5), 463–77.

Cole, J. and Foster, H. 2008. *Using Moodle*. 2nd edn, Sebastopol, CA: O'Reilly Media.

Confederation of British Industry 2008. *Pulling Through: Employment Trends Survey* [online]. Available at: http://www.personneltoday.com/Assets/GetAsset.aspx?ItemID=6794 [accessed: 8 March 2012].

Cole, R.E. 2010. 'Toyota's hyper growth and complexity trap'. *Harvard Business Review Blogs* [online, 23 February]. Available at: http://blogs.hbr.org/cs/2010/02/toyota_the_downside_of_hyper_g.html [accessed: 8 March 2012].

Cook, N. 2008. *Enterprise 2.0: How Social Software Will Change the Future of Work*. Aldershot: Gower Publishing.

Cooper, C. 2005. 'The shape of things to come'. *Director Magazine*, 58(6).

Coulson-Thomas, C. 2007. *Winning Companies, Winning People*. Water Newton: Policy Publications.

Daniel, S. and Reitsberger, W. 1991. 'Linking quality strategy with management control systems: empirical evidence from Japanese industry'. *Accounting, Organizations and Society*, 6(70), 601–15.

Dankbaar, B. 1997. 'Lean production: Denial, confirmation or extension of sociotechnical systems design'. *Human Relations*, 50(5), 567–83.

Datar, S.M., Garvin, D.A. and Cullen, P.G. 2010. *Rethinking the MBA: Business Education at a Crossroads*. Boston, MA: Harvard Business School Press.

Davenport, T. 2005. 'Why office design matters'. *HBR Working Knowledge* [online, 9 September]. Available at: http://hbswk.hbs.edu/archive/4991.html [accessed: 8 March 2012].

Davenport, T. 2009. 'Forwarding is the new networking'. *Harvard Business Review Blogs* [online, 30 September]. Available at: http://blogs.hbr.org/davenport/2009/09/forwarding_is_the_new_networki.html [accessed: 8 March 2012].

Davis, J.H., Schoorman, F.D. and Donaldson, L. 1997. 'Toward a stewardship theory of management'. *The Academy of Management Review*, 22(1), 20–47.

Dawson, P. and Webb, J. 1989. 'New production arrangements: The totally flexible cage?'. *Work, Employment and Society*, 3(2), 221–38.

Day, P. 2010. *Bitter Pills* [online, 12 December: BBC Radio 4 *In Business*]. Available at: http://www.bbc.co.uk/programmes/b00wdjyg [accessed: 12 April 2012].

Dean, J.W. and Snell, S.A. 1991. 'Integrated manufacturing and job design: Moderating effects of organizational inertia'. *Academy of Management Journal*, 34(4), 776–804.

Dean, J.W. and Susman, G.I. 1989. 'Strategic responses to global competition: Advanced technology, organisational design and human resource practices', in *Strategy, Organisation Design and Human Resource Management*, ed. C.C. Snow. Greenwich, CT: JAI Press.

Deiser, R. 2009. *Designing the Smart Organisation: How Breakthrough Corporate Learning Initiatives Drive Strategic Change and Innovation*. San Francisco: Jossey-Bass.

Delbridge, R. 1995. 'Surviving JIT: control and resistance in a Japanese transplant'. *Journal of Management Studies*, 32(6), 803–17.

Delbridge, R. 1998. *Life on the Line in Contemporary Manufacturing*. New York: Oxford University Press.

Delbridge, R., Turnbull, P. and Wilkinson, B. 1992. 'Pushing back the frontiers: Management control and work intensification under JIT/TQM factory regimes'. *New Technology, Work and Employment*, 7(2), 97–106.

Deloitte 2007. *Generation Y: Moving With The Times* [online]. Available at: http://www.deloitte.com/assets/Dcom-Ireland/Local%20Assets/Documents/ie_M_Gen_Y_Client_1007_final(1).pdf [accessed: 8 March 2012].

Deloitte 2009. *Generation Y: Powerhouse of the Global Economy* [online]. Available at: http://www.deloitte.com/view/en_US/us/Services/consulting/consulting-services/human-capital/Talent-Consulting-Consultant-Consultants-Human-Capital/article/a90f49642dff0210VgnVCM100000ba42f00aRCRD.htm [accessed: 8 March 2012].

Denison, D.R. 1997. 'Towards a process-based theory of organisational design: Can organisations be designed around value chains and networks?'. *Advances in Strategic Management* [online], 14, 1–44. Available at: http://www.denisonconsulting.com/Libraries/Resources/Denison-1997-Process-based-Theory.sflb.ashx [accessed: 8 March 2012].

Department of Transport 2011. *Smarter Working and the Public Sector* [online]. Available at: http://www.dft.gov.uk/publications/smarter-working/ [accessed: 31 March 2012].

Dooley, K. 1997. 'A complex adaptive systems model of organisation change'. *Nonlinear Dynamics, Psychology, and Life Sciences*, 1(1), 69–97.

Duffy, F. 2008. 'Lumbering to extinction in the digital age: The Taylorist office building'. *Harvard Design Magazine*, 29.

Economist Intelligence Unit 2008. *The Digital Company 2013: Freedom to Collaborate* [online]. Available at: http://graphics.eiu.com/upload/portal/Digital_company_2013_WP2_WEB.pdf [accessed: 8 March 2012].

Eisner, S.P. 2005. 'Managing Generation Y'. *S.A.M. Advanced Management Journal*, 70(4).

EMC² 2008. *A Journey in Social Media* [online]. Available at: http://chucksblog. emc.com/content/social_media_at_EMC_draft.pdf [accessed: 8 March 2012].

Ennals, R. and McEwan, A.M. 2004. 'Healthy Working Centres: Final Report'. Guildford: South East England Development Agency. Unpublished.

Epstein, M.J. 2005. 'The determinants and evaluation of merger success'. *Business Horizons*, 48, 37–46.

Equal Opportunities Commission 2007a. *Enter the Timelords: Transforming Work to Meet the Future* [online: Equal Opportunities Commission]. Available at: http://bit.ly/boCvQI [accessed: 8 March 2012].

Equal Opportunities Commission 2007b. *Ten Practical Tips for Employers: Transforming Work to Meet the Future* [online: Equal Opportunities Commission].Availableat:http://www.equalityhumanrights.com/uploaded_ files/Employers/tow_tips_leaflet.pdf [accessed: 29 July 2012?].

Erickson, T. and Kellogg, W.A. 2003. 'Knowledge communities: Online environments for supporting knowledge management in its social context', in *Sharing Expertise: Beyond Knowledge Management*, ed. M. Ackerman, V. Pipek and W. Volker. Cambridge, MA: MIT Press.

Espejo, R. 1989. 'The VSM revisited', in *The Viable System Model: Interpretations and Applications of Stafford Beer's VSM*, ed. R. Espejo and R. Harnden. Chichester: Wiley & Sons.

Espejo, R. and Harnden, R. 1989. *The Viable System Model: Interpretations and Applications of Stafford Beer's VSM*. Chichester: Wiley & Sons.

Espejo, R., Schumann, W., Schwaniger, M. and Bilello, U. 1996. *Organisational Transformation and Learning*. Chichester: John Wiley & Sons.

Euromonitor International 2010. 'India's working-age population growing faster than China's' [online, 17 November]. Available at: http://blog. euromonitor.com/2010/11/indias-working-age-population-growing-faster-than-chinas.html [accessed: 15 April 2012].

Ezzamel, M., Lilley, S., Wilkinson, A. and Willmott, H. 1996. 'Practices and practicalities in human resource management'. *Human Resource Management Journal*, 6(1), 63–80.

Farmer, J. 2010. *The Ground Truth*. New York: Riverhead Books.

Fenton-O'Creevy, M. 1996. 'Middle manager: Friend or foe of employee involvement?'. *Journal of Applied Management Studies*, 5(I), 47–62.

Fine, D., Hansen, M.A. and Roggenhofer, S. 2008. 'From lean to lasting: Making operational improvements stick'. *McKinsey Quarterly* [online, November 2008]. Available at: http://www.mckinseyquarterly.com/From_lean_to_lasting_ Making_operational_improvements_stick_2254 [accessed: 8 March 2012].

Fishbein, W. and Treverton, G. 2004. 'Re-thinking "alternative analysis" to address transnational threats'. *The Sherman Kent Center for Intelligent Analysis Occasional Papers*, 3(2) [online]. Available at: https://www.cia.gov/library/kent-center-occasional-papers/vol3no2.htm [accessed: 8 March 2012].

Flood, R.L. and Jackson, M.C. 1991. *Creative Problem-solving: Total Systems Intervention*. Chichester: Wiley & Sons.

Florida, R. 2004. *The Rise of the Creative Class*. New York: Basic Books.

Florida, R. 2007. *The Flight of the Creative Class: The New Global Competition for Talent*. New York: HarperCollins.

Florida, R. 2010. *The Great Reset: How New Ways of Living and Working Drive Post-crash Prosperity*. New York: HarperCollins.

Frey, R. 1993. 'Empowerment or else'. *Harvard Business Review*, 71(5), 80–94.

Garratt, B. 2003. *Fish Rots from the Head. The Crisis in our Boardrooms: Developing the Crucial Skills of the Competent Director*. 2nd edn, London: Profile Books.

Gensler 2008. *2008 Workplace Survey/United Kingdom* [online]. Available at: http://www.gensler.com/uploads/documents/2008_Gensler_Workplace_Survey_UK_09_30_2009.pdf [accessed: 8 March 2012].

Ghoshal, S. 2005. 'Bad management theories are destroying good management practices'. *Academy of Management Learning & Education* [online], 4(1), 75–91. Available at: http://www.corporation2050.org/documents/Resources/Ghoshal.pdf [accessed: 8 March 2012].

Gibbons, J. 2009. *Monkeys with Typewriters: Myths and Realities of Social Media at Work*. Axminster: Triarchy Press.

Gibbons, M., Limoges, C., Nowotny, H., Schwartzman, S., Scott, P. and Trow, M. 1994. *The New Production of Knowledge: The Dynamics of Science and Research in Contemporary Societies*. London: Sage.

Godfrey, G., Dale, B., Marchington, M. and Wilkinson, A. 1997. 'Control: A contested concept in TQM research'. *International Journal of Operations and Production Management*, 17(6), 558–73.

Grace, J., Robson, C. and Pierce, J. 2008. 'Community building within enterprise blogs, an iPhone blog story'. *Proceedings of the ACM 2008 Conference on Computer Supported Cooperative Work*, San Diego, CA, 8–12 November 2008.

Granovetter, M.S. 1973. 'The strength of weak ties'. *American Journal of Sociology*, 78(6), 1,360–80.

Groves, K. 2010. *I Wish I Worked There*. Chichester: Wiley.

Guest, D. 2006. 'Smarter ways of working: The benefits of and barriers to adoption of high-performance working'. *SSDA Catalyst* [online, October 2006]. Available at: http://www.ukces.org.uk/assets/bispartners/ukces/docs/publications/ssda-archive/ssda-catalyst-issue-3-smarter-ways-of-working.pdf [accessed: 8 March 2012].

Gunasekaran, A. 1998. 'Agile manufacturing: Enablers and an implementation framework'. *International Journal of Production Research*, 36(5), 1,223–47.

Gunasekaran, A. and Cecille, P. 1998. 'Experiences of a small company in productivity improvements'. *Production and Inventory Management Journal*, 39(2), 49–54.

Hackman, J.R. and Oldham, G.R. 1980. *Work Redesign*. Reading, MA: Addison-Wesley.

Hagel, J. and Seely-Brown, J. 2010. 'Open innovation's next challenge: Itself'. HBR Blog Network [online, 4 February]. Available at: http://blogs.hbr.org/bigshift/2010/02/open-innovations-next-challeng.html [accessed: 29 July 2012].

Hagel, J., Seely-Brown, J. and Davison, L. 2010. *Power of Pull: How Small Moves, Smartly Made, Can Set Big Things in Motion*. New York: Basic Books.

Hamel, G. 2009a. 'Management moonshots – Part II'. WSJ Blogs [online, 2 March]. Available at: http://blogs.wsj.com/management/2009/03/02/management-moonshots-part-ii/ [accessed: 15 April 2012].

Hamel, G. 2009b. '25 stretch goals for management'. HBR Blog Network [online, 3 February]. Available at: http://blogs.hbr.org/hbr/hamel/2009/02/25_stretch_goals_for_managemen.html [accessed: 31 March 2012].

Hamel, G. 2009c. 'Why companies fail – Part 1'. *WSJ Blogs* [online, 1 June]. Available at: http://blogs.wsj.com/management/2009/06/01/why-companies-fail-part-i/ [accessed: 8 March 2012].

Hamel, G. 2010. 'Empowered individuals and empowered institutions'. WSJ Blogs [online, 20 April]. Available at: http://blogs.wsj.com/management/2010/04/20/empowered-individuals-and-empowering-institutions/ [accessed: 15 April 2012].

Hamel, G. and Breen, B. 2007. *The Future of Management*. Boston, MA: Harvard Business School Press.

Hansen, M. 2009. *Collaboration: How Leaders Avoid the Traps, Create Unity and Reap Big Results*. Boston, MA: Harvard Business Press.

Hansen, M. and Stoner, J. 2009. 'A leaner public sector'. *McKinsey Quarterly* [online, June], no. 4. Available at: http://www.mckinseyquarterly.com/A_leaner_public_sector_2406 [accessed: 8 March 2012].

Hardy, C and Leiba-O'Sullivan, S. 1998. 'The power behind empowerment: Implications for research and practice'. *Human Relations*, 51(4), 451–83.

Harrison, S. and Dourish, P. 1996. 'Re-place-ing space: The roles of place and space in collaborative systems'. Xerox Palo Alto Research Center and Rank Xerox Research Centre, Cambridge Lab (EuroPARC) [online]. Available at: http://www.dourish.com/publications/1996/cscw96-place.pdf [accessed: 9 March 2012].

Hatch, M.J. 2004. 'Dynamics in organisational culture', in *Handbook of Organisational Change and Innovation*, ed. M.S. Poole and A.H. Van de Ven. New York: Oxford University Press, 190–211.

Hayward, B, Fong, B. and Thornton, A. 2007. *The Third Work-life Balance Employer Survey: Executive Summary* [online: BERR Employment Relations Research Series no. 86]. Available at: http://www.bis.gov.uk/files/file42220. pdf [accessed: 8 March 2012].

Heath, C., Luff, P., Morris, S., Hindmarsh, J. and Ratcheva, V. 2000. *The Virtual Organisation: Collaborative Work and Technological Innovation* [online]. Available at: http://www.ukwon.net/files/kdb/da200c9e23fba5ee37bb2acc5aeac639.pdf [accessed: 8 March 2012].

Heckscher, C. 1995. 'The limits of participatory management'. *Across the Board*, 54, 16–21.

Heerwagen, J.H. 2004. 'Does your office feel like a zoo?' [online]. Available at: http://www.creativityatwork.com/articlesContent/May04Heerwagen.html [accessed: 8 March 2012].

Heerwagen, J.H., Kampschroer, K., Powell, K.M. and Loftness, V. 2004. 'Collaborative knowledge work environments'. *Building Research & Information*, 32(6), 510–28.

Hegarty, S. 1995. 'Empowerment turns tradition on its head for the benefit of all'. *Works Management*, 48(11), 24–7.

Herzberg, F. 1987. 'One more time: How do you motivate employees?' *Harvard Business Review* [online, 1 January 2003]. Available at: http://hbr.org/product/one-more-time-how-do-you-motivate-employees-harvar/an/R0301F-PDF-ENG [accessed: 8 March 2012].

Herzberg, F., Mausner, B. and Snyderman, B. 1959. *The Motivation to Work*. 2nd edn, New York: John Wiley.

Heskett, J. 2007. *How Will Millennials Manage?* [online, 2 August]. Available at: http://hbswk.hbs.edu/pdf/item/5736.pdf [accessed: 31 March 2012].

Hill, S. and Wilkinson, A. 1995. 'In search of TQM'. *Employee Relations*, 17(3), 8–25.

Hirsch, W., Garrow, V. and Holbeche, L. 2005. *Supporting Collaborative Working in Business Alliances and Partnerships*. Horsham: Roffey Park Institute.

Hitchins, D. 1997. 'Carry on thinking!'. *Engineering Management*, 7(3), 114–16.

Hofstede, G. 1999. 'The cultural relativity of organisational practices and theories', in *Managing Organisations: Text Readings & Cases*, ed. R.H. Rosenfeld and D.C. Wilson. 2nd edn, Maidenhead: McGraw-Hill, 466–80.

Honold, L. 1997. 'A review of the literature on employee empowerment'. *Empowerment in Organisations*, 5(4), 202–12.

Honore, S. and Schofield, C.P. 2009. *Generation Y Inside Out: A Multi-generational View of Generation Y – Learning and Working* [online]. Available at: http://www.ashridge.org.uk/Website/Content.nsf/FileLibrary/284E3C63840CCC3C802578DF004B5C10/$file/ABSGenYReport2009.pdf [accessed: 31 March 2012].

Hori, Y., Lemann, J.-P., Ma Kam Wah, T. and Wang, V. 2010. 'Facing up to the demographic dilemma'. *strategy + business*, 58 [online]. Available at: http://www.strategy-business.com/media/file/sb58_10105.pdf [accessed: 1 November 2012].

Hoverstadt, P. 2008. *The Fractal Organisation: Creating Sustainable Organisations with the Viable Systems Model*. Chichester: Wiley & Sons.

Hun, S. and Sim, H. 1996. 'Time-based competition: Literature review and implications for modelling'. *International Journal of Operations & Production Management*, 16(1), 75–90.

Huselid, M. 1995. 'The impact of human resource management on turnover, productivity and corporate financial performance', *Academy of Management Journal*, 38(3), 635–72.

Huws, U., Korte, W. and Robinson, S. 1990. *Telework: Towards the Elusive Office*. Chichester and New York: John Wiley.

IBM 2007. *Virtual Worlds, Real Leaders* [online]. Available at: http://www-05.ibm.com/uk/pov/virtual_worlds/ [accessed: 7 March 2012].

IBM 2008. *Global CEO Study: The Enterprise of the Future* [online]. Available at: http://www.ibm.com/ibm/ideasfromibm/us/ceo/20080505/ [accessed: 8 March 2012].

IBM 2010a. *Capitalising on Complexity: Insights from the 2010 IBM Global CEO Study* [online]. Available at: http://www-935.ibm.com/services/us/ceo/ceostudy2010/index.html [accessed: 8 March 2012].

IBM 2010b. *Working Beyond Boundaries: Insights from the Global Chief Human Resource Officer Study* [online]. Available at: http://www-935.ibm.com/services/uk/igs/chro/chrostudy2010/gbe03363usen.pdf [accessed: 8 March 2012].

IBM 2011. *The Social Business: Advent of a New Age*. IBM white paper [online]. Available at: http://www.ibm.com/smarterplanet/global/files/us__en_us__socialbusiness__epw14008usen.pdf [accessed: 7 March 2012].

Jackson, M.C. 1986. 'The cybernetic model of the organisation: An assessment', in *Cybernetics and Systems*, ed. R. Trappl. Dordrecht: Reidel Publishing.

Jackson, M.C. 1989. 'Evaluating the managerial significance of the VSM', in *The Viable System Model: Interpretations and Applications of Stafford Beer's VSM*, ed. R. Espejo and R. Harnden. Chichester: Wiley & Sons.

Jackson, P.R. and Martin, R. 1996. 'Impact of just-in-time on job content, employee attitudes and well-being: A longitudinal study'. *Ergonomics*, 39(1), 1–16.

HR Review 2009. 'Businesses urged to give employees "more autonomy and less intensive management"' [online, 23 March]. Available at: http://www.hrreview. co.uk/articles/hrreview-articles/hr-strategy-practice/businesses-urged-to-give-employees-more-autonomy-and-less-intensive-management/2179 [accessed: 31 March 2012].

Jaokar, A. and Fish, T. 2006. *Mobile Web 2.0*. London: Futuretext.

Johnson Controls 2009. *The Smart Workplace in 2030* [online: Johnson Controls Global Workplace Innovation]. Available at: http://www.johnsoncontrols. co.uk/publish/gb/en/products/building_efficiency/gws/workplace_e-zine/ the_smart_workplace.html [accessed: 8 March 2012].

Johnson, S. 2001. *Emergence*. London: Penguin.

Johnson Controls 2010. *Generation Y and the Workplace Annual Report 2010* [online: Johnson Controls Global Workplace Innovation]. Available at: http://www. johnsoncontrols.com/publish/us/en/products/building_efficiency/gws/gwi/ projects_workplace_innovation/workplace_innovation/future_generation_y_ workplace_innovation.html [accessed: 8 March 2012].

Jones, O. 1997. 'Changing the balance? Taylorism, TQM and work organisation'. *New Technology, Work and Employment*, 12(1), 13–24.

Kahl, M. 2009. 'The new GM – a first look'. *Automotive World* [online, 5 June]. Available at: http://www.automotiveworld.com/news/oems-and-markets/76857-the-new-gm-a-first-look [accessed: 8 March 2012].

Kanter, R.M. 1983. *The Change Masters*. London: Routledge.

Kay, J. 2009. 'Salutory lessons from the downfall of a car maker'. *Financial Times* [online, 3 June]. Available at: http://www.johnkay.com/2009/06/03/salutary-lessons-from-the-downfall-of-a-carmaker [accessed: 8 March 2012].

Kelly, K. 'Gossip is philosophy'. *Wired* [online]. Available at: http://www.wired. com/wired/archive/3.05/eno_pr.html [accessed: 15 April 2012].

Kenney, M. and Florida, R. 1993. *Beyond Mass Production: The Japanese Lean System and its Transfer to the U.S.* New York: Oxford University Press.

Kerfoot, D. and Knights, D. 1995. 'Empowering the "quality" worker? The seduction and contradiction of the total quality phenomena', in *Making Quality Critical: New Perspectives on Organisational Change*, ed. A. Wilkinson and H. Willmott. London: Routledge.

Kinlaw, D.C. 1995. *The Practice of Empowerment: Making the Most of Human Beings*. Aldershot: Gower.

Klein, J.A. 1991. 'A re-examination of autonomy in the light of new manufacturing practices'. *Human Relations*, 44(1), 21–38.

Knowles, M.S. 1986. *Using Learning Contracts*. San Francisco, CA: Jossey-Bass.

Kollewe, J. and Neate, R. 2012. 'AstraZeneca to cut 7,300 jobs'. *The Guardian* [online, 2 February]. Available at: http://www.guardian.co.uk/business/2012/feb/02/astrazeneca-cuts-7300-jobs?newsfeed=true [accessed: 12 April 2012].

KPMG/CIPD 2008. *Labour Market Outlook, Quarterly Survey Report: Focus on Working from Home* [online]. Available at: http://www.cipd.co.uk/NR/rdonlyres/9A93CB46-220F-42AA-8A6E-D3846FAB16D9/0/lmospring2008.pdf [accessed: 8 March 2012].

Lasalle, L. and Friend, D. 2011. 'RIM will take more than a half-billion dollar hit on PlayBook, service outage'. *Canadian Business* [online, 3 December]. Available at: http://www.canadianbusiness.com/article/60032--rim-will-take-more-than-a-half-billion-dollar-hit-on-playbook-service-outage [accessed: 12 April 2012].

Laseter, T. and Cross, R. 2007. 'The craft of connection'. *Strategy + Business* [online], 44. Available at: http://www.strategy-business.com/media/file/enews-01-31-07.pdf [accessed: 8 March 2012].

Laycock, M. and Stephenson, J. 1993. *Using Learning Contracts in Higher Education*. London: Kogan Page.

Lee, R. 2008. 'Keeping the faith: The E2.0 evangelist' [online, 21 March]. Available at: http://rexsthoughtspot.blogspot.com/2008/03/keeping-faith-e20-evangelist.html [accessed: 8 March 2012].

Levi, P. 1989. *The Drowned and the Saved*. New edn, Abacus: London.

Lewin, K. 1951. *Field Theory in Social Science: Selected Theoretical* Papers, ed. D. Cartwright. New York: Harper & Row.

Lewis, K. and Lytton, S. 1997. *How to Transform Your Company and Enjoy It*. 2nd edn, Chalford: Management Books 2000.

Lindberg, P. and Berger, A. 1997. 'Continuous improvement: Design, organisation and management'. *International Journal of Technology Management*, 14(1), 86–101.

Lipscomb, M. and McEwan, A.M. 2001. 'The TCS Model: An effective method of technology transfer at Kingston University, UK'. *Industry and Higher Education*, 15(6), 393–401.

London Business School 2009. *The Reflexive Generation: Young Professionals' Perspectives on Work, Career and Gender* [online]. Available at: http://www.london.edu/assets/documents/facultyandresearch/Gen_Y_The_Reflexive_Generation_The_Report.pdf [accessed: 8 March 2012].

Lowell, L., Matson, E. and Weiss, L.M. 2007. 'Harnessing the power of informal employee networks'. *McKinsey Quarterly* [online, November]. Available at: http://www.mckinseyquarterly.com/Harnessing_the_power_of_informal_employee_networks_2051 [accessed: 8 March 2012].

MacLeod, D. and Clarke, N. 2009. *Engaging for Success: Enhancing Performance Through Employee Engagement* [online]. Available at: http://www.bis.gov.uk/files/file52215.pdf [accessed: 8 March 2012].

Malik, O. 2009. *The Evolution of Blogging* [online, 13 August]. Available at: http://gigaom.com/2009/08/13/the-evolution-of-blogging/ [accessed: 8 March 2012].

Manz, C.C., Mossholder, K.W. and Luthans, F. 1987. 'An integrated perspective of self-control in organisations'. *Administration & Society*, 19(1), 3–24.

Marchington, M. 1995. 'Fairy tales and magic wands: New employment practices in perspective'. *Employee Relations*, 17, 51–66.

Marmot, M. 2006. 'Health in an unequal world'. *The Lancet* [online, 5 December]. Available at: http://www.who.int/social_determinants/publications/health_in_an_unequal_world_marmott_lancet.pdf [accessed: 8 March 2012].

Martin, C. and Tulgan, B. 2006. *Managing the Generation Mix*. 2nd edn, Amherst, MA: HRD Press [online]. Available at: http://downloads.hrdpressonline.com/files/7320080417162646.pdf [accessed: 8 March 2012].

Martin, R. 2007. *The Opposable Mind: How Successful Leaders Win Through Integrative Thinking*. Boston, MA: Harvard Business School Press.

Markov, R. 2008. Unpublished Master's thesis. Kingston University and the Academy of National Economy, Moscow.

Matthews, R. 2010. *A Meta Model of Organisational Strategy* [online]. Available at: http://robindcmatthews.com/lecdocs/documents/31/original_the%20meta%20model%20october%202010.pdf [accessed: 8 March 2012].

McAfee, A. 2009. *Enterprise 2.0: New Collaborative Tools For Your Organisations' Toughest Challenges*. Boston, MA: Harvard Business Press.

McArdle, L., Rowlinson, M., Proctor, S., Hassard, J. and Forrester, P. 1995. 'Total Quality Management and participation: Employee empowerment, or the enhancement of exploitation?', in *Making Quality Critical: New Perspectives on Organisational Change*, ed. A. Wilkinson and H. Willmott. London: Routledge.

McCarthy, I. and Menicou, M. 2002. 'A classification schema of manufacturing decisions for the GRAI enterprise modelling technique'. *Computers in Industry* [online], 47, 339–55. Available at: http://motresearch.bus.sfu.ca/Papers/GraiSchema2002.pdf [accessed: 28 July 2012].

McCrindle Research 2006. *New Generations at Work: Attracting, Recruiting, Retraining & Training Generation Y* [online]. Available at: http://www.libraries.vic.gov.au/downloads/Public_Libraries_Unit/newgenerationsatwork.pdf [accessed: 8 March 2012].

McEwan, A.M. 1999. '*A Systems Approach to Empowerment* in Manufacturing Enterprises'. Cranfield University: Unpublished PhD thesis.

McKinsey Quarterly. 2009. 'The Crisis: A New Era in Management'. *The McKinsey Quarterly*, 1.

Meyer, P. 2010. *From Workplace to Playspace: Innovating, Learning and Changing Through Dynamic Engagement*. San Francisco, CA: Jossey-Bass.

Milczarek, M., Schneider, E. and González, E.R. 2009. *European Risk Observatory Report: OSH in Figures: Stress at Work – Facts and Figures* [online: European Agency for Safety and Health at Work]. Available at: http://osha.europa.eu/en/publications/reports/TE-81-08-478-EN-C_OSH_in_figures_stress_at_work [accessed: 9 March 2012].

Mills, P.K. 1983. 'Self-management: Its control and relationship to other organisational properties'. *The Academy of Management Journal*, 8(3), 445–53.

Mitev, N. 1996. 'Empowerment, change and information technology: Socio-technical design and business process re-engineering', *Personnel Review*, 25(4), 56–66.

Moffat, A. and McLean, A. 2010. 'Merger as conversation'. *Leadership & Organisation Development Journal*, 31(6), 534–50. Available at: http://www.emeraldinsight.com/journals.htm?articleid=1881488 [accessed: 29 July 2012].

Moon, J. 1999. *Reflection in Learning and Professional Development*. London: Kogan Page.

Moore, P. 2009. *Memorandum from Paul Moore, Ex-head of Group Regulatory Risk, HBOS plc* [online: UK Parliament Website]. Available at: http://www.publications.parliament.uk/pa/cm200809/cmselect/cmtreasy/144/144w243.htm [accessed: 8 March 2012].

MSNBC 2010. 'No easy answer to why Toyota accelerators stick' [online, 28 January 2010]. Available at: http://www.msnbc.msn.com/id/35110966/ns/business-autos/ [accessed: 9 March 2012].

Murray, J. and Shah, R. 2010. *Nurturing BlueIQ: Enterprise 2.0 Adoption in IBM* [online]. Available at: https://www-950.ibm.com/files/app?lang=en_US#/person/100000R0P5/file/9e211d17-b003-4e60-81ba-611dce7d9174 [accessed: 8 March 2012].

Myerson, J., Bichard, J. and Erlich, A. 2010. *New Demographics, New Workspace: Office Design for the Changing Workforce*. Farnham: Gower.

Nadler, D. 1977. *Feedback and Organisation Development: Using Data-based Methods*. Reading, MA: Addison-Wesley.

National Commission on the BP Deepwater Horizon Oil Spill and Offshore Drilling. 2011. *Report to the President: The Gulf Oil Disaster and the Future of Offshore Drilling* [online]. Available at: http://www.oilspillcommission.gov/sites/default/files/documents/FinalReportIntro.pdf [accessed: 9 March 2012].

Nayar, V. 2010. *Employees First, Customers Second: Turning Conventional Management Upside Down*. Boston, MA: Harvard Business School Publishing.

Nonaka, I., Toyama, R. and Konno, N. 2000. 'SECI, *ba* and leadership: A unified model of dynamic knowledge creation'. *Long Range Planning*, 33, 5–34.

Noteboom, C. 1998. *Roads to Santiago: Detours and Riddles in the Lands and History of Spain*. London: Harvill Press.

Oakland, J. 1997. 'Interdependence and co-operation: The essentials of Total Quality Management'. *Total Quality Management*, 8(2–3), S31–S35.

Olie, R. 1994. 'Shades of culture and institutions in international mergers'. *Organisation Studies*, 15(3), 381–405.

Orange Future Enterprise Coalition 2007. *Beyond Boundaries: The Emerging Work Culture of Independence and Responsibility* [online]. Available at: http://www.orangecoalition.com/whitepapers/ [accessed: 8 March 2012].

Osborne, C.S. 1998. 'Systems for sustainable organisations: Emergent strategies, interactive controls and semi-formal information'. *Journal of Management Studies*, 35(4), 481.

Osterwalder, A. and Pigneur, Y. 2010. *Business Model Generation: A Handbook for Visionaries, Gamechangers, and Challengers*. Hoboken, NJ: John Wiley & Sons.

Ouchi, W.G. 1977. 'The relationship between organisational structure and organisational control'. *Administrative Science Quarterly*, 22, 95–113.

Palmberg, K. 2009. 'Complex adaptive systems as metaphors for organizational management'. *The Learning Organisation*, 16(6), 483–98.

Palmisano, S. 2006. 'The globally integrated enterprise'. *Foreign Affairs* [online], 85(3), 127–36. Available at: http://www.ibm.com/ibm/governmentalprograms/samforeignaffairs.pdf [accessed: 8 March 2012].

Payne, J. and Keep, E. 2003. 'Re-visiting the Nordic approaches to work re-organisation and job redesign: Lessons for UK skills policy', *Policy Studies*, 24(4), 205–25.

Pearson, N., Lesser, E. and Sapp, J. 2010. *A New Way of Working: Insights from Global Leaders* [online: IBM Institute for Business Value]. Available at: http://www-935.ibm.com/services/uk/bcs/pdf/HCMA_new_way_of_working-Insights_from_global_leaders-Executive_Report.pdf [accessed: 8 March 2012].

Peppard, J. and Rylander, A. 2006. 'From value chain to value network: Insights for mobile operators'. *European Management Journal*, 24(2–3), 128–41.

Peters, T. and Waterman, R.H. 2004. *In Search of Excellence*. 2nd edn, London: Profile Books.

Pettigrew, A.M. and Fenton, E.M. 2000. *The Innovating Organisation*. London: Sage.

Picken, J.C. and Dess, G. 1997. 'Out of (strategic) control'. *Organisational Dynamics*, 26(1), 35–48.

Pidd, M. 1996. *Tools for Thinking: Modelling in Management Science*. Chichester: Wiley & Sons.

Polanyi, M. 2009. *The Tacit Dimension*. Re-issue edn, Chicago, IL: University of Chicago Press.

Poole, D. and Sheehan, T. 2006. *Strategies for Managing the Brain Drain: Implications for Knowledge Management* [online: Arup]. Available at: http://www.arup.com/_assets/_download/F01A0F5F-19BB-316E-40ED890DF0885EB3.pdf [accessed: 8 March 2012].

Porter, M.E. 1985. *Competitive Advantage*. New York: The Free Press.

Price, F. 1993. 'Perspectives: Educated power'. *TQM Magazine*, 5(3), 5–6.

Puybaraud, M.C. 2010. *Flexible Working 2010* [online]. Available at: http://www.johnsoncontrols.com/content/dam/WWW/jci/be/global_workplace_solutions/global_workplace_innovation/flex_working/Flexible_Working_2010.pdf [accessed: 9 March 2012].

Puybaraud, M.C. and McEwan, A.M. 2007. 'Adapting to the dynamics of a global workforce'. *KM Review*, 10(5), 30–33.

Puybaraud, M.C. and McEwan, A.M. 2008. 'Knowledge Management and Enterprise Social Networking'. Unpublished white paper for Johnson Controls Global Mobility Network.

Puybaraud, M.C. and McEwan, A.M. 2009a. 'Shrinking Social Distance'. Unpublished white paper for Johnson Controls Global Mobility Network.

Puybaraud, M.C. and McEwan, A.M. 2009b. 'Workplace to Zero?'. Unpublished white paper for Johnson Controls Global Mobility Network.

Puybaraud, M.C. and McEwan, A.M. 2010. 'Understanding Culture in the Workplace'. Unpublished white paper for Johnson Controls Global Mobility Network.

PWC 2009. *12th Annual Global CEO Survey* [online]. Available at: http://www.pwc.com/en_TH/th/publications/assets/12th_annual_global_ceo_survey.pdf [accessed: 8 March 2012].

PWC 2010. *13th Annual Global CEO Survey* [online]. Available at: http://www.pwc.com/gx/en/ceo-survey/download.jhtml [accessed: 8 March 2012].

PWC 2012. *15th Annual Global CEO Survey* [online]. Available at: http://www.pwc.com/gx/en/ceo-survey/pdf/15th-global-ceo-survey.pdf [accessed: 12 April 2012].

PWC 2010. *Emerging Multinationals: The Rise of New Multinational Companies From Emerging Economies* [online, April]. Available at: http://www.pwc.fr/assets/files/pdf/2010/04/pwc_emerging_multinationals.pdf [accessed: 8 March 2012].

QAA 2008. 'The framework for higher education qualifications in England, Wales and Northern Ireland' [online: The Quality Assurance Agency for Higher Education]. Available at: http://www.qaa.ac.uk/Publications/InformationAndGuidance/Documents/FHEQ08.pdf [accessed: 9 March 2012].

QAA 2010. *Masters Degree Characteristics* [online: The Quality Assurance Agency for Higher Education]. Available at: http://www.qaa.ac.uk/Publications/

InformationAndGuidance/Documents/MastersDegreeCharacteristics.pdf [accessed: 8 March 2012].

Radnor, Z., Walley, P., Stephens, A. and Bucci, G. 2006. *Evaluation of the Lean Approach to Business Management and its Use in the Public Sector* [online]. Available at: http://www.scotland.gov.uk/Publications/2006/06/13162106/0 [accessed: 8 March 2012].

Randolph, W.A. 1995. 'Navigating the journey to empowerment'. *Organisational Dynamics*, 23(4), 19–32.

Rehder, R.R. 1992. 'Sayonara, Uddevalla?'. *Business Horizons*, 35(6), 8–18.

Robb, F.F. 1984. 'Cybernetics in management thinking'. *Systems Research*, 1(1), 5–23.

Robinson, R. 1997. 'Loosening the reins without losing control'. *Empowerment in Organizations*, 5(2), 76–81.

Robson, C. 1993. *Real World Research*. Oxford: Blackwell Publishers.

Rock, D. 2009. 'Managing with the brain in mind'. *strategy + business* [online, 27 August]. Available at: http://www.strategy-business.com/article/09306?gko=5df7f [accessed: 8 March 2012].

Rodrigues, C.A. 1994. 'Employee participation and empowerment programs'. *Empowerment in Organisations*, 2(2), 29–40.

Sandberg, A. 2007. 'The Uddevalla experience in perspective', in *Enriching Production: Perspectives on Volvo's Uddevalla Plant as an Alternative to Lean Production*, ed. A. Sandberg. Digital edn, Farnham: Gower. Available at: http://freyssenet.com/files/Enriching%20Production%20-complete%20book.pdf [accessed: 8 March 2012].

Schaffers, H., Brodt, T., Pallot, M. and Prinz, W. 2006. *The Future Workspace: Mobile and Collaborative Working Perspectives*. Enschede, The Netherlands: Telematica Instituut [online]. Available at: http://www.ami-communities.eu/pub/bscw.cgi/d163187/The%20Future%20Workspace.pdf [accessed: 8 March 2012].

Schein, E.H. 1996. 'Culture: The missing concept in organisation studies'. *Administrative Science Quarterly*, 41(2) 229–40.

Schein, E.H. 2009. *The Corporate Culture Survival Guide*. 2nd edn, San Francisco, CA: Jossey-Bass.

Schoderbek, P.P., Skefalas, A.G. and Schoderbek, C.G. 1975. *Management Systems: Conceptual Considerations*. Dallas, TX: Business Publications.

Schon, D. 1991. *The Reflective Practitioner: How Professionals Think in Action*. New edn, Aldershot: Ashgate.

Seider, C., Lafferty, S. and Lee, S. 2008. *Go Mobile, Grow*. IBM Institute for Business Value [online]. Available at: https://www-304.ibm.com/easyaccess/fileserve?contentid=142404 [accessed: 7 March 2012].

Selto, F.H., Renner, C.J. and Young, S.M. 1995. 'Assessing the organisational fit of a just-in-time manufacturing system: Testing, selection, interaction and systems models of contingency theory'. *Accounting, Organisation and Society*, 20(7–8), 665–84.

Senge, P.M. 1993. *The Fifth Discipline: The Art and Practice of the Learning Organisation*. London: Century Business.

Sewell, G. and Wilkinson, B. 1992a. 'Empowerment or emasculation: Shopfloor surveillance in a Total Quality organisation', in *Reassessing Human Resource Management*, ed. P. Blyton and P. Turnbull. London: Sage, 97–115.

Sewell, G. and Wilkinson, B. 1992b. 'Someone to watch over me: Surveillance, discipline and the just-in-time labour process'. *Sociology*, 26(2), 279–82.

Shah, R. 2010. *Social Networking for Business: Choosing the Right Tools and Resources to Fit Your Needs*. Upper Saddle River, NJ: Wharton School Publishing.

Shapiro, E.C. 1998. *Fad Surfing in the Boardroom: Reclaiming the Courage to Manage in the Age of Instant Answers*. Oxford: Capstone Publishing.

Shaw, D.R., Snowden, B., Christopher, P.H., Kawalek, P. and Warboys, B. 2004. 'The viable systems model applied to a smart network: The case of the UK electricity market'. *Journal of Information Technology*, 19, 270–80.

Silverman, R.E. 2011. 'Latest game theory: Mixing work and play'. *The Wall Street Journal* [online, 9 October]. Available at: http://online.wsj.com/article/SB10001424052970204294504576615371783795248.html [accessed: 12 April 2012].

Simons, R. 1995. 'Control in an age of empowerment', *Harvard Business Review*, 73(2), 80–88.

Snook, S., Nohria, N. and Khurana, R. (eds). 2011. *The Handbook for Teaching Leadership: Knowing, Doing, and Being*. Thousand Oaks, CA: Sage Publications.

Stacey, R.D. 1996. *Complexity and Creativity in Organisations*. San Francisco, CA: Berrett-Koehler.

Stalk, G. 1988. 'Time – the next source of competitive advantage'. *Harvard Business Review*, July–August, 41–51.

Stalk, G. and Hout, T.M. 1990. *Competing Against Time: How Time-based Competition is Reshaping Global Markets*. New York: Free Press.

Sterman, J. 2006. 'Learning from evidence in a complex world'. *American Journal of Public Health* [online], 96, 505–14. Available at: http://web.mit.edu/jsterman/www/LearningFromEvidenceFinal.pdf [accessed: 8 March 2012].

Sutton, R. 2007. *The No-asshole Rule: Building a Civilised Workplace and Surviving One that Isn't*. London: Sphere.

Sutton, R. 2010. 'Most claims of originality are testimony to ignorance and most claims of magic are testimony to hubris'. *Bob Sutton Work Matters* [online, 20 January]. Available at: http://bobsutton.typepad.com/my_weblog/2010/01/

most-claims-of-originality-are-testimony-to-ignorance-and-most-claims-of-magic-are-testimony-to-hubr.html [accessed: 8 March 2012].

Tamkin, P., Cowling, M. and Hunt, W. 2008. *People and the Bottom Line*. Institute for Employment Studies [online: Department for Business, Innovation and Skills]. Available at: http://www.bis.gov.uk/assets/biscore/corporate/migratedd/publications/d/dius_iip_448.pdf [accessed: 8 March 2012].

Tannenbaum, A.S. 1968. *Control in Organizations*. New York: McGraw-Hill.

Tarnowski, L. 2009. *How to Manage Gen Y Expectations* [online]. Available at: http://www.changeboard.com/content/1499/how-to-manage-gen-y-expectations/ [accessed: 15 April 2012].

Taylor, R. 2002. *Managing Workplace Change* [online]. Available at: http://www.leeds.ac.uk/esrcfutureofwork/downloads/fow_publication_5.pdf [accessed: 8 March 2012].

Taylor, W.C. and Labarre, P. 2006. *Mavericks at Work: Why the Most Original Minds in Business Win*. London: HarperCollins.

Tett, G. 2009. *Fool's Gold: How Unrestrained Greed Corrupted a Dream, Shattered Global Markets and Unleashed a Catastrophe*. London: Little, Brown.

The Economist 2008. *A Survey of Mobility: Nomads at Last* [online, 12 April]. Available at: http://www.economist.com/node/10950394 [accessed: 29 July 2012].

The Economist 2010a. 'India's surprising economic miracle' [online]. Available at: http://www.economist.com/node/17147648 [accessed: 9 March 2012].

The Economist 2010b. 'The power to disrupt: A special report on innovation in emerging markets' [online, April]. Available at: http://www.economist.com/node/15879393 [accessed: 8 March 2012].

The Work Foundation in association with BT 2009. *Changing Relationships at Work* [online]. Available at: http://www.theworkfoundation.com/Assets/Docs/BT_final270109b.pdf [accessed: 8 March 2012].

Thompson, K.R. 1998. 'Confronting the paradoxes in a Total Quality environment'. *Organizational Dynamics*, 26(3), 62–72.

Totterdill, P, Exton, O., Exton, R. and Sherrin, J. 2009. 'Workplace Innovation Policies in European Countries'. Unpublished UK Work Organisation Network report to Korea Workplace Innovation Center.

Toshiba and flexibility.co.uk 2012. *The Complete Guide to Flexible Working* [online]. Available at: http://www.flexibility.co.uk/guide/Content/CompleteGuide.pdf [accessed: 7 March 2012].

Towers Perrin 2007. *Closing the Engagement Gap: A Road Map for Driving Superior Business Performance* [online]. Available at: http://www.towersperrin.com/tp/getwebcachedoc?webc=HRS/USA/2008/200803/GWS_Global_Report 20072008_31208.pdf [accessed: 8 March 2012].

Trompenaars, F. and Hampden-Turner, C. 1997. *Riding the Waves of Corporate Culture*. 2nd edn, London: Nicholas Brealey.

Twentyman, J. 2009. 'Businesses start to take Web 2.0 tools seriously'. *Financial Times* [online: 27 January]. Available at: http://www.ft.com/cms/s/0/d28887ea-eb49-11dd-bb6e-0000779fd2ac.html [accessed: 29 July 2012].

United Nations 2002. *World Population Ageing: 1950–2050* [online: United Nations Population Division]. Available at: http://www.un.org/esa/population/publications/worldageing19502050/ [accessed: 9 March 2012].

United Nations 2009. *World Population Ageing 2009* [online: United Nations Population Division]. Available at: http://www.un.org/esa/population/publications/WPA2009/WPA2009_WorkingPaper.pdf [accessed: 9 March 2012].

Vaara, E., Tienari, J. and Santti, R. 2003. 'Metaphors as vehicles of social identity-building in cross-border mergers'. *Human Relations*, 56(4), 419–51.

Van de Ven, A.H. and Delbecq, A.L. 1974. 'A task-contingent model of work-unit structure'. *Administrative Science Quarterly*, 19(1), 183–97.

Very, P., Lubatkin, M. and Calori, R. 1996. 'A cross-national assessment of acculturative stress in recent European mergers'. *International Studies of Management & Organisation*, 26(1), 59–86.

Wagner, D. 2007. 'Managing an age-diverse workforce', *Sloan Management Review*, 48(4), 9.

Walker, D. 2009. *A Review of Corporate Governance in UK Banks and Other Financial Industry Entities: Final Recommendations* [online]. Available at: http://webarchive.nationalarchives.gov.uk/+/http://www.hm-treasury.gov.uk/d/walker_review_261109.pdf [accessed: 8 March 2012].

Warr, P. 2002. 'The study of well-being, behaviour and attitudes', in *Psychology at Work*, ed. P. Warr. 5th edn, London: Penguin Books.

Warwick Manufacturing Group. *Transforming Capability Support Materials: The Puttick Grid* [online]. Available at: http://www.docstoc.com/docs/76796576/Puttick-Grid---Welcome-to-the-University-of-Warwick [accessed: 31 March 2012].

Weber, Y. 1996. 'Corporate cultural fit and performance in mergers and acquisitions'. *Human Relations*, 49(9), 1,181–202.

Weerakoon, T.S. and Lai, K.-H. 1997. 'Organization performance: Empowering the workforce'. *Total Quality Management*, 8(2–3), S305–S309.

Weick. K. 1979. *The Social Psychology of Organising*. Reading, MA: Addison-Wesley.

Weick, K. 2001. *Making Sense of the Organisation*. Oxford: Blackwell Publishing.

Wenger, E. 2006. *Communities of Practice: A Brief Introduction* [online]. Available at: http://www.ewenger.com/theory/ [accessed: 29 July 2012].

Westley, F., Zimmerman, B. and Quinn Patton, M. 2007. *Getting to Maybe: How the World is Changed*. Toronto: Vintage Canada.

White, D., Zheltoukhova, K., Reid, B. and Chiasson, M. 2011. *Letting the Barbarians Through the Gates? Harnessing the Power of Social Media*. The Work Foundation. Available at: http://theworkfoundation.com/DownloadPublication/Report/293_Letting%20the%20Barbarians%20through%20the%20Gates.pdf [accessed: 8 March 2012].

White, M., Hill, S., Mills, C. and Smeaton, D. 2004. *Managing to Change? British Workplaces and the Future of Work*. Basingstoke: Palgrave Macmillan.

Wickisier, E.L. 1997. 'The paradox of empowerment – a case study'. *Empowerment in Organisations*, 5(4), 213–19.

Wilkinson, A. 1998. 'Empowerment: Theory and practice'. *Personnel Review*, 27(1), 40–56.

Willmott, H. 1995a. 'The odd couple? Re-engineering business process and managing human relations'. *New Technology, Work and Employment*, 10(2), 89–98.

Willmott, H. 1995b. 'Will the turkeys vote for Christmas? The re-engineering of human resources', in *Examining Business Process Re-engineering: Current Perspectives and Research Directions*, ed. G. Burke and J. Peppard. London: Kogan Page.

Womack, J.P., Jones, D.T. and Roos, D. 1990. *The Machine that Changed the World*. New York: Rawson Associates.

www.ukparliament.co.uk 2009. *Memorandum from Paul Moore, Ex-head of Group Regulatory Risk, HBOS plc* [online, 1 April]. Available at: http://www.publications.parliament.uk/pa/cm200809/cmselect/cmtreasy/144/144w243.htm [accessed: 31 March 2012].

Zhu, Z. and Huang, H. 2007. 'The cultural integration in the process of cross-border mergers and acquisitions'. *International Management Review*, 3(2), 40–44.

Index